ARTHURIAN STUDIES XX

READING THE MORTE DARTHUR

ARTHURIAN STUDIES

ISSN 0261–9814

READING THE MORTE DARTHUR

Terence McCarthy

D. S. BREWER

First published 1988 by D. S. Brewer
240 Hills Road, Cambridge
an imprint of Boydell & Brewer Ltd
PO Box 9, Woodbridge, Suffolk IP12 3DF
and of Boydell & Brewer Inc.
Wolfeboro, New Hampshire 03894-2069, USA

ISBN 0 85991 269 8

British Library Cataloguing in Publication Data

McCarthy, Terence
    Reading the Morte Darthur –
    (Arthurian studies, ISSN 0261-9814 ; 20)
    1. Fiction in English. Malory, Sir Thomas
    – Critical studies
    I. Title II. Series
    823'.2
    ISBN 0-85991-269-8

Library of Congress Cataloging-in-Publication Data

McCarthy, Terence.
    Reading the Morte Darthur / Terence McCarthy.
        p. cm. – (Arthurian studies : 20)
    Bibliography: p.
    ISBN 0-85991-269-8 (alk. paper)
    1. Malory, Thomas, Sir, 15th cent. Morte d'Arthur. 2. Arthurian
    romances – History and criticism. I. Title. II. Series.
    PR2045.M36 1988
    823'.2--dc19   88-12086
    CIP

∞ Printed on long life paper
made to the full American Standard

Printed in Great Britain by St Edmundsbury Press, Bury St Edmunds, Suffolk

Contents

ACKNOWLEDGEMENTS

No one can study Malory without being aware of the formidable contribution of Eugène Vinaver, and most people are glad to rely on the work of Derek Brewer and Peter Field. I have borrowed ideas from other writers without always taking time to acknowledge their help. They will not, I hope, be offended: my list of further reading is, in itself, an acknowledgement of my most obvious debts.

Some aspects of this book took shape as a series of lectures given to students preparing the *Agrégation* in Dijon (I thank them for listening indulgently), and I aired a few views expressed here in an essay André Crépin of the University of Paris (IV) once requested (I thank him for his discreet encouragement at all times). David Lodge has kindly given me permission to quote from his novel *Small World*. Derek Brewer and Richard Barber read my book in manuscript form and were good enough to suggest improvements, but they are not responsible for the flaws that remain. I have no need to acknowledge anyone's help there.

A number of friends and colleagues helped directly (by correcting typescript) and indirectly (by offering encouragement and the pleasure of their company): I would like to thank in particular Françoise Pellan, Margaret Tomarchio and Andrew King.

My greatest debt is to three people who had nothing to do with the writing of this book at all, and no doubt I should not be mentioning them here. They appear more fittingly in my dedication. The debt I owe is one of those that can only be mentioned, never repaid.

Dijon
February 1988
Terence McCarthy

FOR MY MOTHER AND SISTER
AND IN MEMORY OF
MY FATHER

Preliminaries

READING THE MORTE DARTHUR

I could begin by praising the *Morte Darthur*. After all, it has been read and admired for five hundred years; it has inspired writers in English from Spenser to Steinbeck; and it has become one of the major landmarks of English literature. All this should be encouraging news to those who are turning to Malory for the first time. The *Morte Darthur* is undeniably a great book.

At the same time, however, it is one which is surrounded with controversy, a book which invites division and prejudice. By no means all specialists of medieval literature show much enthusiasm for the *Morte Darthur*; literary histories often pay it scant attention; and even newcomers to Malory have difficulty approaching his book with an open mind.

The present study is intended for newcomers. It is an introduction to Malory written for those who know nothing about the *Morte Darthur* – although, in a way, that is an audience which does not exist. Indeed, this is our first problem. People who have never read a word of Malory come to his book with at least some prior knowledge. They may not know much, but they have almost certainly heard of the sword in the stone; the wizardry of Merlin; Excalibur; the Round Table; Lancelot and his love for Queen Guenevere; the destruction of the kingdom and Arthur's mysterious death. They may not be able to identify with precision other characters, such as Morgan le Fay, Mordred, or Galahad, but the names – and much else in the book, perhaps – will somehow have a familiar ring.

Prior knowledge is no drawback in itself, of course, but where that knowledge comes from can be. The Arthurian legends exist independently of any one literary version – Malory had no monopoly on Arthur – and the information we have picked up, complete with our impressions – good or bad – of that information, may have nothing to do with Malory at all. But this will not stop us, when we turn to the *Morte Darthur*, bringing our preconceptions along. And since most people receive their first (and, perhaps, only) taste of the Arthurian legends in childhood, the preconceptions are likely to be all the more firmly rooted. Those who have retained their childlike enthusiasm will be looking forward to rediscovering a world that once held them captive. But those who feel they have put away childish thoughts will not turn to Malory at all, unless they have been told to. They will express resentment and scepticism that what was once childhood bedtime reading can form the basis of serious, academic, literary study. They will not appreciate spending time on things they have grown out of.

To readers of both categories, however, the enthusiastic and the disgruntled, the *Morte Darthur* is likely to appear an odd book. They will probably not find what they expected, not all they hoped for and not quite what they dreaded. If you come looking for elegant knights and ladies, and those memorable love stories, you will find them of course; but somehow they are never allowed much space before we are back off out to the battlefield. What is more, with the story of Lancelot and Guenevere it is like arriving at the theatre in the middle of act three: the whole thing is half way through before we have had time to get settled in.

If, on the other hand, you have recollections of endless, tiresome adventures, of brainless boobies ever ready to pick a fight, you will find these too; but you will also see that Malory's knights have more wisdom and restraint than childhood abridgements had space for. There may be little philosophy or deep thought, but there is much common sense and sternness of purpose. They are not just overgrown boy scouts; the finest of them are men of diplomacy and judgment, and the others, at worst, resemble Jane Austen's Lady Bertram: they do not think deeply, but, guided by Sir Thomas, they think justly on all important points.

Childhood recollections can distort – for good or bad – and it is therefore the first duty of newcomers to Malory to keep an open mind. They may not have read his book before, but they are probably far more biased than they think. Those who approach the *Morte Darthur* with misgivings should try to dominate their prejudices and become more receptive to what the book actually contains as opposed to what they imagine, or seem to remember, it contains. But the same advice is not inappropriate for those who welcome the prospect of studying the *Morte Darthur*. Indeed, instead of encouraging their enthusiasm it would be tempting to curb it. If they let themselves be governed by their expectations, they, too, might miss the best of Malory and be disappointed.

The *Morte Darthur* is a book of action and adventure, not a book of thought. It is full of unexplained and inexplicable customs, magic and mystery, love and hate, nobility, villainy and the highest ideals. Among its characters are the heroes and heroines of the greatest love stories in the western tradition, although love here is a catalyst for a number of public events rather than the centre of attention itself; Malory takes it for granted that we are fairly *au courant* anyway. We meet men who are paragons of integrity or show a dashing lack of moral concern. When Lancelot's lady jailer offers him the keys to his cell if he first lets her taste the pleasures of his handsome body, he chooses to stay in prison, while the teenaged Arthur no sooner sets his eyes on a fetching maid than – with her consent, of course – he 'had ado with her.'

There is much sobriety in the *Morte Darthur*, but much gentle comedy too, although some of our amusement is perhaps ill-founded, a failure merely to appreciate a world where logic must be sacrificed to action. We smile at what they take in deadly earnest. If we are able to accept the world on its own terms, it is full of fascination and charm, but even if we cannot banish an ironic smile, the charm does not disappear, for the *Morte Darthur* can survive parody. However quaint and mindless things may seem if we wilfully misunderstand, there is still much to admire and regret the loss of. There are ideals we can all revere. The book appeals to some of the most basic and powerful sentiments: patriotism, loyalty, truth, mercy, goodness, humility and decency; it appeals to our better selves, before disillusionment set in, before self-interest and social profit made us compromise.

Malory's book is full of vivid incident, characters who come alive immediately, however briefly we see them, and unforgettable scenes of haunting beauty. Malory's prose seems plain, unobtrusive and spendidly unpretentious, as when a king's absence is explained with no more formality than 'He ys oute. He ys nat at home', but there are passages where the cadences are unmistakeable, extremely moving and branded in our minds. Lancelot seeing the dead Guenevere 'wept nat gretely but sighed'; while the Maid of Astolat's dying complaint has all the assurance of one who has abandoned herself to death and for whom the reproof of a priest is too trivial to shake her purpose:

'Why sholde I leve such thoughtes? Am I nat an erthely woman? And all the whyle the brethe ys in my body I may complayne me, for my belyve ys that I do none offence, though I love an erthely man, unto God, for He fourmed me thereto, and all maner of good love comyth of God. And othir than good love loved I never sir Launcelot du Lake. And I take God to recorde, I loved never none but hym, nor never shall, of erthely creature; and a clene maydyn I am for hym and for all othir. And sitthyn hit ys the sufferaunce of God that I shall dye for so noble a knyght, I beseche The, Hyghe Fadir of Hevyn, have mercy uppon me and my soule, and uppon myne unnumerable paynys that I suffir may be alygeaunce of parte of my synnes. For Swete Lorde Jesu,' seyde the fayre maydyn, 'I take God to recorde I was never to The grete offenser nother ayenote Thy lawis but that I loved thys noble knyght, sir Launcelot, oute of mesure.

And of myselff, Good Lorde, I had no myght to withstonde the fervent love, wherefore I have my deth!'

The *Morte Darthur* is not an intellectual book: we are called upon to feel, to commit ourselves, to take sides (the image of an army or a team is appropriate), not to analyse or to reason. We are on Lancelot's side not because in all logic he is in the right, but because he is the best. Malory tells us that Arthur's army is 'oure noble knyghtes of mery Ingelonde' and we lend them our support with all the heartfelt, if mindless, allegiance to a team because it is *our* team.

The *Morte Darthur* is not a book where everything is pared down to the essentials; it is not spare, dense, tightly packed and economically structured, and – perhaps unfairly, for it is a medieval book – it has come under attack for this. But it is a generous book: big, inefficient, sprawling, leisurely, in a way an image of the fortunes of the knights who fill its pages. It is as loose-fitting and comfortable as an old garment. It is a book which demands (and usually gets, in one way or another) a massive emotional response. There are those who find it a noble book, a plea for all that is fine, trustworthy, and upright; just as there are those who think that all this commitment to knight errantry without a trace of irony, discrimination, or detachment is somewhat trivial.

If Malory had examined the gap between pretention and achievement, if he had scrutinised the chivalry of a man who lies through his teeth to defend the virtue of an adulterous queen, as Lancelot, they say, does, his book might have commanded more respect. But Malory questions nothing; he swallows his chivalry whole. The idea of how to survive without too much compromise in a corrupt world never crosses his mind. All Lancelot tries to do is to keep corruption hidden and brazen it out. The only disillusionment Malory expresses is with his own contemporary society. The ethic of the Arthurian world he subscribes to wholly, with a confidence which is inspiring and which we would willingly share, but his book, ultimately, has no intellectual fibre to offer when the more immediate pleasures begin to pall. It is full of surface brilliance and appeal, it is noble and uplifting, if you like, and exciting too, but it is flimsy, insubstantial and lacking in weight.

I am not sure there is much to say against arguments of this kind. One agrees or not; it is a question of sympathy. Each reader must decide for himself. And yet behind the excitement of a book full of action, there is, I would suggest, much seriousness of purpose. Malory relates with enthusiasm the deeds of his knights not only because he loves action, but because his centre of interest is conduct. The French – as often – have a word for it: Malory is interested in what they call *moeurs*, behaviour, but also morals. He has a clear perception of the values that count, and if he views chivalry without scepticism, he can only be accused of triviality if you have already decided in advance that chivalry is palatable only if taken with a good pinch of salt – yet another example of the lack of open-mindedness we bring to the *Morte Darthur*.

Malory's enthusiasm for Arthurian chivalry is not gushing and naive. He knows that Arthurian society was not perfect and he makes no attempt to hide the shoddiness of certain members of the court. His is not dewy-eyed nostalgia for a golden age, the old soldier's vain reverie about things past, but a clear-sighted awareness that, for all its faults, Arthurian chivalry embodied an ideal far superior to anything that survives today. Malory's enthusiasm measures the force of that mature conviction.

But there are areas in which Malory cannot be defended altogether and there is little point in encouraging a newcomer to be open-minded if we refuse to admit at least this. The *Morte Darthur* is a book of great variety but it is also an uneven book. Its leisurely pace is one of its charms, but there are times when it is more than leisurely, it begins merely to ramble. Malory can labour things too. When we have the impression that he has given us the feel of a battle, for example, by describing a few representative encounters, he goes on to give us more, and then more, and then more. His documentary urge to record great deeds is, as we shall see, a vital part of his outlook, but even the most indulgent reader can find it tiresome.

For those who are unfamiliar with it, the *Morte Darthur* can seem purposeless in structure, full of splendid material – it is true – but full, also, of incidents of a far lower rank; knights we frankly care little for, adventures we yawn our way through. It is, after all, a vast book, and one in which it is extremely easy to get lost. The first task, therefore, of an introductory study of the *Morte Darthur* is simply to help the newcomer find his way through and around, with the conviction that the book is well worth the effort. There are those who – patronisingly – concede that the *Morte Darthur* is a treasure house of details but an indifferent whole, a book to be dipped into from time to time. Others, however, find it hard to dismiss a book which has such an undeniable impact. Without being blind to its faults, they think that those faults have perhaps been overstated somewhat if the *Morte Darthur* – alone of all medieval prose romances – has survived as a living book for five centuries. A popularity so extensive claims and merits our open-minded attention.

1

How to Read the Morte Darthur

The reasonable assumption that we should start reading the *Morte Darthur* at page one and continue to the end is perhaps not the best line of approach when turning to Malory for the first time. His book has, it is true, a beginning, a middle, and an end. It begins where we would expect and the ending is the ending we have probably all heard about, but there is simply far too much middle for the uninitiated reader to cope with. Before he can hope to reach a satisfactory reading of the *Morte Darthur*, the newcomer needs to know – in a very literal sense – how to read it.

Despite occasional superficial resemblances, the *Morte Darthur* is not a novel. It is as much an anthology as a long work of prose fiction, and the relationship of the parts to the whole is unlike that in many other books. As they stand, the various sections are arranged in what is no doubt the best reading order from a chronological point of view, but there is much to be said for not trying to read the *Morte Darthur* chronologically at all – especially for a newcomer. Its unity – is the *Morte Darthur* a single book at all? – is a much-debated issue and one we will need to glance at later (my remark that Malory's book has a beginning, a middle, and an end begs more questions than might be thought); for the moment it is sufficient to say that there are parts of the *Morte Darthur*, whole sections even, which the new reader could afford to overlook. As he rereads the book, he will begin to see the role these sections play, but, first time through, they may well detract his attention from larger issues. The traveller who is anxious about making a series of connexions and worrying whether he will ever reach his destination is in no mood to enjoy the scenery from the window of the train. The same is true if we travel in Malory's world. This does not merely involve the removal of curiosity and suspense; it entails the ready acceptance of a pace which may seem unusual to twentieth century readers. More than leisurely, it can appear rambling and inefficient.

One of the paradoxes of the *Morte Darthur* is that although in many ways its impact is unforgettable, much of the incidental narrative is –

quite frankly – extremely hard to remember. Attention has often been drawn to the inconsistencies of the book: a knight killed in battle in one section turns up none the worse for wear later on. But I would wager that no one except a scholar has ever noticed these inconsistencies while reading. It is hard enough trying to remember all the major events we have read about, let alone the fate that befell a few minor characters.

Nor is this merely the result of our undisciplined attention. As twentieth century readers we have acquired, whether we like it or not, habits which make us expect a strict sense of unity or relevance in a work of prose fiction. With Malory we must learn to shed these habits. His book is not a farrago of unnecessary incidents of debatable relevance (though even the most indulgent critic will admit that there are some); the nature of the book is entirely different.

The *Morte Darthur* is created splendidly in the image of the arbitrary adventures of the knights that people its pages. The book as a whole moves slowly and relentlessly forward but, like its knights, we are continually being sidetracked, re-routed and even de-routed. This is not because Malory is incompetent and cannot keep to the point, but because his book does not have quite the sort of narrative point we have come to expect. The *Morte Darthur* is dominated more by action than by consequence, more by story than by plot. What is happening is more urgent than what is going to happen *next*. Cause and effect are not absent from the book – they are, indeed, memorably present – but they are not all, and we must learn to curb our impatience. We will have taken our first step towards an understanding of the *Morte Darthur* when we realise that the road to Camelot is long and adventurous. If there were signposts along the way, the most frequent would no doubt be 'detour ahead'.

The newcomer to Malory, therefore, needs to be guided through the book, needs to be encouraged, if necessary, not to read from cover to cover – at least for the first time. It is only when we see where we are going, as we realise what the various parts contribute to the whole, that we can begin to find our way. Let us say that for twentieth century readers it is easier to read the *Morte Darthur* for the first time if we have already read it before. This impossibility is not mere nonsense, and I propose therefore to present the various sections of the *Morte Darthur* and guide the reader through them in an attempt to show their basic characteristics and the part they play in the book as a whole. This will inevitably involve a certain amount of narrative summary, but the summary is not intended (and I hope will not be taken) as a substitute for reading the *Morte Darthur* itself; rather it aims to provide the overall acquaintance one would acquire from a first reading in order to make what will in fact be a first reading more like a second.

Such a guide through Malory's Arthurian world will inevitably impose a simplification, will in many ways betray the spirit of the whole book. The *Morte Darthur* will appear perhaps clearer, smaller, more accessible, more tightly structured than it really is; less rambling but also less leisurely, less varied, rich, and inclusive. But few guidebooks can do justice to the infinite variety of the places they seek to recommend, and especially those written for first-time visitors with, perhaps, a limited amount of time at their disposal. A guidebook inevitably makes a city seem smaller than it really is, but the first-time visitor needs to be shown something of manageable proportions. As major landmarks are pointed out he can begin to appreciate the lay-out of the city and get the feel of the place as a whole. He will of course miss a lot, but there will always be time to see more – and more fully – on a return trip. And by that time he will have no need of someone to guide him at all.

Malory's book is indeed, not unlike a major city: not only because of its size and complexity, but also because it is multifaceted. A capital city has its elegant district, its student quarter, its commercial area, its Chinatown. There are districts even which correspond to no one's image of the city, and yet there they are. In the same way, Malory's book seems to change character as we move around in it. At times we are well and truly in the kingdom of romance, as in Book I, but then we pass into the world of epic and military chronicle (Book II). In Book III we are back in romance; in Book IV we enter the world of folktale; in Book VI Malory takes us into the world of religious mysticism and regrets he ever came; and in Book V, I am not sure that he knows (sometimes) where he is. But the guide, however many simplifications he is forced to impose *en route*, can at least hope to show the way around.

The Overall Structure

Malory's two most important editors – William Caxton and Professor Vinaver – have had a great influence on the physical appearance of the *Morte Darthur*, which varies considerably according to the edition we use. In 1485, Caxton published a single work, which has come to be known as *Le Morte Darthur*, divided into twenty-one sections or books, and subdivided into chapters. In 1947, Vinaver, working with a recently discovered manuscript of Malory's book (the only one that has survived), was convinced that what Malory had written was not one book but eight, and produced an edition of the seperate tales, which he published (together) as the collected works of Sir Thomas Malory. How Malory himself would have organised his work for presentation – if the matter ever crossed his mind – is something we do now know, and we are obliged to use these (now) traditional divisions in order to refer to Malory's text. What we can say, however, is that the *Morte Darthur* itself – however it is presented in print – has a clear overall structure.

Malory tells the story of the rise and fall of Arthur's kingdom. The establishing of the king's authority at home and abroad and the founding of the Round Table community with its code of chivalry represent the upward movement of the wheel of fortune, a familiar medieval image referred to several times in the *Morte Darthur*. This section corresponds to Vinaver's Books I and II, Caxton's Books I to V. The age of glory of Arthurian chivalry, the period when the wheel seems motionless because at its height, is the middle section of the *Morte Darthur* (Books III to V, Caxton Books VI to XII), and the steady downward movement comes as loyalties become divided and private rancour leads to public strife (Books VI to VIII, Caxton Books XIII to XXI).

This overall structure seems straightforward enough but it cannot, of course, account for everything the *Morte Darthur* contains. It is to be borne in mind as the ultimate, but not necessarily the immediate, justification for the various parts of the narrative, which are often best appreciated for themselves. The *Morte Darthur* is a vast book in which Malory sought not to prove any precise point but to record faithfully the life and events of a certain world now vanished. It is as rich as life and, like life, its incidents do not necessarily lead anywhere. Indeed, such is the richness of incident in the *Morte Darthur* that however much the newcomer bears in mind the overall pattern, the complexity of the moment can be so bewildering that he easily gets swamped. A closer look at the different parts of the whole might be useful. Some of the shorter books are fairly straightforward and require no more than a few preliminary remarks; the longer ones need a little more attention. The presentation of Book I (Caxton I to IV) will give me the opportunity of mentioning a number of general points.

Most studies of Malory use the standard edition of the *Morte Darthur* edited by Professor Vinaver, and therefore follow the divisions (I to VIII) he proposed. This does not imply by any means that everyone agrees with his theory of eight separate books, and most people happily continue to refer to one work called the *Morte Darthur*, divided into eight books, a diplomatic compromise between Vinaver's arrangement and Caxton's. For convenience, I shall use Vinaver's divisions and all quotations will be taken from his one-volume Oxford text (second edition 1977) called *Works*. References will be given by page and line number, but I will also quote the Caxton book and chapter numbers, which, although they are less precise, will enable readers with other editions to trace the passages I quote.

PART ONE: THE RISE OF ARTHUR'S KINGDOM

The *Morte Darthur* begins by focusing our attention on Arthur. That it should do so seems natural for us, but this is not where the Arthurian legends themselves begin. Malory has stripped away all the early material, but since it is his version that has influenced English culture for the last five hundred years, most of us are unaware of the originality of his approach. His centre of attention is defined at once and modern readers feel instantly at home: this is where we expected it all to begin.

BOOK I.

THE EARLY PHASE: WAR AND PEACE

The opening pages of the *Morte Darthur* relate briefly the circumstances leading to the conception and birth of Arthur. Igrayne, the virtuous Duchess of Cornwall, rejects the unlawful advances of King Uther, who is ready to jeopardise the peace of his realm for a beautiful woman, and with her husband secretly hastens from court. Uther's frustration brings him to his sick bed, and Merlin, the king's wizard counsellor, is contacted to find a solution to the situation. Merlin has the means of (and no qualms about) arranging access to the lady's bed and agrees to do so on condition that the child conceived there be, in due time, handed over into his safe keeping. The king readily agrees to this singular condition at which not an eyelid is batted. Since the Duchess's husband happens to be killed a matter of hours before Uther and Igrayne come to bed, there is nothing to prevent their later healing the political strife by marrying and hence assuring that their child, though conceived out of, is born in wedlock. Arthur is duly born, delivered over to Merlin, and brought up by Sir Ector. The opening pages of Malory's book get straight down to business, and we soon reach an event which must, in some form or other, be familiar to most readers: the sword in the stone.

Uther dies, anarchy reigns as various barons vie for the throne, and, on the advice of Merlin, the Archbishop of Canterbury summons the nobility of the land. There appears – it is as simple as that – a block of stone with a sword stuck in it: whoever can remove the sword from the stone will be king. The strongest in the land fail; the boy Arthur, innocently trying to provide his stepbrother with a sword (he finds the doors shut when he returns home to collect one they had forgotten) alone succeeds, accidently at first, then repeatedly with intent. The *Morte Darthur* is off to a good start.

The narrative is brief, clear, and straightforward, and we are eager for more.

The Romance World

But these early pages are not merely giving us a digest of the biography of a royal prince; we are being clearly introduced to the Arthurian world itself. And for the reader, getting the feel of this world is perhaps as important as being able to remember all the facts. From the beginning Malory presents many of the themes and much of the atmosphere that we will encounter throughout the *Morte Darthur*. However much of a problem reading the whole of his book might be, few readers find the opening a trouble. We are led swiftly and willingly into the world of romance.

It is a world we recognise at once, a world of mystery and unexplained meanings. We are constantly given the impression that events have a significance even though that significence is not always (perhaps cannot be) expounded. We never quite learn who Merlin is and what are the limits of his power. He begins his career by playing pander to the king's unlawful lusts, and yet at the same time, he is using those lusts to take charge of the wider-reaching destinies of the land. Why does Merlin have to confiscate Arthur when Uther and Igrayne are happily married at the time of the birth? In the broader scheme of events we can suppose that Merlin foresaw the early death of Uther and realises (as Malory's readers in the last quarter of the fifteenth century would) the danger young princes were in with ambitious lords in the realm. Merlin, that is, is safeguarding the royal line.

Or is he more specifically safeguarding Arthur, whose conception he knew about and even orchestrated? Without Merlin there would be no Arthur. Before the child is conceived, Igrayne's husband is killed, so that Arthur, contrary to the plan as Uther imagined it, is not a child of adultery. Is the Duke's death a mere coincidence, an integral part of Merlin's plan, or part of a more far-reaching pattern of providence or destiny? For certainly the legitimacy of Arthur's claim to the throne is a vital element. And is Igrayne aware of these things too? She is, we are told, wise, but is her silence when she realises that she has slept with someone other than her husband the practical expression of a prudent policy of 'least said soonest mended', or is she aware of the larger issues involved?

We do not know the meaning of things, but as we read we constantly feel that there is a meaning. Throughout the *Morte Darthur* we will see that Malory insists on the historicity of the Arthurian world: his knights are not mere knights of legend, they fought historical battles and took part in events in places he can specifically name. But Malory would never claim that the Arthurian world was totally like ours. It was not so impoverished; it was a world of heightened significance.

It is also a world with a law and logic of its own, not one which can be analysed according to the reasoning or morality of our modern age. Few of us would have much confidence in a king who was ready to hand over a royal infant in order to satisfy his sexual desire (and we would no doubt raise an eyebrow over his readiness to swear on the gospels to keep his part of the bargain in this adulterous scheme). But no one in Malory questions the king's wisdom or sanity – nor his morals for going after Igrayne in the first place. He says he will agree with Merlin's plan if the demands are not unreasonable, and when Merlin asks for the child to be handed over, no one sees anything unreasonable in the request. And when the time comes to hand Arthur over, no one tries to go back on their promise. Uther does not say: 'O come now Merlin, you weren't being serious', and Igrayne, unaware of the initial bargain, hands over her royal issue without a qualm. The madness of the situation is an integral part of the sense of meaning contained in the narrative. The bed trick does not fit any of the categories of our narrow morality (any more than it does later, at the conception through similar methods of another child of destiny: Galahad), and because the court pander is in control of the fortunes of the realm, it seems perfectly appropriate that the Archbishop of Canterbury should work on his advice.

The Arthurian world is one which is fraught with a sense of meaning but for which we are rarely offered an explanation. We are told how things happen, but never why, as though the reasons were self evident. So, Arthur was brought up in safety, but the ignorance of him which assured his survival – no one knew there was an heir to kill – is the basic obstacle to the throne. Evidence is needed not only to prove his claim, but to show that a claim exists, and the sword in the stone provides the evidence. Why it should, we are never told, for there is no logical link between drawing swords from stones and inheriting royal titles, but it remains a powerful image: Arthur's right to the throne is beyond question. None of his other qualities has any relevance: it is not because he is the strongest, the boldest, the most virtuous, or the all-round best that he succeeds, for he is not, and he will not succeed in similar tests later. Nor do we feel it is an initiation rite, a test of his manhood, since all the men fail where he alone succeeds. The sword in the stone proves what would not have needed proof if his life had not needed safeguarding, quite simply, who his father was, and therefore his kingship. Arthur is a man born to be king, and the sword is an image of his destiny – as it will be with Balin a little later, and with Galahad towards the end of the Morte Darthur. They too draw swords and gain access to their fate.

When Arthur has succeeded (and everyone else failed) in drawing the sword on successive feast days and his kingship is finally recognised, the new monarch, forgiving, because he understands, his people's reluctance to accept him, organises a great celebration. But not everyone is willing to admit his claim to such an important throne, and the kings of a number of surrounding realms decide to wage war. The rest of Book I therefore describes the series of wars by which Arthur imposes his authority on his neighbours, with the help of wise counsel and loyal support, and, once peace has been achieved, the first adventures of the new kingdom, those of Balin, Torre, Pellinor, Gawain, Ywain, Marhalt, and Arthur himself. All this seems reasonable enough, and yet the newcomer soon grows uneasy: only too speedily he finds that Malory's treatment of the wars is often a wearisome catalogue of military events, a far cry from the romance world he thought he had entered, and the following adventures, though pleasant enough, are inconsequential to the extreme. The first knight we meet – Balin – dies at the end of his story. Neither the martial spirit nor the aimlessness is quite what we bargained for.

We should bear in mind two things: the adventures represent the ideal of behaviour which in peace time forms the basis of this world. A Knight must ride in search of action. Secondly, the chronicle-like presentation of war is a reminder that for Malory the story he is telling is firmly rooted in history.

Historical Record

Important deeds need recording. However far-fetched the deed may appear to us – with the arrival on English soil of the Saracens for example – we are none the less dealing with a world of historical import. The reality of events (albeit heightened) is one of Malory's great concerns and not only does Merlin, the wizard-counsellor, oversee events in the land, he is also the one in charge of recording great deeds. With Bloyse, his master, he sees a broader context of historic destiny. Who took part or lost his life in which encounter is of vital importance for the record, however dreary it may be to our half-hearted interest. There is much to give pleasure in the pages of the *Morte Darthur* – and Malory would be glad to hear us say so – but as court historian he has another job to do also. He cannot pander to our lighter tastes all the time; he writes for our instruction as well as our pleasure.

Book I documents, therefore, a number of important incidents in the early history of Arthur's reign: the young king's wedding to an exceptional princess, and her not inconsiderable dowry, the Round Table; and the providing of Arthur's magic sword, Excalibur, in circumstances of haunting beauty. And it is because Malory is aware that the events he is describing are part of a clearly defined whole that he regularly refers ahead to future incidents, things we have not as yet read about, but which we have probably heard of, things which therefore help to give solidity and a context to the beginnings of the story: Arthur's death and his punishment for the incestuous begetting of Mordred; Lancelot's love for Guenevere, who is therefore an unwise choice for a royal bride; references to Lamorak, Perceval, Lancelot, Tristram, King Mark, and the Grail. Even if the references mean little to us, they give the impression that the events Malory is relating are indeed the beginnings of something important. As yet we may not quite know where we are going, but we know we are going somewhere: the sense of movement forward, within a clear framework, is important.

Modern readers, however, frequently lose patience with Malory's historical bent, and in particular with his battle descriptions. He tends to go into repetitive detail and is only too ready to swamp us with lists of names, victims or participants. This is an essential aspect of the attempt to give a semblance of an authentic historical record, but it is something of a problem for the reader. Malory the military historian inevitably gives detailed accounts of battles, but the reader cannot be expected to appreciate them as anything else. Lists, after all, make rather poor literature. And yet if we fail to recognise the importance of the lists, we miss an essential aspect of Malory's point of view.

Our impatience, of course, is an expression of our lack of sympathy for the military ideal. Malory writes – let us say – like a retired colonel in a London club, endlessly reliving battles over brandy and cigars (one suspects that Malory's fighting days were over too). The general outline of a campaign will not do; there is no question of giving a few details to brush in the essentials before going on to more important things. Malory's approach is similar. He is not wasting our time with the battles, he is relishing them. His descriptions are the blow by blow account of the passionate sportsman.

The battles and lists are a vital part of the military historian's art. Great deeds cannot remain unspoken, for the greatness of Arthur's kingdom resides here. Furthermore, a list is even more than a record, it is a testimonial, a measure of the greatness of the events being described. To say that thirty knights were killed in battle is one thing; to tell us who those knights were specifies the horror of the massacre. To say that Guenevere was abducted while in the company of ten Maying knights (as she is in Book VII) does not fully describe the situation. But when we realise that those knights were not the inexperienced young men who usually rode with the queen, but were Sir Pelleas, Sir Kay, Sir Ozanna le Cure Hardy, etc., we see how threatening the situation was, and how obsessed with his project her kidnapper must have been to mount such a major operation. His outnumbering the Queen's men is not merely a sign of his cowardice, it shows the lengths to which he had to go. If Sir Pelleas, Sir Kay, Sir Ozanna le Cure Hardy, etc., failed to save her, who could have succeeded? No one could possibly criticise palace security.

Those of us who are not battle enthusiasts inevitably find Malory's lists something of a trial, but it is not hard to understand how he saw them, especially if we consider tournaments of another kind. A sports report of Wimbledon which gave no more than the name of the champion would be worthless for the tennis fan. He wants to know who played whom in the final, and the score. And the players the finalists beat on their way to the last round (with scores and details of the match) are also vital. It is impossible to gauge the glory of the man who wins if we know nothing of the men who lose.

Malory's lists work in exactly the same way. They are not only historical records, they are a precise measure of the author's scale of values. If they were removed not only would the *Morte Darthur* have less of a semblance of historical authenticity, but the edge would be taken off the point Malory is making. It does not matter if some of the names mean little to us – perhaps some of them meant little to a medieval audience – the fact that names are listed at all inevitably makes an impact.

Lists are important in the *Morte Darthur* because names themselves are important. Since a knight's life is devoted to seeking adventures to perform so that his name will be associated with glorious deeds, identity and reputation are closely linked. The knight who conceals his identity is therefore in danger of appearing suspect. Words addressed to Merlin (in a category of his own, of course) reveal the attitude: 'Hit ys evyll sygne . . . that thou arte a trew man, that thou wolt nat telle thy name' (46.10–11; II.8). Knights frequently go about in disguise – a dangerous game to play because it can lead to trouble – and voluntarily set up a difference between who they are and who they appear to be. This inevitably gives them a certain superiority over others, whom they can identify without being recognised. The ability to name someone gives you a certain advantage, even authority, over him, as Lancelot sees, in Book III when he helps a lady because she knows his name (169.33; VI.16). When a knight reveals his name he confides himself, puts himself at the mercy of the other, lays himself open, perhaps, to attack, or guarantees his safety. There is a certain logic to all this in a world where soldiers wear armour. The device on one's armour is a statement of one's name because the armour itself conceals one's identity. But armour too can be disguised; nor can a knight hope to recognise every device. Throughout the *Morte Darthur*, then, knights are asked to reveal their names. It is inevitable, for a name leads an individual towards his fate, and especially in the context of rivalry, combat, war, or adventure. A name is a password or a provocation, a part of the delicate balance of power.

Adventure

The earliest adventures of the Arthurian knights are described as taking place within this initial period when Arthur was consolidating his kingdom. They are important as representative episodes revealing the code which is the basis of the Arthurian ideal. Knights are devoted to adventure, to seeking the events that fortune will bring. They put themselves at the mercy of chance: their lives are dedicated to risk not prudent domesticity, for their readiness to face the unknown means flaunting prudence. Their devotion to action is so total that they appear at times wilful and unreasonable. Naive too, since a knight gives himself wholeheartedly and instantly to the cause. We might wish to cross-examine some of the distressed damsels who come in search of aid a little more thoroughly before abandoning everything merely to recuperate a lost dog, but such niggling is unworthy of a knight. Action not interrogation becomes him; 'he sayth but lytil, but he doth much more' (80.43; IV.5) is the spirit.

The story of Balin is a clear example of the impetuous devotion to adventure. Balin draws a sword destined for the knight most clearly 'withoute velony other trechory and withoute treson' (38.20–21; II.1) and sets out to seek his fate, refusing to surrender the sword even when he is told that he will kill the man he loves most with it. Catastrophe dogs Balin all the way until in the end he kills (and is killed by) his own brother, his dearest friend. The story ends in death and, in itself, therefore, leads nowhere (Balin's sword, however, is kept by Merlin for 'Launcelot other ellis Galahad, hys sonne' (58.26; II.19) and Malory, by referring to events yet to come, connects the theme of Balin's story with later developments). But the story of Balin shows us, at the very beginning of the *Morte Darthur*, the importance of the notion of adventure. Reason and prudence are not as essential as an unquestioning devotion to action. When warned of the danger involved if he keeps the sword, Balin does not ask for a few hours to think it over; without hesitation he replies: 'I shall take the aventure . . . that God woll ordayne for me' (40.3–4; II.2). When towards the end of the *Morte Darthur*, Lancelot uses the same words to Guenevere, Malory is echoing not Balin's words but the important concept of which the Balin story was the first example (cf. 622.27–28; XVIII.9). The reader who feels that these early adventures are not leading anywhere should realise – as he enjoys them for themselves – that they are in fact leading us to a clear appreciation of the Arthurian ethic.

The same is true of the series of aventures centred on Gawain, Torre, Pellinor, Yvain, and Marhalt. The new reader may find them, however pleasant, rather unsettling because they seem to lead nowhere. In fact they show clearly that adventure is in itself the *raison d'être* of the kingdom at peace. Each of the knights is in the service of a lady and the patterned nature of their adventures (two sets of three; Gawain being in each) seems to be highlighting a significance which never becomes apparent – except that knightly endeavour in the service of ladies is in itself important. Each individual adventure may seem inconsequential (the detail we are given at 109.9–10; IV.28 takes some beating: 'And sir Marhalte and sir Uwayne brought their damesels with hem, but sir Gawayne had loste his damesel.'), but what it illustrates is the very basis of knightly chivalry, the oath which Arthur makes his knights swear each Pentecost:

> never to do outerage nothir mourthir, and allwayes to fle treson, and to gyff mercy unto hym that askith mercy, upon payne of forfiture of their worship and lordship of kynge Arthure for evirmore; and allwayes to do ladyes, damesels, and jantilwomen and wydowes socour; strengthe hem in hir ryghtes, and never to enforce them, uppon payne of dethe. Also, that no man take no batayles in a wrongefull quarell for no love ne for no worldis goodis
>
> (75.38–44; III.15)

The oath comes as a conclusion to the first set of adventures; it is the basis of the second and, indeed, of the rest of the *Morte Darthur*. We shall need to return to it.

Continuations and Beginnings

Book I, then, while presenting the birth and consolidation of the Arthurian kingdom, presents – through examples – the concepts which are important for an understanding of the kingdom. That Malory sees the beginnings in the light of a continuation can be seen in his regular references ahead to characters and incidents which are (to varying degrees) common knowledge and which help provide a context. The wider implicatons are also clear in that from the beginning Malory draws attention to the factors which will eventually destroy – internal rivalry and ill-will. Danger is in the background from the start; this is (and will remain) a world where jealousy is rife. One knight's success provokes resentment among the others. 'Many knyghtes had grete despite at' Balin (39.36; II.2) when unas-

suming though he looked, he was able to draw the sword; and Bagdema-
gus, whose son Meliagaunt is to cause much trouble later, is furious when
Torre is elected to the Round Table rather than himself (80.35 ff.; IV.5).
More importantly, it is in Book I that we meet the villainess of the piece,
the murderous and lecherous Morgan le Fay, with her machinations and
devious ways, using and abusing everyone, profiting from her position as
Arthur's half-sister, and endlessly trying to sow the seeds of discord. She
is a fascinating character whose every appearance enlivens the narrative
and whom, infuriatingly, no one seems capable of taking in hand. Constantly exploiting everyone else's virtue and totally devoid of virtue herself, it is at once a measure of the generosity and the weakness of the
realm that Arthurian courtesy can extend to her.

Book I also introduces us to a character whose villainy will be more disruptive because it is less blantant, more dangerous because it is much
nearer to honour, for he plays the honourable game: Gawain. His adventures show him failing in the key points of chivalry, and though this may
not attract the reader's attention at the beginning of the book, in the overall structure of the *Morte Darthur* it has a greater force. The reader should
keep an eye out for Gawain. In his second set of adventures, during which
we are introduced to the agreeable character Sir Pelleas, Gawain's shoddiness of behaviour is evident: he is a calculating lecher. Most important of
all, when King Pellinor joins the Round Table, Gawain is envious and
says: 'Yondir knyght ys putte to grete worship, whych grevith me sore, for
he slewe oure fadir kynge Lott. Therefore I woll sle hym . . . with a swerde
that was sette me that ys passynge trencheaunte' (63.9–12; III.4). Gawain is
a complex figure, a valiant knight of great achievement, who can be both
magnanimous and diplomatic, but he can also be a troublemaker and it is
worth pointing out that he starts his career in the *Morte Darthur* as he fin-
ishes it, seeking family vengeance.

We are introduced to some important characters, but Book I remains
Arthur's book, a book about kingship. He is the rightful heir and as such
the only one able unite the kingdom beneath him, for it is impossible to resist a true king. And a true king must have a queen of course, fittingly a
woman of exceptional beauty, who plays an essential part in the unification of the realm (hence the irony of her later guilt), because it is she who
brings the Round Table as her dowry.

Till the kingdom is established, however, there is somthing almost
primitive about the Arthurian world. Arthur is a chieftain (the word is
used of him only in this part of the book) with a serious task of unification
to undertake. He fights alongside his men and asks them to take no risks
he is not willing to take himself. He is appreciated for his democratic notion of kingship (36.23–25; I.25) not admired as a monarch presiding over
the elegances of his court. This is not a realm in which the queen gives pri-

vate dinner parties for her husband's knights or goes out Maying with them (as she does later), it is a harsher world where the king, Herod-like, resorts to slaying infant males to avoid the destiny which is the price of his sin. It is a world where strange forces are at work and where military strategy is in the hands not of a battle-tried warrior but of a wizard. Arthur remains down- to-earth enough to appreciate the arrival of reinforcements, in spite of all Merlin's power (12.25–27; I.9), but victory seems none the less to depend on supernatural aid. Later, these dark forces will disappear from the *Morte Darthur*. Once Merlin is dismissed the rest of the work is less overtly magical, even though Merlin's early presence has already conditioned our response. And when the Arthurian kingdom no longer needs to rely on supernatural aid, when it has strength of its own, we feel that there are still forces present somewhere, hidden away perhaps, but ready, if ever they were needed – as at the very end when the queens come to take Arthur off to Avalon.

A Note on Magic

The haunting image of Arthur's departure with the queens reminds us that some of the most powerful scenes in the *Morte Darthur*, those that have captured the imagination of thousands, are concerned with magic: the sword in the stone, or the other sword, taken from (and returned to) the waters. And yet readers of the *Morte Darthur* must soon get used to the fact that the realm of magic is one in which Malory shows little interest. Magical events occur, it is true, right until the end, but after Book I they do so infrequently (and are perhaps all the more evocative for that).

More typical is the way that Malory contains his magic. He writes about a kingdom far superior to the one we know, and we should not be surprised if incidents at times go beyond the limits of our personal experience. Magical events, that is, are little more than a reflexion of the fact that everyday occurrences in Camelot were a shade less everyday than now, and consequently Malory somehow takes it all for granted. It is for this reason that he can do without Merlin's services once the kingdom is established. There are occasional references back to Merlin's providential guidance later in the *Morte Darthur*, but his active presence is dispensed with scarcely before the *Morte Darthur* gets under way. His mischievous wizardry does not appeal to Malory; the author is much happier when Merlin's advice is a judicious mixture of common sense and prediction, the fruit of a wider and wiser vision of human destiny.

Of course, the magic remains: spells and enchantments; magic horns and invisible knights; and miraculous healings which can be the result of mysterious skills – as in the Gareth story – or of spiritual virtue – as in the Urry episode of Book VII. But then the *Morte Darthur* splendidly confuses the religious and the profane; we are not always sure whether the supernatural soliciting is ill or good. The Archbishop of Canterbury works on Merlin's orders and Morgan le Fay learnt her sorcery, we are told, in a nunnery!

But more central and more pervasive than the magical devices is the atmosphere of hidden significance which pervades the book. When he receives Excalibur, for example, Arthur is asked whether he likes the sword or its scabbard best (36.9 ff.; I.25). The strangeness of the question might well have given Arthur a hint as to the answer expected of him, but with soldierly unsubtlety he expresses a natural preferance for the sword. He is wrong to do so however, for the scabbard can provide even greater protection. Why this should be so we do not know; it defies all logic and, ultimately, the unexplained superiority of the scabbard provokes as great a sense of wonder as the magic sword itself. What sort of a world is this? There are doors, we feel, which would give access to other realms if only we could find the key. But we never can.

The Logic of Adventure

The *Morte Darthur* is full of deeds but singularly lacking in explanation, analysis, and opinion. Malory offers few comments of his own because action is at the centre of his book not interpretation. His duty is to record not to explain or justify and it is for this reason that no attempt is made to reconcile the logic of the Arthurian world with that of our own. We might enquire why a deed needs to be done, help granted, or a quest undertaken, but in Malory's world any pretext is good enough if an adventure is in the offing.

It is a knight's duty to seek adventure. The ideal life of chivalry is eventful; something is always happening; there is never a dull moment. Hence the Grail quest later is something of a bore for Gawain because there are no adventures to be found (a sign, he does not realise, of his own sinful state). When a knight rides off to see what life has to offer in the way of incident, he is devoting himself to what turns up, to chance, and, inevitably, to risk. A life given over to adventure is, of necessity, given over to chance: something that happens 'by adventure' happens by chance.

The chivalric life is essentially active. A knight cannot sit around waiting for something to turn up – there can be no Sir Micawber in Camelot – he must go out looking for adventure. And since chance can be fortunate or not, looking for adventure is often the same as looking for trouble. Much of the woe Malory's knights suffer they bring upon themselves; but then action is more important than circumspection. Let sleeping dogs lie is a proverb which never reached Camelot.

Adventure is the knight's duty, an obligation stronger than any logic. When Balin is warned of the danger ahead, without the slightest hesitation he declares himself adamant: he is ready to take the adventure anyone in his right mind would have been only too glad to jettison. But there can be no reason here. The nearest we get to an explanation of why something was or should be done is 'for the custom was such that time' – the unanswerable non- explanation, the simple reminder that no justification will be given, that in this world logic and reason are banished. Adventure, chance, and risk are reasons unto themselves. They are all that counts in this closed world with rules of its own in which no one is ever heard to ask the question why – except Dinadan, whom we will meet in Book V.

To modern readers, of course, it is a mad world, and the folly of Arthurian chivalry is an easy butt for our irreverence. There are all those distressed damsels loitering in forests ready to pester the first knight who rides by with the most unreasonable request. None of the knights dreams of compromising his gallantry by even hesitating to help, and as they ride off having immediately and unquestioningly taken the adventure, none of them seems to be wondering what a nice girl like that was actually doing in the forest alone. It would have been rather caddish after all to ask if she was carrying any ID.

Knights themselves can be just as unreasonable. Some of them arrive at court and without the slightest explanation or introduction request a boon. The requests are at times no more than odd, more of a nuisance than anything else, like Gareth's request for board and lodge for a year in Book IV; others are singular, to say the least. Palomides, taking advantage of a favour he was promised at the Cornish court, promptly declares he intends to take Isolde away with him (264.21 ff.; VIII.30). Sheer madness of course, but the consequent need to rescue the queen is a first rate adventure.

There are times when a request is made and the proviso 'if it is reasonable' is at least mentioned, but this is mere bluff, no more than a formality. There is no reason to believe that a glimmer of sanity is creeping in. No one would sacrifice an adventure to mere reason, and when we recall that handing over the heir to the throne strikes no one as unreasonable, we see that the proviso has little meaning at all. The requests system can have no logic; it exists merely to open the door to adventure. In the *Morte Darthur*, logic and adventure are incompatible terms.

Knights regularly challenge others for no reason at all. Occasionally they recall that it is improper to fight other Round Table knights – occasionally, but not always. They are even ready to wake a sleeping knight to fight with him, often only to be beaten. Serves them right, we feel, but there can be no regrets for them. It is part of the constant rough and tumble of adventure, and they have no time to weigh up the pros and cons of a situation if it promises action. Theirs not to reason why, theirs but to do and – if, by adventure, things turn out badly – die.

BOOK II
THE ROMAN CAMPAIGN: WAR AND WORSHIP

The second main division of Malory's book, and the final stage in the rise of Arthur's kingdom, is important from three points of view: it establishes Arthur's reputation abroad; it gives scope for military achievment in active combat; and it lays emphasis on the (for us pseudo-) historical career of the king. It is a section of the *Morte Darthur* the newcomer might well prefer to postpone to a later reading.

Alternatively, he might care to browse through it for a while and see how its epic spirit and alliterative style are unlike the rest of Malory's book. It is a section which has few admirers and although I think that, for all its singularity, it serves a clear purpose, the uninitiated reader is likely to find this world of rousing military endeavour, described with strange vocabulary and thumping rhythms somewhat tiresome. There will be time to come back to it later. When we see how it fits into the whole, it may even begin to have a certain rugged appeal and colour our general impression of Arthur as a king. For the moment it is perhaps sufficient to indicate the part it plays in the overall structure.

There is a gap of some years between the events of Book I and those of Book II: the young knights of Book I now have sons of fighting age, while the young knights of Book II like Lancelot, were babes in arms back in Book I. Messengers arrive demanding that Arthur acknowledge the Emperor of Rome as overlord by paying tribute to him. Arthur takes umbrage, learns from the chronicles that he has a right to the Imperial title, settles matters at home, and crosses into Europe determined to assert himself and his claim. After fighting foes both human and superhuman, he is crowned Emperor by the Pope, distributes rewards to his men and returns to England supreme:

For his myght and prowesse is most to be doubted seen the noble kynges and grete multytude of knyghtes of the round table to whome none erthely prynce may compare.

(Caxton only, V.8)

To establish this is evidently the purpose of Book II. It is not sufficient that Arthur should have asserted his authority over local rivals and worked out an efficient domestic policy. No hero can remain a big fish in a little pool and for Arthur's kingship to have any meaning he must earn an international reputation. It will not do to be famed only for courtesy and nobility; Arthur must make it known that he is not to be meddled with.

For a soldier there is an obvious link between reputation and active combat. No one can make a career out of war games; even today you can show great promise out on manoeuvres, but you are not likely to win many medals there. Since Arthur has (in Book I) established peace and order at home, he has robbed his knights of the best opportunity of increasing their honour. A foreign campaign is, therefore, ideal and Sir Cador of Cornwall expresses what provides the matter and the motto for Book II when the Emperor's message arrives: 'The lettyrs of Lucius the Emperoure lykis me well, for now shall we have warre and worshyp' (114.12–13; not in Caxton). What Malory calls worship is what we call honour, and it is an important notion throughout the Morte Darthur. A knight's first duty is to be 'besy and aboute to wyn worshyp' (695.18–19; XX.15), that is, to win a reputation, to make a name for himself. We will need to come back to this more than once.

Book II takes a more overtly military interest in Arthur's career. His men are itching to fight 'for som of hem fought nat their fylle of all this fyve wyntyr' (141.6–7; not in Caxton). Most modern readers tend to find Book II dreary business, but Malory seems to take an evident soldier's delight in narrating events and he reveals his wholehearted authorial commitment to the English cause by a number of references to 'oure knyghtes', 'oure noble knyghtes of mery Ingelonde' (125.7–8; not in Caxton).

A hero of romance can measure up to giants and fight fictitious foes, but a king of England also takes part in historical battles fought in real places that a historian can name, and earns titles we have all heard about. Book II is important in that it continues along the lines of certain parts of Book I in asserting the historicity of Arthur. The Roman campaign owes much to the epic in spirit but also to the chronicle, and although modern readers might object, with C. S. Lewis, that we have no more than 'vast contradictions of known history scrawled across a whole continent', in many ways this is no more than modern impatience. For right or wrong, the pseudo-history gives a historical turn; it may invite contradiction but it none the less colours our response.

The Arthur of romance becomes therefore a historical king with a historical claim to the title he sets off to conquer. And his campain is described with a fine eye for the details of a genuine war. The king does not merely rush off to Rome in a surge of literary enthusiasm; his counsellors offer military solidarity in precise terms: they say how many soldiers they can provide and who will be paying their wages.

The army is made up of soldiers who need to be fed (136.20 ff.; V.9), because this is no longer play but the brutal business of warfare. The violence is the violence of real battle, and although the numbers of dead are somewhat overstated, as is characteristic of traditional literature, we must not take Malory to task. These battles were exceptionally bloody because they were exceptional battles. Numerical exaggeration was also a common habit among genuine historians at that time, and we must not forget that Malory is writing about a world of heightened significance. No one is shocked at massive shaughter, which not only measures the extent of one's victory but also the rightness of one's cause: in Book I, when thirty thousand of the enemy are massacred, Arthur 'kneled downe and thanked God mekely' (79.34–35; IV.3).

The Roman campaign is not just an ordinary war, not just a battle between two equally arrogant rulers as Arthur's dream, as he crosses the channel, suggests. As the rest of the known world joins forces with Lucius, the combat becomes that of a contest between David and Goliath, and right is clearly on the side of Arthur. The Emperor's army, 'all hys horryble peple' (117.19; not in Caxton), clearly come to represent the forces of evil, and when we learn that they are taking advantage of the services of giants, we realise not that the narrative is overstepping the bounds of reality, but to what extent we are stepping outside the world of military honour. Arthur's cause seems all the more justified as we see him fighting against the forces of barbarism. Just as he has brought peace, order, and justice to England, so too he must establish his influence over Europe. Arthurian foreign policy is not merely a question of conquest and colonisation, but a process of liberating and civilising, the ethics of the Arthurian code radiating outward. Arthur's single-handed victory over the giant of St Michael's Mount, who ravishes women and devours children, does not merely make him the heroic giant-slayer; far more is involved. The giant is a personification of everything the Pentecostal oath sets out to eradicate.

The motives of the war remain, of course, subservient to the war itself and Book II puts the emphasis firmly on the excitement of military action. What may make it unpalatable to literary intellectuals obviously constituted its essential charm for Malory. During the war a number of knights distinguish themselves, including Gawain and the newly knighted Lancelot. Lancelot is mentioned several times and singled out for praise to prepare for future developments, but no one knight steals the limelight as yet. Book II remains Arthur's book and Arthur's victory; the king is still the centre of attention.

The epic spirit of military bombast is not to everyone's taste and the version of the *Morte Darthur* Caxton published in 1485 contains only a summary of the tale (hence the absence of certain quotations above). In the version printed by Caxton the language of the original is greatly standardised and the material severely abridged. It is less barbaric, less vivid, and more formal. Whatever its merits, the shorter version also reveals a trace of boredom. The new reader might prefer the abridged version or, quite simply, cut his losses, leave Book II for later, and go straight on to Book III.

PART TWO: THE GLORY OF ARTHUR'S KINGDOM

In the long middle section of the *Morte Darthur* (Books III to V, Caxton's Books VI to XII), Malory shows us the practical aspects of ideal chivalry as he records the deeds and adventures of the golden age of the Arthurian fellowship. Our attention is taken from Arthur, whose preeminence has now been fully established, and whose court has become, therefore, a point of reference, the place where adventures begin and (rightly) end. Any society is only as great as its individual members, and the exploits of the leading knights are at once a testimony to their personal merit and a reflexion of the glory of the community to which they belong. Malory records the deeds of Lancelot, Gareth, Tristram, Lamorak, Palomides, and others, and though the book he devotes to Lancelot is the shortest of the tales, it soon becomes evident that Lancelot is the best knight of them all. The middle section of the *Morte Darthur* begins and ends with adventures specifically devoted to Lancelot, but he is present in the background throughout. Lancelot is the one who knights Gareth and is dearer to him than his own brothers; and Lancelot is the one whose company and approval Tristram constantly seeks. In knighthood and achievement he is a regular point of comparison, a sourse of inspiration to them all, the knight whose friendship they all strive for and whom they wish to emulate – although his preeminence can also arouse jealousy and resentment.

The Arthurian world is at its height but it is never perfect. The seeds of destruction remain within, not only because of the rivalries which inevitably result from the competitive spirit of knightly achievement (it is not always fellow-feeling which animates this fellowship of knights), but also because the chivalric and amatory adventures of one knight can be an offence to the family honour of another. They can even, in theory, be an offence to the community as a whole, and essential to the glory of Lancelot is (as we all know) his devotion to the queen. When this perfectly proper and admirable attachment oversteps the bounds of public allegiance through private devotion, Lancelot, the strongest link in the social chain, becomes the most vulnerable, the symbol of perfect loyalty and disloyalty at the same time. At the end of the middle section it is Lancelot's love for Guenevere which leads him (mistakenly and under enchantment) into the bed of another lady, who conceives Galahad, the perfect knight, the image both of his father's perfection and vulnerability, who will achieve what his father can no longer attain.

The middle section of the *Morte Darthur* is extremely long and, towards the end, in the Tristram book, varies a great deal in quality and relevance. Certain adventures are so loosely connected and dealt with in such summary fashion that their inclusion is hard to justify at all. Some arouse no more than a modicum of interest even in the most indulgent reader. What it is important to bear in mind is that collectively the adventures of the middle section testify to the diversity, richness, and complexity of Arthurian life. We see the community in various lights, not all of which are flattering, although the general impression is, undeniably, that of a world superior by far to our own.

Malory goes to great lengths to record the deeds of the Round Table community not only because its deeds were glorious, but because they are also a measure both of Arthur's achievement in unifying the land and establishing the Round Table fellowship in the first place, and, therefore, of the weight of the tragedy to come. Without the middle section, that is, neither the rise nor the fall would have its full significance. Long and unwieldy though it is, it is the middle section that holds the *Morte Darthur* together.

On first reading, however, this might be far from evident, and the accumulation of adventures might merely tire our patience. If a newcomer's attention wavers, he might be excused for skipping, selecting passages according to his own tastes, reading a reasonable amount and, rather than losing heart, moving on. There will be time to return later.

BOOK III

LANCELOT: LOVE AND WORSHIP

The opening of the middle section is not likely to be a problem for anyone: from the unfamiliar and (perhaps) uncongenial spirit of Book II, the brief book devoted to Lancelot takes us back to the kind of Malory most readers enjoy. This is not a chronicle of endless battles, it is a book of adventure, combat, gallantry, treachery, love, enchantment and virtue. Malory offers us the whole gamut of chivalry through the itinerary of a knight whom we have all heard of and whom we immediately sympathise with and respect. We met Lancelot briefly during the Roman campaign, in which he ended up with a fine military record. Book III shows his preeminence in knightly achievement: he can only be beaten through treason or enchantment. These two hazards are casually mentioned by Malory as if they constituted an inevitable part of the Arthurian world. They do.

Lancelot sets out to seek adventure and Book III, although brief, offers a wide variety. It includes some gentle comedy – although the young Lancelot is not always sufficiently sure of himself to appreciate the joke, as when he has to fight off the amorous advances of a fellow knight into whose bed he has come by error. Lancelot feels more at ease when he is master of the situation. When he borrows Kay's armour he creates a situation in which there is a gap between a knight's real ability in combat and his apparent ability. The incidents of mistaken identity lead to a certain amount of harmless amusement.

Book III establishes Lancelot's preeminence. He alone suceeds where others fail, as he does against the fearsome Tarquin, who has daunted so many other Round Table knights. Lancelot's success is not surprising, however; he makes light work even of giants. More important, the adventures of Book III help to situate Lancelot precisely in relation to the knighthood oath, for the great majority of his adventures here are specifically undertaken in the service of ladies. A knight must be, first and foremost, a gallant man, and one who is not cannot be a knight. Hence Lancelot's indignant outburst on hearing of the behaviour of Sir Perys de Forest Savage: 'What?. . . is he a theff and a knyght? And a ravyssher of women? He doth shame unto the Order of Knyghthode, and contrary unto his oth. Hit is pyté that he lyvyth!' (160.10–12; VI.10). And as Lancelot succeeds where Sir Perys so dismally fails, we have an object lesson in knighthood and a practical application of the oath.

The figures of Tarquin and Perys are important and one of the ladies Lancelot helps sums them up in one sentence: 'lyke as Terquyn wacched to dystresse good knyghtes, so dud this knyght attende to destroy and dystresse ladyes, damesels and jantyllwomen' (160.29–31; VI.10). De-

stroying good knights and distressing ladies, these are the great sins of the
Arthurian world, and it is important to see Lancelot taking a firm stand
against them both.

The service of ladies is, for Malory, in no way a frivolous or effete occupation for a fighting man, and a knight can get into some unpleasant
scrapes in his endeavour to serve them. Just as there are knights – like
Perys – who have, but do not deserve, the title of knight, so there are
ladies who are ladies in name only. They too can deceive; they too can
watch to distress good knights, and a man must know how to handle
them. Their designs can be far from lady-like for some of them are no better than they ought to be. And together with Lancelot's excellence in the
service of women is an important statement of his virtue. Book II shows us
the link between worship and war; Book III's motto could be love and
worship.

To ride in the service of ladies does not make Lancelot a ladies' man.
Quite the contrary, he seems ill-at-ease in feminine company (no doubt
part of his youthful inexperience). His physical prowess has inevitably
earned him a reputation and made him sexually desirable, but Lancelot
will not hear of such things. He is as reluctant to admit his reputation as
the Gawain of *Sir Gawain and the Green Knight*. He rejects the pursuit of
amatory pleasure: he has better things to do. Lancelot is not the romantic
young lover; in affairs of the heart and the flesh his attitude is abstemious
and ascetic.

Malory emphasises Lancelot's virtue as an essential aspect of his success in arms, but it is also something which has very real spiritual manifestations: he is able to perform miracles – the healing of a knight in the
Chapel Perillous incident and, later (in Book VII) the healing of Sir Urry.
The relationship between virtue (specifically chastity) and knightly
achievement will be an important theme in a later book; it is important to
notice its introduction in Book III, particularly because it is here that
Malory begins to deal with the relationship between Lancelot and Guenevere. The love of Lancelot for the queen does not herald an abandonment
of virtue – as a Victorian might think – rather it is brought to our attention
in circumstances in which Lancelot's virtue is made abundantly plain. In
this way, Malory specifies the nature of his central romance theme.

Lancelot, it is said, loves Guenevere. Lancelot claims that he cannot
stop people talking, but he has nothing to say on the subject. The relationship is presented, however, as something which already exists. It certainly
seems to be common knowledge (we are not surprised, we have heard of
it too). Lancelot, that is, enters the *Morte Darthur* with his reputation as
Guenevere's lover ready-made, and Malory gives us no elucidation of the
matter. The lovers meet, get to know each other, and fall in love off stage.
Their private relationship is an important element throughout the book,

but it is something Malory takes for granted, and when it is mentioned for the first time, it is hotly denied by the hero.

The strength of the legend is such, of course, that we do not believe Lancelot's denial (and anyway, Merlin has let us into the secret in Book I). Lancelot is being diplomatic; he is lying about his relationship with the queen because, although a gentleman should not lie, a gentleman should certainly not compromise the reputation of a lady – expecially one who is both married and a queen. And the lie is unimportant for the question is improper in the first place. Knights are bound by their chivalry to help ladies; satisfying the curiosity of ladies is not part of the bargain.

Nor is it part of Malory's task to satisfy our curiosity, and he introduces the Lancelot/Guenevere theme shrouded in ambiguity. It may be that in Book III Lancelot can deny being Guenevere's lover because as yet he is not. All the gossip at court is a reflexion of the potential of their relationship but not of its actual state. At any rate, few of us, I believe, have the impression that Lancelot is a hardened fornicator with a ready denial on his lips and equally ready to spin a glib yarn about his being far too busy to think of a wife and far too devout to think of illicit sex. There are knights in Camelot only too ready to satisfy a lonely lady, but Lancelot is not one of these. He could be, since few knights seem to set much store by sexual purity, but he is not. His prowess has made him something of a sex symbol, but he remains chaste. And it is, I think, important to read Book III with this in mind. Malory is establishing Lancelot's reputation and character: not only does he excel other knights in combat, his attitude to love is also superior. He does not share their merry acceptance of carnal pleasure and he reminds us – as Malory introduces the Lancelot/Guenevere relationship – that love must be less important than worship. To what extent this translates Lancelot's *real* attitude is not made clear (except that it is clearly none of our business) but it places the central love theme firmly in the context of virtue, fidelity, and singlemindedness. Malory will have much to say about this later; it is worth bearing in mind that it is here in Book III that he begins his presentation of what he calls 'vertuouse love'.

BOOK IV

GARETH: LOVE AND ALLEGIANCE

Having presented his favourite knight in Book III, Malory turns his attention to Gareth, his second favourite. We do not, however, leave Lancelot behind; a few years older now, and a benevolent elder brother figure, he remains importantly in the background. Indeed it is his role in Book IV that is one of its major elements: Gareth begins his knightly career under the auspices of Lancelot.

The newcomer to Malory is not likely to find Book IV a problem and in a sense it is even more accessible than Book III, more immediately appealing. The adventures of both books make pleasant reading, but we are likely to feel greater warmth towards Gareth. Lancelot's purity is, of course, admirable; Gareth's somewhat warmer, lower humanity is more endearing. Nor is it, I believe, a weakness in the overall structure of the book that for the moment we should identify less willingly with Lancelot. Later, when Gareth is not so central to the action, our fond recollection of him at a time when Lancelot does have our full sympathy will be important.

There is one aspect of the Book of Gareth, however, which comes as something of a surprise: although Arthur, Lancelot, Gawain and other leading Arthurian characters are present, this charming and unusually self-contained story at times does not seem quite to belong to the *Morte Darthur*. We seem to leave the world of romance and step into the world of folktale, for the story is structured according to patterns reminiscent of folklore.

A fine-looking young man arrives unknown at Arthur's court and the arrival – seen in itself as a marvel – is the beginning of a series of adventures. The young man asks for board and lodging and consciously humbles himself. In mockery he is given a name and in mockery he spends a year in the kitchens of Camelot. His self-abasement is an essential part of the scheme to prove his worth, but both Lancelot and Gawain readily see the innate qualities of the young man, to whom they behave in a brotherly manner. For this tale is indeed the exile and testing of the young brother, who must set out to prove his valour. Gareth is the younger brother of Gawain, who is unaware of the fact, and this is both essential for the sake of the story, and also an expression of the emotional rupture at the heart of the tale. Lancelot is brought in by the ties of affection and nobility – not merely of blood – to replace the real brother, to provide an ideal of behaviour the young Gareth can adopt.

The insults of the court follow Gareth on his adventures since the lady he is assigned to help sees none of his innate nobility, and the series of adventures – overcoming four knights each wearing different colours – becomes a statement of Gareth's worth and, as the lady comes to realise it, a revelation of that worth. Just as Lancelot's adventures were undertaken for ladies, so Gareth's exploits are specifically devoted to the service of a lady (the sister of the one who accompanies him), with whom, he falls in love the moment he sees her. As with Lancelot, so too with Gareth, his virtue, not only his valour, must be tested, and the young man nobly refuses to take advantage of a young lady sent to his bed ostensibly as a reward, in fact as a test. But Gareth's virtue is more frail than Lancelot's and when, later, he is united with his own lady, they are only too ready to anticipate the wedding ceremony. It is here that magic must be brought in to safe-guard honour where the flesh proves only too willing to compromise it. When Gareth and his lady try to come to bed, Gareth is attacked and wounded by a knight who, though beheaded, is restored to life. Gareth learns his lessons slowly, and when the knight attacks him again during a further attempt to sleep with his lady, he cuts him into a hundred pieces. To no avail, since the lady's sister has the power to put the knight together again. But although Gareth is technically innocent after the test of his vir-tue, the wound becomes a reminder of his moral infirmity and a hind-rance in his desire to win future renown.

Once Gareth has proved his worth in exile he must be found again and reintegrated into the group. His mother arrives at Arthur's court to claim Gareth and protests at their ill-treatment of her son, the king's own nephew. This revelation is essential for the story and its pattern; not the slightest attention is paid to convincing motivation. Queen Morgause complains that they have treated her son badly, but this is not a world in which anyone troubles to remark that if she had let them know he was coming there would have been no problem, nor if she had seen to the up-bringing of her progeny in a more rigorous manner the situation would not have arisen in which even Gawain was unable to recognise his sibling.

Gareth is not to be found easily, of course; the narrative pattern re-quires delay. When he is finally brought before them all at a tournament a magic ring hampers their discovery of him by changing the colour of his armour. Colours were important in the revelation of his qualities, now they are important in the revelation of his identity. Inevitably all goes well, the characters are united, and the agreeable tale ends in joy as the knights Gareth has overcome arrive to pledge allegiance to him and turn the insults that accompanied his first arrival into acclaim.

The Arthurian world contains its share of the improbable but it is not usually improbable in this patterned way. But the Gareth book makes pleasant reading and the hero is thoroughly agreeable. That he should be so is important. I would not suggest that with other heroes, Tristram for instance, Malory did not care whether we felt any sympathy for them, but I believe our sympathetic feelings for Gareth were intentionally aroused. Malory took the unusual step of including a whole book about Gareth be-cause he had the importance of future events in mind. It may well have been late in writing the *Morte Darthur* that he did so, when the link be-tween Gareth, Lancelot and Gawain is about to become dramatically im-portant. Thinking of the fraternal allegiances that play a vital part at Gareth's death, Malory saw the relevance of describing those that play a vital part in Gareth's life. For what matters most in Book IV is Gareth's relationship to Lancelot. It is Lancelot not Gawain whose affection is regularly stressed. Both Gawain and Lancelot defend Gareth from the mockery of Kay and show him kindness, but Lancelot's generosity is far more meaningful, Malory tells us, in that he and Gareth are not blood relations. That Gawain does not as yet know the identity of his brother is no excuse; the mere fact of their kinship makes Gawain's generosity less noteworthy. Gareth specifically asks Lancelot to knight him, and it is Lancelot's company Gareth seeks. On the other hand, when he realises the vengeful nature of his brother, such a driving force later, he withdraws from him.

In many ways the Gareth story is more orderly and more clearly rounded off than other parts of the *Morte Darthur*; there are fewer digressions and loose ends. In tone it is somewhat different, too, with its much franker sense of a happy ending. There may be the occasional hint of gloom, but the world portrayed is essentially untroubled. It is a world in which heads can roll and be restored, where bridegrooms are kept off the battlefield in expectation of the wedding night, and where family honour *can* be saved.

Indeed, part of the warmth of tone of Book IV is due to the fact that the concept of the family is of greater importance here than anywhere else in the *Morte Darthur*. Kinship is a central theme of the book and hence Gareth wins worship and finds love in the context of a family. Gawain and Lancelot both offer fraternal affection, Morgause upbraids the court for failing in its family duties, and Gareth must be sought and found by the family that failed to recognise him and allowed him to leave. Meanwhile Gareth discovers love, and a future brother and sister-in-law who are bent on preserving the honour of the new family he is entering. He is the only major knight allowed to marry and he chooses specifically to do so. His worship wins him both a place in his own family and a family of his own. We hear no more about the second; the division at the heart of the first is important throughout the *Morte Darthur*. The folktale pattern of sibling rivalry which seems to make the Gareth tale stand apart from the others, at the same time assures its relevance to the whole book.

It is, in itself, a preparation for later events to have a tale devoted to Gareth at all. However much prior Arthurian knowledge we have, Gareth is not a hero we are expecting to find a whole book devoted to. In Malory there is triumvirate of knightly achievement regularly referred to as a touchstone of excellence, and Gareth is not one: Lancelot, Tristram and Lamorak. Malory devotes whole books to Lancelot and Tristram; in all logic we might have expected a book of Lamorak, but there is not one. Instead, surprisingly, there is a whole book for Gareth. Once Book IV draws to a close Gareth returns to the background. When he appears again our affection for him is rekindled, but he is no longer the exceptional young man he is in his own book. Here, he is (as he is not later) invincible, not even beaten by Lancelot with whom his fight (they are unaware of each other's identity of course) results in a stalemate. Book IV is Gareth's book. We may wonder why, but the question is irrelevant while there are adventures to be enjoyed. Later, in the wider scheme of the *Morte Darthur*, we will understand: we need a life of Gareth because his death means so much.

BOOK V
TRISTRAM: LOVE AND FORTUNE

Although the story of Tristram and Isolde had already been assimilated into the body of Arthurian writings it remained none the less a separate branch. Malory, however, chose to include the series of adventures centred more or less closely around Tristram in his overall history of the Arthurian kingdom, and his Tale of Sir Tristram takes its place as part of the continuation of the age of chivalric glory. The tale contains much agreeable material, and as Malory draws it in, he is able to use Tristram's fame and achievement and his well-known, undying love for Isolde as a reflexion of the major themes of his whole book. We move in part, of course, to another kingdom, Cornwall, an inferior realm with a ruler of dubious integrity and – as one would logically expect, therefore – where knighthood is not based on firm principles. Cornish knights are proverbially braggarts and cowards. Cornwall is a shoddy parallel to Arthur's kingdom, a statement of ordinary life that measures the splendour of the English achievement. Tristram begins his career *in* Cornwall, but he is never *of* it, and his tale is the process and route by which he comes to win membership of the Round Table, to which in achievement and sympathy he rightly belongs.

Problems

A parallel of this nature is not difficult for the reader to appreciate, but the problem with Book V is simply that Malory perhaps tries to fit too much in. The tale as a whole seems far too long (the first subdivision alone is longer than the whole of Book III) and though by now we are growing accustomed to a leisurely, almost purposeless narrative line, there are, we feel, limits. A summary of the incidents of the book would run to considerable length and even a descriptive list of the main events would be both too long and varied for us to feel we can have an overall view of the book. The Tristram section is like a city without a tower, one we can never hope to dominate at a glance. Finding one's way about is not an easy matter and, to make things worse, even the central story of Tristram and Isolde seems to have a poor hold on Malory's interest. It soon becomes clear that Malory has turned to Tristram more for the mass of adventures that can be accumulated round a knight of such outstanding fame than for the precise incidents which – at least in twentieth century minds – have established that fame. We have a greater feeling of inconsequence to the extent that the knight who is, in theory, holding the narrative together is something of an excuse himself. The book tells us nothing of Tristram's fate even; Malory mentions that much later, and by the way. Perhaps more unsettling for the reader is that Tristram himself betrays little interest in his own destiny. He may be the hero of one of the greatest love stories in the world, but at one point he makes it clear that he remains by Isolde's side out of duty rather than passion. When invited to set off on an adventure he declares: 'Alas! . . . and I had nat this messayge in hande with this fayre lady, truly I wolde never stynte or I had founde sir Launcelot' (263.1–3; VIII.28). When Malory turned his attention to the French book of *Tristan* he found not so much an ideal text to translate, but an ideal pretext.

There is another aspect of the Tristram book that the reader may find somewhat troublesome, another sign that the material has been incompletely assimilated. Amorous adventures inevitably play a considerable part, but the morality of Book V is disturbingly unsettled. Book III shows us Lancelot as a young man of exceptional virtue, an ascetic, a knight who knows that achievement is based on self denial and discipline. Even if his position is a diplomatic lie, he is a man of extreme discretion. Gareth's behaviour is more frankly human and he has to be protected from sexual misdemeanour, but he does know how to control his passions and at the end openly chooses marriage rather than the illicit joys of amorous affairs. Tristram, on the other hand, is something of a frank libertine. He begins well enough by rejecting love in favour of knighthood, but as soon as he is sexually initiated he refuses himself nothing. Despite his pledge to Isolde, we see him scheming his way to the bed of a married woman, who turns out to be little better than she ought to be, and although he seems to reform later, the reader's memory of his early sexual career remains. It is hard for us to share Lancelot's regret that 'so noble a knyght as sir Trystrames is sholde be founde to his fyrst lady and love untrew' (273.32–33; VIII.36) when we know that Isolde is not exactly Tristram's first love at all.

The love of Lancelot and Guenevere is regularly shrouded in ambiguity; the private affair never quite becomes public knowledge. Even at the end an element of doubt remains: Lancelot is trapped in Guenevere's *chamber*, there is no proof of anything else. With Tristram and Isolde there is no ambiguity. They are caught 'nakyd a-bed' together and the splendour of their love is something to be proclaimed openly. It is at times difficult to draw the line between lovers who are not ashamed of being in love and those who are shameless.And in the court of Cornwall there is even an element of sexual effrontery. Morgan le Fay, Arthur's trouble-making half sister, sends a magic horn to Camelot to confound Lancelot and Guenevere. All ladies who drink from the horn will spill the contents if they have been unchaste. Fortunately the horn is de-routed and comes to King Mark. Of the hundred ladies who drink, only four manage to do so cleanly. Mark, in an unseemly show of righteous indignation, is all for condemning the adulteresses to the death they deserve, but his counsellors pooh-pooh the idea. This is Cornwall of course, but the atmosphere of fashionable corruption (one can almost hear the ladies sniggering behind their hands), obviously due to continental influence, fits uneasily with the general sexual morality of Arthurian England.

The Tristram book, then, is long, so full of inconsequence that even the central story is accorded little enthusiasm, and fits the overall moral order of the *Morte Darthur* uneasily. It could perhaps be suggested that since the beginner already has the more straightforward stories of Lancelot and Gareth to represent the age of Arthurian glory, he could leave Book V till later. This is certainly true for many of the incidental narratives. We could certainly wait to learn about the careers of, say, Alexander the Orphan or Sir La Cote Male Tayle. It is none the less true that certain aspects of the Tristram book are important for an appreciation of the *Morte Darthur* as a whole. It would be best to take stock of them *en route*.

Parallels

First of all, it is in the Tristram book that we see an element of risk entering the Lancelot/Guenevere relationship. Before, people at court may well have been talking, but that was all. Now, Morgan le Fay is positively seeking to cause trouble by publicly revealing the nature of the affair. In the background of the adulterous relationship of Tristram and Isolde that is, there is another relationship of a similar nature in which the dangers of revelation are becoming apparent.

More important than this are the events in the life of Lancelot which we discover in the course of Book V and which bind the whole book together. Lancelot is not only regularly in the background as a point of reference for Tristram, as he was for Gareth in Book IV, but elements of Tristram's story also point up certain aspects of Lancelot's (later) career.

The reader will be struck by the closeness between the Tristram story and the central themes of the *Morte Darthur*. There are frequent points of resemblance even if these never constitute a systematic parallel. In each case we have a young man of exemplary valour and achievement in the service of a king who has a rightful claim to that service – Arthur because of his previous help to Lancelot and because of his deserving, Mark through family allegiance. In each case the young man loves the king's wife, who (though the theme is secondary) also has another – and troublesome – admirer: Meliagaunt and Palomides. Tristram's first rescue of his lady is in a context of moral murk, but later he (like Lancelot in Book VII) rescues the queen when she has been abducted by her other admirer and when (though this is on another occasion for Lancelot) the king is unable to help because of his legal position. Incidental details are not unalike in the careers of both men. Bloodstains on sheets betray sexual activity in each case, and there is an interlude of harmony disturbed by the scheming of a member of the family, who is responsible for the final revelation: he has been lying in wait and takes a dozen men with him to trap the lovers. There are times when one feels that the opening of the Tristram book reads like a trial run for Books VII and VIII and there are even similarities of phraseology:

> And thus they lyved with joy and play a longe whyle. But ever sir Andret, that was nye cosyn unto sir Trystrams, lay in a watche to wayte betwyxte sir Trystrames and La Beale Isode for to take hym and devoure hym.
>
> (267.31–34; VIII.32)

and:

> Thus they lyved in all that courte wyth grete nobeles and joy longe tymes.
> But every nyght and day sir Aggravayne, sir Gawaynes brother, awayted quene Gwenyver and sir Launcelot to put hem bothe to a rebuke and a shame.
>
> (699.17–21; XIX.13)

Tristram and Isolde may live on a lower plane, but their story provides a clear foil to that of Lancelot and Guenevere.

Mainly of Tristram

The size of the Tristram book remains a daunting proposition for the newcomer, who might wish to relegate much of it to a later reading, but it is important at least to recognise the major preoccupations of the tale. A knight must test his courage in the adventures to which fortune leads him, and the proof of courage and the accumulation of adventure is, we feel, as important a guideline through the book as the career of any one knight. The central characters and key incidents are worth getting to know and it would be wise to read at least representative sections – perhaps the first and the penultimate parts, 'Isode the Fair' and 'Lancelot and Elaine'. The new-comer will notice that the Tristram book betrays a certain looseness of or-ganisation and a shifting centre of attention, even though this is by no means noticeable at first.

Indeed, the reader's first impression of the Tristram book is that he is about to be given a more thoroughly comprehensive account of this hero than of the others, since Book V opens with Tristram's birth and child-hood. Arthur is the only other character whose childhood is important and, like Arthur, Tristram is born into a world of political rivalry, a world in which Merlin is on hand to protect the royal line, a world in which a royal prince will never know a mother's love. From boyhood the generos-ity and warmheartedness of Tristram are evident and he even pleads for the life of the stepmother who seeks to poison him. He is a young man of great accomplishment, the epitome of all the knightly graces, but also ex-ceptionally courageous. When his uncle, king Mark of Cornwall, is or-dered to pay tribute to the king of Ireland or find a knight to champion his cause, Tristram, not yet a knight, is eager to take up the challenge even though some people feel it is a task for a knight of Lancelot's calibre. 'Be ruled as youre corrage woll rule you' (234.9–10; VIII.5), says Tristram's father as he leaves to help his uncle, and the advice becomes a motto to him. Like the young Lancelot he is too busy in knightly achievement to be interested in love, although it is wounds received during his combat with the king of Ireland's champion, Marhalt, whom we met in Book I, that leads him to Isolde: she alone can heal him. Before returning to Cornwall, Tristram vows fidelity to Isolde.

There is a wealth of incident in these early pages of the Tristram book; much to interest the reader and little to disturb him. But once Tristram re-turns to Cornwall, his career takes an unhappy turn. His relationship with his uncle King Mark has so far been harmonious; now, jealousy and ri-valry take over, but not as the two of them compete for the noble love of Isolde. The king and his nephew are both trying to conduct a clandestine affair with the same married woman. The incidents of this first triangular love affair foreshadow those of the Isolde relationship: just how openly can Tristram serve his lady, how can he reconcile the demands of love and feudal allegiance? But here the whole business is thoroughly shoddy. Mark begins a moral decline from which he will never recover, but even Tristram's shining armour begins to appear somewhat tarnished. With his early amorous adventures in mind it is not easy for us to see him as 'peereles and makeles of ony Crystyn knyght' (268.19–20; VIII.33).

Mark's plan to marry Isolde is linked, from the start, with his ill-feeling toward Tristram, who, he hopes, will be killed when he goes to Ireland to bring the lady back. As everyone knows, Tristram and Isolde drink a love potion by accident and although Isolde and Mark are duly married, the love of Tristram and the queen remains unaltered. The relationship of Lancelot and Guenevere is taken for granted more than it is stated, it is a private devotion which reinforces the power of public allegiance; the love of Tristram and Isolde is, from the first, more openly declared and the plots to trap them together are realised with much greater ease. When Tristram is forced to leave the country after he and Isolde have been caught, he meets another lady called Isolde, almost forgets the first until Lancelot writes sharply to him about his duties, and then lives with the lady in sexual innocence.

The irreverent reader might at this point begin to wonder whether someone had not been watering down that love potion. Tristram never seems to live up to the role he traditionally plays, never shows quite the interest in Isolde we expected. Or rather Malory prefers to concentrate on more active business. Consequently, at this point he interrupts the story to introduce us to two other knights: Lamorak and La Cote Male Tayle. Lamorak is an important figure. His name is a regular point of reference in knightly achievement. He is one of the three best knights in Malory's world, after Lancelot and Tristram, and his personal story of family vengeance is tied up with later events. La Cote Male Tayle's story is a pleasant adventure, but for those who enjoyed reading about Gareth there is – complete with its 'damesell Maledysaunte' – more than an element of déjà vu.

The interruption in the story of Tristram and Isolde is, however, and indication of the writer's interests. 'Sir Trystram, of whom this booke is pryncipall off' (411.3–4; X.50) may be the subject in hand, but certainly not exclusively so. Book V encompasses other things and is certainly not a book devoted to the love story as such. After introducing Lamorak and La Cote Male Tayle, Malory returns to Tristram, who is sailing back to Cornwall, but he is blown off course and in the narrative so are we. It is the adventures that count, Tristram's and those of other knights; there is little left to say about the love story. What is important is that Tristram remains unwelcome in Cornwall. His relationship with Isolde inevitably makes him an outcast there, even though in a way that relationship is merely a symptom of a much more fundamental division of sympathy. He is, of course, welcome at Arthur's court, but then this is the motivating force of much of Book V: Tristram is made a knight of the Round Table and finds his true home, his allegiance to Arthur being far stronger than his family ties to King Mark. As in Book IV, the ties of honour are stronger than the ties of blood.

After a period in which Tristram runs mad out of grief at his suspicions of Isolde's infidelity, Lancelot eventually sets the lovers up *en ménage* in his castle of Joyous Gard, and the castle gives its name (in Vinaver's edition) to one section of the book. But the title is misleading; even here we are not being offered an interlude devoted to the lovers. We see nothing of their life there; it is merely the next stage in their itinerary and greater attention is paid to Tristram's daily hunting exploits. The new reader needs, I think, to be warned of this. We must not expect too much of Book V. We have all heard of the story of Tristram and Isolde and at the beginning it looks as though Malory is going to tell it to us. But no. The story is – inevitably – mentioned, and then taken for granted. A royal historian who decided to write a monograph on the public career of Edwad VIII (overseas visits, official functions, etc.) might deal similarly with the Mrs Simpson affair. He would have no cause to describe the elegant houseparties and romantic intrigue. If we turned to the book as a definitive version of the famous love story we would no doubt feel frustrated, as it is easy to feel frustrated with Malory's Tristram book if we approach it in the wrong way. We expect more where Malory probably thought he had already given us enough. We presume that the Book of Sir Tristram means the Book of Tristram and Isolde. We are wrong. As Malory reminds us, it is only in part the book of Tristram even.

Because of its size, Book V inevitably lacks the integrity of the other two parts of the middle section. Tristram is never quite the hero of his own book. This is in part because Malory is interested both in a host of minor characters and incidents, and also in some of the major figures for more than their present role: their importance in the overall history is what counts. More than this, Lancelot wanders through the Tristram book constantly casting a shadow. He is, as always, a point of knightly reference. His excellence is one of the ties that binds the fellowship together, but he is also the weak link in the chain, and as the age of glory comes to a close, it is the story of Lancelot that takes over.

The new reader may prefer to leave much of the Tristram book to a second reading. When he returns, and until then he should bear in mind that the love story will never be central to the narrative, that much of the book should be read for the delight of the moment without trying to fabricate any strict relevance (like the delightful tale of Alexander the Orphan, which, however much it measures Mark's treason, is important for itself), and that certain major figures are important: in particular Mark, Lamorak, Dinaden, Palomides and Lancelot. A few comments on the role of these characters in Book V – and in the light of the *Morte Darthur* as a whole – might be appropriate before we pass on.

Villainy: King Mark

In the logic of a triangular love story it would be sufficient to make the
husband a cruel and thoughtless older man for the young lovers to have
our sympathy. In the Tristram story, Mark is much more than this: he is
the positive blackguard who (almost) makes us overlook the illicit nature
of the love of Tristram and Isolde, and throughout the book he forms a
clear contrast to the uprightness of the hero. His role in Book V, however,
is inevitably a reflexion on the action of the *Morte Darthur* as a whole, and
Mark is, most of all, a regular point of comparison for Arthur, who is
everything Mark is not. When Arthur is ordered to pay tribute to a self-
appointed overlord, he gets his men together and sets off to wage war on
the insolent Emperor; the craven Mark looks to others for help. He is a
man afraid, a weakling who resorts to treachery and devious action as his
only hope of success (he will come to mind later when we meet Meliagaint
in Book VII). He is a living illustration of the vital need for stable kingship:
his incompetence in his role is inevitably mirrored in his realm. Arthur's
kingdom is full of valour because the king is a man of deeds; Mark's
knights are full of talk, well-known for the cowardice which finds its inspiration on the throne. Mark is a man of seeming and deceit, 'a fayre
speker, and false thereundir' (365.31–32; X.15), in league with Morgan le
Fay, a troublemaker, worse, a destroyer of good knights, and he is so because he is entirely dominated by his personal animosity towards Tristram. His own private concerns motivate his every action; the stability of
the realm (something his barons are forced at times to recall to his attention) means nothing. He is the picture of corrupt kingship, the man who
uses public power for personal gain. He is, in this sense and importantly,
the black to Arthur's white: Arthur is the king who silences all private
doubt to save the kingdom. The portrait of King Mark is not merely therefore an essential aspect of one book of the *Morte Darthur*, it is part of
Malory's wider, almost political vision.

Vengeance: Lamorak

Lamorak is another character whom we meet in Book V but whose importance is felt in the *Morte Darthur* as a whole. He is a character whose
reputation is already well established before we ever see him in action. In
Book IV he is frequently mentioned as one of the three best knights in the
world whose prowess outstrips all others, but his activities are almost exclusively narrated in Book V (a sign perhaps that Malory wrote his Gareth

book after Book V, which explains why in Book IV he refers to the out-standing reputation of a knight of whom, as yet, we have not heard).

Lamorak's first deed in the book is motivated by spite (the sending of the magic horn to Cornwall rather than Camelot), and he frequently seems haughty and a bit too sure of himself. He appears to have an on and off rivalry with Tristram, but his most important role is amatory: like his two fellow knights in excellence, Lancelot and Tristram, his love injures family peace. Lamorak loves Queen Morgause of Orkney and she him, but the queen's numerous grown-up offspring, Gawain, Gaherys, Agravain and Mordred, do not take kindly to the liaison since they suspect Lamo-rak's father, Pellinor, of killing their father, Lott. The antagonism between Lamorak and the Orkney clan – although Gareth is regularly excluded from the plot – is a theme which runs throughout Book V. One of the bro-thers (Gaherys) even kills his own mother when he finds her in bed with her lover and the whole affair comes to a head when the brothers gang up on Lamorak and in most unknightly conditions slaughter him, despite Arthur's attempts to stem his nephews' thirst for vengeance. Lamorak fights alone against four. They slay his horse before killing him in the back. The murder is sly and underhand, carried out 'in a pryvy place' (428.7; X.58), and it is this dirty deed which convinces Gareth that his bro-thers are to be shunned. He keeps himself apart from them, and most no-ticeably later, in Book VIII, when the stand he takes leads to his death. Lamorak, then, is a reminder that corruption does exist in Camelot and that there are forces of discord which, though kept in check at present, are close to the surface. The story of Lamorak makes us aware of the frailty of Arthurian chivalry.

Mockery: Dinadan

In theory, so too does Dinadan, a character who anticipates our mockery of the knightly code. In the French books Malory was adapting Dinadan plays a prominent part. He is the knight who remains sceptical and his constant stream of criticism exposes the sublime quixotry of the Arthurian ethic. Since Malory refuses to endorse any attacks on chivalry, he allows Dinadan to play only a small part, but he is present none the less, ever ready to puncture ideals: love and knightly encounter are more trouble than they are worth. On one occasion Tristram and he are told they will have to fight two knights if they want to lodge in a particular castle. (312.17 ff.; IX.24). Tristram is evidently thrilled: there could be no more splendid a place. Not only does it provide accommodation, but excite-ment and adventure are thrown in at no extra charge. Dinadan's heart sinks. He would prefer to look elsewhere. Having to fight for a bed is not his idea of five-star accommodation.

Until Dinadan comes on the scene however there is no criticism of this kind at all; Malory and his knights are wholeheartedly devoted to the Arthurian ideal. And even for the modern reader perhaps, Dinadan arrives too late. We have already spent our irrelevant irony and by now have learnt to accept the Arthurian world on its own terms. In any case, Dinadan's logical approach to life, his constant debunking of ideals and artificial codes is something Malory does not sympathise with and so he deviates the presentation of Dinadan somewhat. Dinadan becomes the man with the sense of humour, the talker, the comic, the knight the others appreciate for his brand of fun. He enjoys a joke and even gets away with calling Lancelot an 'olde shrew' (407.22; X.47). He is a popular man with a sharp eye for what is bogus but he is also – and this is what counts – a fine fighter. Tristram thinks particularly highly of him.

Whatever he may say against knighthood, Dinadan is an excellent specimen of knighthood himself. His wit parades itself as a grudge against chivalry, but he is too good a knight for us to take him seriously. He grumbles at some of the assumptions of knighthood, but his disenchantment can be no more than a pose, for when the situation gets tough we see at a glance that Dinadan is as good a knight as any of them. He may be verbally irreverent but in deed he lends chivalry his entire support.

The ideal knight 'seyth but lytil, but he doth much more' (80.43; IV.5). Since Dinadan is not lacking in deeds it does not really matter that he talks too much. At any rate, it is only talk. Everyone knows he does not really mean what he says. No one suggests that if he cannot stop grouching he should resign from the Round Table, and he never mentions retiring. It is just his way.

La Bête Noire: Palomides

The adventures of Palomides also thread their way through Book V, providing a theme which holds the book together. Palomides, the Saracen, is a man of outstanding achievement and one of the most redoubtable knights, able even to unhorse Tristram and Lamorak; but most of all he is in love with Isolde. His love, of course, is not returned and although it is the driving force of all his valorous achievements (without Isolde he would have accomplished nothing he says) it is also a constant source of antagonism and of personal suffering. Palomides is a foil to Tristram, and even to Lancelot, whose understanding of Palomides' situation shows how close his own experience is:

'Well,' seyde sir Launcelot, 'I se, for to say the sothe, ye have done mervaylously well this day, and I undirstonde a parte for whos love ye do hit, and well I wote that love is a grete maystry. And yf my lady were here, as she is nat, wyte you well, sir Palomydes, ye shulde nat beare away the worshyp!'

(449.31–35; X.71).

Palomides is a complex, tortured character. His love for Isolde and jealousy of Tristram lead him into disreputable conduct at times. He is not always able to distinguish between earnest and play in knightly combat, and so eager is he to steal the show from Tristram in the eyes of Isolde that he gives free rein to his ill-will, resorts to untruth, and, when challenged, is ready to brazen it out. And yet his torment lies not only in his failure to obtain Isolde, but also in the emnity he is forced to feel for Tristram, whom he would willingly love. Knightly achievement forces admiration and Palomides hates Tristram against his better wishes.

In the same way, Palomides' valour demands respect even though he is not a Christian. His infidel stature makes him even more fearful, his knightly prowess is not kept in check by the power of Christian sentiment, it lacks a proper humanising basis and can too readily deteriorate into cruelty. But this does not cut him off. Indeed, there is concern lest he should die unchristened and his fellow knights urge him to accept the true faith. But at heart and in deed Palomides is Christian already – just as at heart and in deed Tristram belonged to the Round Table. He feels merely that he must prove himself further and earn more of a reputation before he can merit baptism, just as Tristram felt unworthy (despite his reputation) to join the Round Table.

Palomides vows therefore to achieve seven victories for Christ before considering that he is ready for baptism, and Book V draws to a close with the christening of this colourful figure, who tails Tristram through the book like another, more violent, version of himself, but who also introduces us to the theme of knightly achievement undertaken, in a real sense, for the Christian cause. This is a subject we are about to come up against. In Book VI it introduces the beginning of the end. In this way, the figure of Palomides does not merely enrich the narrative in adventure, but also prepares us for future developments.

Continuations and Beginnings: Lancelot

The most obvious future development, of course, is provided by the subject matter of the final section of the Tristram book: Lancelot and Elaine.

Lancelot has been present throughout the book; it is as though Malory cannot tell a story without referring to his favourite knight. Lancelot is the clearest standard of excellence, his opinion and approval cannot be ignored and are, indeed, an important guide for the young Tristram. Tristram's endeavour to meet Lancelot becomes in itself an essential stage in his itinerary.

Our encounters with Lancelot also provide further information in his biography, some of which will play an important part later. We learn of Meliagaunt's hatred for Lancelot and his love for Guenevere which will dominate the action for a while in Book VII, and we see the various plots to publicise Lancelot's love for the queen; in Book VIII the Orkney clan continue their aunt Morgan's evil work. Not all that we see has overtones of doom and we discover even that Lancelot has a rollicking sense of humour and makes a laughing stock of Dinadan, much to the appreciation of the court. But such moments of joy are few and rather more central to the story is the irony by which the incidents which testify to Lancelot's greatness are those which reveal his imperfection. When Lancelot comes to the castle of the Grail King, Pelles, the king, aware that Lancelot will father Galahad on his daughter, is eager to contrive the conception. The task seems impossible since Lancelot is so faithful in his love for Guenevere, but the lady Bruson is able to use this exclusive devotion to lead him, under a spell, into Elaine's bed.

Lancelot is tricked into betraying Guenevere – we know from Book III that he can only be overcome by treason or enchantment – but the act of betrayal is, in many ways, his finest achievement: Galahad is born, the image both of his father's perfection and his father's fallibility. Because Lancelot loves the queen with an adulterous love, his son is conceived and born out of wedlock to a young woman who sacrifices her maidenhood – no one questions her purity for a moment – for a higher cause. The arrival of Galahad will ultimately herald the downfall of the Arthurian kingdom – it can go no higher. His conception was plotted as carefully as that of Arthur, with which the whole adventure began, but in this case wizardry has been replaced by spiritual overseeing.

The birth of Galahad inevitably provokes disharmony between Lancelot and the queen, and especially since the moral weight of Elaine and her child is such that Lancelot cannot merely refuse to acknowledge paternity, however much he feels ashamed. Guenevere for once proves forgiving (a habit she gets out of later), but not when the bed trick is played again by lady Bruson on the occasion of Elaine's visit to court some years later. Guenevere this time is patrolling the royal corridors and discovers Lancelot in the other woman's arms. Lancelot is appalled to find himself in such a situation and his distress leads to a period in which he, like Tristram, runs mad.

Elaine is sent from court, although not before she speaks her mind to Guenevere with a frankness and authority no one else ever musters, and Lancelot is eagerly sought for. There are a good number of adventures till he is found (at great expense; Guenevere spent twenty thousand pounds) and healed by the power of the Grail. The introduction of the Grail makes it clear that the book of knight errantry is taking on a more sober tone; other things are in store. We have met all the leading characters. Bors and Perceval have recently appeared. We only have to wait for Galahad to grow up.

PART THREE: THE FALL OF ARTHUR'S KINGDOM

The wheel of fortune begins its downward movement in Book VI where, ironically, the one quest that the whole of the Round Table undertakes, the one which therefore reflects their perfect unity, is the one which will disunite them and prove their imperfection. They set out on the spiritual quest of the Holy Grail and those who return (for not all of them do) come back to a land where the private rancours of different clans are about to challenge the harmony of the realm, and where, as a result, Lancelot is no longer able to reconcile his private and public loyalties. Rivalries and resentments like those Arthur quelled when he was young begin to rear their head and the kingdom is once again divided. The Round Table code shows itself unable to resist the pressure of internal strife and Arthur's great work of unification finally collapses.

The threat to the realm was present, lying dormant, when Arthurian chivalry was at its height because one essential element of the glory of that age was Lancelot's love for the queen. It was the inspiration of his greatness which, in turn, reflected glory on the community. But his love, though beneficial, is suspect. What inspires him to loyal service as a knight is, at the same time, the most eloquent statement of his disloyalty.

The middle section of the *Morte Darthur* shows the increasing danger implicit in their love. At first there are only rumours: smoke without fire perhaps, for people will, after all, talk, as Lancelot is well aware. Later the affair seems to be common knowledge (Isolde is entirely *au courant*) and Morgan le Fay seeks merely a pretext for public revelation. At the end of the middle section there can be no doubt: Galahad is the living proof that the fire of love well and truly exists, even though there is still no revelation of that love, for in the public eye Guenevere has nothing to do with the conception of Galahad. As long a Morgan's plots are foiled and rivalries are held in check, Lancelot's love has no other consequence than success in arms and glory to the realm. In Part Three his love is seen in another light, seen for what it is, and the consequence of adultery is knightly failure and political destruction.

Three books constitute the final section of the *Morte Darthur*. Two of them (the last two) pose no problem at all. They are the best and best known parts of Malory and many people read them first anyway. The other section, Book VI, is understandably one of the least popular of Malory's tales. Certain aspects of it, at least, are important.

BOOK VI
THE GRAIL: SIN AND WORSHIP

We have come across the Grail before. It has been mentioned several times, and at the end of Book V Lancelot was healed by it. In Book VI all 150 Round Table knights go off in search of it and three of them attain a vision of it. No one at any point asks the question modern readers invariably ask: what is the Grail? Indeed their total familiarity with the object increases our sense of mystery. This is appropriate since it is a mysterious object.

The origins of the Grail are obscure, lost in the depths of legend and folklore, but it is an object which has captured the European imagination. It became identified as a cup from the Last Supper used by Joseph of Arimathea to catch the blood of the agonising Christ. The Grail was brought to England and entrusted to a line of kings who were to guard it in the Castle of Corbenic till the destined Grail knight appeared. But its identity as an object is less important than the state of grace and intense religious experience it symbolises. The knights are not setting off to find something they can bring back to court in their saddle bag; the quest of the Holy Grail is a search for the divine presence. Once found, there is – in a literal sense for two of them – no going back. All the Round Table knights set out on the quest, but Book VI concentrates on the adventures of Galahad, Perceval, and Bors (who succeed), Gawain (whose dismal failure reflects that of Arthurian knighthood in general), and Lancelot (whom Malory will not allow completely to fail).

The object of this quest may be different but the adventure begins like so many others: a maiden arrives at court and makes a request; the king expects to see an adventure before sitting down to his meal; when the adventure arrives it is in the form (once again) of a sword in a stone; before the knights finally leave there is one last day of jousting organised. This

may well be the highest adventure the Round Table knights have undertaken, but the elements are familiar to us all.

Of Other Worlds

The context, however, is decidedly new and there is an almost oppressive
sense of significance. No mockery heralds the arrival of the unknown adolescent who is to succeed in the adventure; Galahad is no Balin, Gareth, La
Cote Male Tayle or, even, Perceval, and he is brought before the court by
nuns. Moreover, Arthur's words of farewell as his knights set out, with
their patterned repetition have all the urgency of a final good-bye:

> 'Now . . . I am sure at this quest of the Sankegreall shall all ye of the
> Rownde Table departe, and nevyr shall I se you agayne holé togy-
> dirs, therefore ones shall I se you togydir in the medow, all holé to-
> gydirs! Therefore I woll se you all holé togydir in the medow of
> Camelot, to juste and to turney, that aftir youre dethe men may
> speke of hit that such good knyghtes were here, such a day, holé to-
> gydirs'.

(520.39–44; XIII.6)

The reader, however, soon becomes uneasy in that we seem to be moving in an entirely different world, a world of religious mysticism in which
pseudo-history becomes hagiography. The characters of the Grail book
are all familiar, the elements of the narrative remain the same, but the context is quite strange. As the story goes on there will be much to capture
our imagination: mysterious ships, sumptuous rooms, and beautiful, dangerous women. But the change of context heralds a change of ethos and
the readers' patience is tested by the extremely severe religious doctrine.
Until now, a knight errant could expect to come across a castle from time
to time in which to seek lodging. Now, castles are few and far between
and the forests of England are positively bristling with convents, while the
number of hermits per square mile, all ready to interpret your dreams or
tell you where you went wrong is staggering.

For the adventures of Book VI are never arbitrary, not merely exciting
exhibitions of knightly prowess, they are fraught with meaning and full of
religious symbolism designed to expose a knight's decadence or (more
rarely) his deserving: his spiritual life or death is at stake. When the explanations are succinct, the reader does not demur, but the hermits of the
Grail book can be loquacious and the moralising may seem tiresome. One
suspects that Malory felt the tedium too: he does not always ensure that
his hermits explain themselves with clarity. Malory, of course, could not

possibly have left such an important and well-known episode out of his history, but when he left the world of romance for that of spiritual experience, he did so – it would seem – with a heavy heart. Yet he felt the compulsion and the underlying logic of the whole story, which demands the Grail Quest.

Book VI, sees the recognition of the notion of sin. Till now, the knights we have met were (or were not) upright, courageous, gallant, dependable, honest, just – in a word, knightly. They were usually good men, of moral fibre, though not, of course, saints. They were, after all, men. In Book VI ideal knighthood now embraces (and demands) chastity, and so all the men we once took to be heroes now turn out to be failures. The sort of acts that once passed unnoticed, that were indeed, everyday aspects of knightly adventure, are now singled out for castigation. Life was once so cheap, heads were lopped off without a qualm. Now, killing another man is a sin: 'For ... as synfull as ever sir Launcelot hath byn, sith that he wente into the queste of the Sankgreal he slew never man nother nought shall, tylle that he com to Camelot agayne; for he hath takyn upon hym to forsake synne' (563.16–19; XVI.5). The rules of the game have been suddenly changed and without warning. The new reader might well get lost, irritated, or bored. Many people are tempted to skip.

Virginity and chastity are unfashionable virtues and it is hard to muster much enthusiasm for knights who succeed in a quest because they are clean virgins (like Galahad and Perceval) or (like Bors, who has known the pleasures of the flesh on one occasion only) repentant and totally chaste. When chastity is a guarantee of success, modern readers tend to lose interest in success. We tire of the endless attacks on knights we once admired. They cannot hope to succeed now that their exploits are being judged from an entirely different point of view, according to a set of religious principles we (and they) had no reason to suspect counted for so much. It is almost as though they are being victimised. We do not begrudge Galahad, Perceval, and Bors their victory, or imagine that it is undeserved; basically, we just do not care. Nor can we feel much regret or emotion for the death of Galahad or Perceval. They go to a better world, no doubt, but they have never warmed our hearts. 'She was too good for me' says Juliet's nurse, with scarce a tear as she recalls the death of her own child. Perhaps the loss of Galahad strikes us in much the same way.

Contradictions

The basic difficulty with Book VI is that in many ways it comes too late. By now we have wholeheartedly accepted the premises of Arthurian chivalry, and we have just spent some considerable time reading all about its age of glory. This is no time to tell us that it is worth nothing. And yet Book VI tries to do precisely that: it introduces us to a world of spiritual experience in which earthly chivalry – 'knyghtes dedys in worldly workis' – is infinitely inferior to heavenly chivalry – 'knyghtly dedys in Goddys workys' (531.25–26; XIII.14). On this scale of values, Galahad, totally devoted to spiritual matters, is the perfect knight, and Gawain, who has forgotten knightly deeds and virtuous living, the most corrupt:

> And sir Galahad ys a mayde and synned never, and that ys the cause he shall enchyve where he goth that ye nor none suche shall never attayne, nother none in youre felyship, for ye have used the moste untrewyst lyff that ever I herd knyght lyve.
>
> (535.9–12; XIII.16)

Gawain is cleverly characterised in the Grail book. The quest bores him. Adventures are in rather short supply and he loses patience, failing to see that the lack of adventure is a reflexion on himself. When a man of God later tells him this and explains the reasons for his failure, Gawain listens politely. When the good man tries to continue Gawain points out that he would willingly listen to more, but he really doesn't have time. It is interesting that Book VI continues the portrait of Gawain as a corrupt knight, but there is more than a suspicion that the description here is a little biased.

The morality of Book VI is most troublesome, however, and most fascinating in relation to Lancelot. The arrival of Galahad represents the demotion of Lancelot since the son is the living proof of the father's sin. In a world where the passport to success is virginity or at the very least chastity, Lancelot, who has 'bene the devillis servaunte four and twenty yerys' (562.38–39; XVI.4), can scarcely hope to be among the medal winners. Indeed, the French version of the Grail quest that Malory was translating here (perhaps a little too closely for the comfort of his own ethic) condemns Lancelot without hesitation. In earthly adventures Lancelot always won; in this world he is out of his depth.

Malory's version of this idea is more complex. Of course Lancelot is sinful and that sin must disqualify him from total success, but apart from his love for Guenevere, Lancelot is the best of them all. Galahad, Perceval and Bors are in an entirely separate category; where all the others are concerned, Lancelot is by far the best, the best of the sinful, he is told: 'for of a synner erthely thou hast no pere as in knyghthode nother never shall have' (555.11–12; XV.4). Malory's commitment to Lancelot (and ours too) is such that he refuses to abandon him here. His Grail book is more tolerant than the French, and this warm understanding of weakness in a great man is something we readily sympathise with. Malory admits that Galahad is perfect and gives him his reward, but he prefers to turn his interest to another category, the sinful, and concentrates on what is best there. It is this which guides Malory's moral distinctions in the final tales: Lancelot is the 'trewest lover, of a synful man, that ever loved woman' (725.21; XXI.13), and Guenevere turned to a life of penance as sincerely 'as ever ded synfull woman in thys londe' (717.43–718.1; XXI.7)

Malory refuses to abandon earthly chivalry, which he sees as a legitimate part of the Grail quest: 'For he shall have much erthly worship that may bryng hit to an ende' says Bors (564.8–9; XVI.6) In the same way he stresses the fact that Lancelot's success in earthly adventure is itself God given, even though Lancelot admits that he was inspired by his love for Guenevere in all the exploits he undertook. A hermit urges him to forsake the Queen and to avoid wickedness, but the penance he is given is not to take to a life of religious devotion, not to reject the earthly chivalry that is so inferior; he is enjoined to 'sew knyghthode and to do fetys of armys' (540.12–13; XIII.20). For earthly chivalry, properly pursued, is in itself fine. And it is so because, as Lancelot explained earlier (161.1 ff.; VI.10) there is a close link between virtue and knightly achievement. Those who are impure 'be nat happy nother fortunate unto the werrys.' Logically, therefore, Lancelot's preeminence in earthly chivalry is a statement of his moral superiority. Indeed, for Gawain it puts him in the same category as Galahad, Perceval, and Bors, 'for they four have no peerys' (558.26; XVI.1). Nor is it merely that Gawain is so corrupt himself that he has an exaggerated reverence for even a modest virtue, since Malory, too, presents Lancelot in this way, and is reluctant to admit his failure in the quest. Lancelot's vision of the Grail may be partial, but it is enough to make him one of the four knights whose adventures are placed on record:

> And whan they had etyn the kynge made grete clerkes to com before hym, for cause they shulde cronycle of the hyghe adventures of the good knyghtes. So whan sir Bors had tolde hym of the hyghe adventures of the Sankgreall such as had befalle hym and hys three felowes, which were sir Launcelot, Percivale and sir Galahad and hymselff, than sir Launcelot tolde the adventures of the Sangreall that he had sene. And all thys was made in grete bookes and put up in almeryes at Salysbury.
>
> (607.31–38; XVII.23).

Malory's story of the Grail quest is not quite the traditional version, because his brand of spirituality is more practical, less other-worldly. The quest may well point up the weaknesses of earthly ideals, but it does not destroy the ethic altogether. Malory may momentarily turn his eyes towards heaven, but his feet remain firmly on the ground. For a knight to be a good Christian he must be a good knight. The Arthurian world may be

why?

imperfect, but it is the best of the sinful. That something better exists, Malory will not deny. It is simply not his subject.

BOOK VII
LANCELOT AND GUENEVERE: VIRTUE AND PRUDENCE

Everyone agrees that Books VII and VIII are the finest of Malory's tales. Separate editions of them have been published and they are the only parts of the *Morte Darthur* some people read. The final two books present a series of connected events. This is congenial to modern taste since we are used to reading novels. We should realise, however, that the method is not typical of Malory's work as a whole. The rather arbitrary connectiveness of the central tales produces a leisurely pace and an expansiveness appropriate to the depiction of an age of glory. There is no need to rush things; we can take our time getting an overall picture. The sense of inevitability of the final tales, where things happen because of other things (often arbitrary in themselves), gives a much greater feeling of speed. This is not a slow process of decline; once the wheel has passed its highest point – the point of apparent immobility – the weight of events will pull it quickly down.

Although there was a movement from rumour to certitude, the relationship of Lancelot and Guenevere remained in the background of the central section of the *Morte Darthur*. It was never allowed to disturb the public surface of events because the insinuations of Morgan le Fay and King Mark were discredited on account of the unreliability of the source. The final part of the *Morte Darthur* takes the same movement from rumour to certitude but concentrates on the public sphere. The Grail book tells us the lovers are guilty; Books VII and VIII are the public revelation of that guilt. And yet at the same time Malory is not interested in merely punishing Lancelot and Guenevere for their sin. Its wages may well be the death of the flower of kings and knights but their contribution is shown to be at once central and incidental. Of course there would have been no political collapse if their adultery had not provoked disruption; but it took a lot more than adultery to destroy the realm. However reprehensible the behaviour of the lovers may be, Malory lays the emphasis clearly on the far more destructive guilt of the others, and, in the face of such villainy, on the great virtue of Lancelot and the queen. Their love, admittedly, caused trouble, but Malory takes time to describe and justify it; it is, he says, virtuous love.

Book VII is divided into five parts. In the first, Lancelot is unable to do without Guenevere, although he had vowed to in the Grail quest, but decides to conceal their affair by paying attention to other ladies and apparently proclaiming his indifference to the queen. His ruse is unfortunately so convincing that even Guenevere is taken in, and having banished Lancelot, she flaunts her own indifference to him by organising a private dinner for other knights. Sir Pinel seizes the opportunity to settle an old score – past vendettas are coming alive again – and poison Sir Gawain, but another knight dies instead, and the queen is accused of murder. The lovers are reconciled when Lancelot comes to save the queen. If they had never quarrelled, if Guenevere had been more reasonable (but then she would not have been Guenevere) trouble-makers would have been robbed of an opportunity to act.

In the second section, Lancelot thoughtlessly gives encouragement to a young woman who loves him, by accepting a token from her to complete the disguise he has decided to wear. The maid's love provokes Guenevere's jealousy, but it is unrequited love and Elayne dies for Lancelot. It is a moving story of romantic love in which the traditional roles are reversed – the lady takes the initiative and languishes for love – and which reminds us of the sexual attraction of valour. At a time when his behaviour is about to come under attack, Lancelot is shown not to be a cheap adulterer, but a man whose moral superiority can totally subjugate the honest love of a pure maiden. The story of the Maiden of Astolat is a celebration of Lancelot's merit.

The subject of the third section is a tournament. Lancelot's success in combat is all the more remarkable in that he has recently been accidentally wounded by a lady hunter (another parallel with the earlier career of Tristram). The tournament also brings Gareth back to our attention.

In the fourth episode Lancelot rescues Guenevere from the clutches of Meliagaunt (her admirer from the Tristram book), but injures himself trying to enter her bedroom. The bloodstains on the bed (another reminder of Tristram) suggest to the caddish Meliagaunt that Guenevere has betrayed Arthur with one of her guards, who were wounded while trying to stop Meliagaunt from kidnapping her. Lancelot has no difficulty disposing of this carelessly formulated accusation and the lovers are saved again. In case the reader feels that Lancelot and the queen are lucky here but steeped in guilt, Malory takes the trouble to introduce this section with a long passage exlaining the virtue of their love not its sordidness.

The final section is another total vindication of Lancelot. None of the Round Table knights is able to heal the Hungarian knight Sir Urry, whose wounds have been festering ever since his last victim's mother put a curse on him seven years before. Lancelot arrives, tries reluctantly and, through the power of prayer, is able to heal the knight. In Book III his prowess was the external manifestation of an inner virtue which enabled him (in the

Chapel Perillous episode) to perform a miracle. We may have thought that Lancelot's inner virtue had become somewhat tainted by now – and Lancelot himself seems none too sure – but Malory obviously does not agree. When Urry is healed, Lancelot weeps 'as he had bene a chylde that had bene beatyn' (688.35–36; XIX.12). It is a touching scene, and all the more so in that Malory offers no explanation of those tears. Perhaps Lancelot is relieved that his sucess has concealed the fact that his virtue is no longer intact; perhaps he is aware of how much he could achieve if only it were. But we do not know. All we can say is that although the wheel of fortune is on its way down, for a moment it stops and almost seems to rise again. Book VII comes to a close – ominously – with Lancelot's finest hour.

BOOK VIII

THE DEATH OF ARTHUR: TRUTH AND ALLEGIANCE

Malory's final book needs little introduction: some of the incidents are well known even if we have read nothing of the *Morte Darthur*. There are passages of great excitement (as when Lancelot has to fight his way out of the queen's chamber), moments of haunting beauty full of a sense of meaning we can somehow never explain (as when Excalibur must be returned to the waters), and scenes that are intensely moving (as when Guenevere sees Lancelot for the last time and sends him away). Anyone coming to Malory for the first time will find nothing troublesome here.

The events form a logical and clear sequence: Agravain and Mordred goad Arthur into laying a trap for Lancelot and the queen; the lovers are caught together in compromising circumstances; Guenevere is brought to trial and Lancelot accidentally kills Gareth, present at the execution but unarmed in protest at the whole business, when he rides in to save the queen. Gawain's vengeance is roused by the death of the best of his brothers, and he forces Arthur to declare war on Lancelot, who returns Guenevere to the king when the Pope orders them to restore peace. Gawain refuses to allow Arthur to seek reconciliation and dies from wounds received in single combat with Lancelot, while another brother, Mordred, continues the work of disruption by claiming the throne and the queen left in his charge. The final battle is sparked off accidentally by the killing of an adder: in an uneasy truce soldiers are sensitive to a carelessly drawn sword. Arthur and Mordred kill each other, Guenevere takes to a nunnery and banishes Lancelot forever when he visits her; they, she says, have caused all this disaster. He imitates her assumption of a life of devotion and they die without meeting again. The kingdom is given to Constantine and Lancelot's companions follow his example into a life of devotion and religious crusade.

When knights are no longer motivated by a code of honour but by private feelings of hate, the situation inevitably deteriorates and the relentless decline into disorder is the result of a mixture of ill luck and ill will. Arthur is no longer able to keep his nephews under control and in Mordred – half nephew, half bastard son of incest – the image of an old, long forgotten transgression rears its head. Gawain loses all self control and diplomacy on the death of Gareth – the image of his better, guileless self – and abandons himself to a thirst for vengeance which is totally destructive. The ties of loyalty that bind him to Arthur, his uncle and his king, become part of a blackmailer's pact: if Arthur and Lancelot become reconciled his own allegiance will be forfeited. And Mordred's villainy is beyond words. He who provoked the initial crisis by daring to assert (with inadequate proof) the impropriety of Lancelot's love for the queen and his consequent treason to the crown, now usurps the crown and (but Guenevere is too wise) tries to take to bed the wife of the king, his uncle, and his own father. At the end Guenevere banishes Lancelot from her sight because they two have brought about all this chaos; by the time we read these words it is hard for us to believe them. Lancelot is the only one who, to the last, fights to save the realm.

The realm of course is not totally destroyed and another king comes to the throne. But we are not interested. All the knights we have admired are gone, and the end of Malory's book is, in a real sense, the end. There is nothing left, no further volume for another historian to write. Life may well continue, but in little, the sort of life we all live and know only too well. Certainly nothing to write about.

A READING LIST

The preceding guide was designed to give the reader an overall acquaintance with the *Morte Darthur*, to provide an idea of what the book is about and what it is like. It is meant to help the reader approach and find his way about in Malory, but it cannot replace a first hand, personal knowledge of the book. The *Morte Darthur* is vast and the newcomer need not worry about reading it all at once, nor about reading it in chronological order.

A number of selections from the *Morte Darthur* have been published and it might be tempting to recommend the reading of one of these; but I think it is always better for the reader to do his own selecting. It would not be a bad idea for him to open the *Morte Darthur* and continue reading as long as he is enjoying it. When his attention begins to waver, it is perhaps time to pass on to something else. In many ways this is rather Malorian advice since Malory seems to have worked in much the same way: he often cuts the matter short and turns elsewhere.

If I were asked which passages I would suggest to provide the reader with a reasonably representative selection from the *Morte Darthur*, perhaps I would propose the following, aware, as I do so, that some people will find me blind to essentials and my list exceedingly thin or unnecessarily long. No advice at all, of course, can help the student who wants to know what is the minimum he has to read.

Book I: The first three sections (Caxton's Books I to III) – though readers might well wish to hurry through the account of Arthur's early wars (though it is here that Arthur receives Excalibur) and go straight on to the Balin story. Read the story of Torre and the others for as long as you wish, till you get the feel of the book and would like to move on.

Book II: Read the first few pages and then browse.

Book III and IV: All

Book V: The first (long) section (Caxton's Book VIII) and the last but one (Caxton's Books XI and XII).

Book VI: Sections one and two (Caxton's Book XIII), and sections four, five, and nine if you can (Caxton's Book XV and XVI up to chapter 5, and the second half of Book XVIII).

Books VII and VIII: All.

It is not necessary to read the selections in this order; it is not as though we have never heard of Arthur and the Round Table knights before. Since Books VII and VIII are the finest and the most immediately accessible, some readers might prefer to begin here, reading everything else in flashback.

Those who would like a modicum of chronology, could try reading the beginning of Book I, Book III, and Books VII and VIII before turning to the rest. In this way they will see both Arthur and Lancelot as young men before reading of their final conflict. It is up to each reader to choose his method. Anyone who feels tempted to give up before reaching Books VII and VIII has chosen the wrong method, should immediately leave what he is reading, and proceed there at once.

Before going any further with this book, the reader should now turn to the *Morte Darthur*. From now on I will take it for granted that he is at least acquainted with the major incidents of the book, though there will always be enough page references for him to refresh his memory if necessary.

My discussions will often concentrate on the final tales, because these are both the best and the most frequently read and studied. It is also there that the central issues become particularly clear.

2

A Reading of the Morte Darthur

LOVE AND LICENCE

A character in David Lodge's novel *Small World* gives a useful definition of romance:

> Real romance is a pre-novelistic kind of narrative. It's full of adventure and coincidence and surprises and marvels, and has lots of characters who are lost or enchanted or wandering about looking for each other, or the Grail, or something like that. Of course, they are often in love too . . .

This offers a very reasonable assessment of the *Morte Darthur* and the final sentence is singularly appropriate. For in Malory, love is both a *sine qua non* and an afterthought, at once the first thing we recall, and something we suspect Malory was not very interested in.

At times it is not easy to isolate the author's attitude at all. Indeed, two of the most famous passages about love in the *Morte Darthur*, to which attention is often drawn, seem strangely inconsistent with the story. One is, admittedly, put into the mouth of a character (Lancelot), but the other is a direct statement by the author. The first is a denial of the importance of love in comparison with knightly endeavour, and the second is a definition of love in those days which seems to be contradicted by almost all the amorous goings on we are witness to. It is a statement of a theory which most knights in Malory seem to fail to put into practice. We will consider both passages in a moment.

The Arthurian legends contain two of the greatest love stories of all times, stories of great power which were obviously suitable material for the constantly developing interest during the medieval period in personal experience and the analysis of feeling. Over the years the concentration on the refinements of courtly sentiment became excessive and the genre went out of fashion or – according to Joachim du Bellay and Chaucer's Nun's

love is subsumed in category of all earthly experience.

Priest, at least – was relegated to a (light-headed) feminine audience. When Malory chose to give his version of the Arthurian legends, he naturally adopted the central love stories, but since he was not interested in the private affairs of lovers, but rather in their social behaviour, he removed much of the love intrigue and rescued the material from excess. An apparent lack of interest in love, that is, places the stories firmly at the centre of his work. The relationships of Lancelot and Guenevere or Tristram and Isolde are important in the *Morte Darthur* because there were far-reaching public consequences, and Malory therefore gives them pride of place. But he turns a blind eye to the trivialities of what the lovers did in private and we rarely see them alone. What is more, Malory introduces the love of Lancelot and Guenevere in its fully fledged state. By Book III they are already lovers (in reputation at least), but we have been shown nothing of their first meeting, let alone the first kiss of a relationship which is to shake and unsettle the Arthurian world.

The martial spirit of Malory's book leaves little scope for the investigation of private behaviour. Not much of Tristram's time is spent with Isolde, and even when they are comfortably *en ménage* in Lancelot's castle we are rarely in their joint presence. We are not surprised perhaps: we recall that the love potion was scarcely dry on Tristram's lips before he was expressing regret that his obligations to Isolde prevented his riding off in search of Sir Lancelot (263.1–3; VIII.28). Malory and his knights are more interested in fighting than in amatory experience. Nothing could be more alien to the spirit of Malory's book than the pacifist slogan of the 1960s: make love not war.

If anything, Malory proposes the opposite slogan: make war not love. Lancelot rejects both wives and mistresses and declares:

> But for to be a weddyd man, I thynke hit nat, for than I muste couche with hir and leve armys and turnamentis, batellys and adventures. And as for to sey to take my pleasaunce with peramours, that woll I refuse: in prencipall for drede of God, for knyghtes that bene adventures sholde nat be advoutrers nothir lecherous, for than they be nat happy nother fortunate unto the werrys; for other they shall be overcom with a sympler knight than they be hemself, other ellys they shall sle by unhappe and hir cursednesse bettir men than they be hemself. And so who that usyth peramours shall be unhappy, and all thynge unhappy that is aboute them.
>
> (161.2–11; VI.10).

With our modern taste for psychological interpretation we might suspect that Lancelot is something of an overgrown adolescent, not really interested in girls yet (or still frightened of them), or that he has been listening too closely to the advice of the team coach, encouraging celibacy in his men to keep them at fever pitch before the big match. Of course, Lancelot is in a corner here. A lady has mentioned the rumour that he is having an affair with the queen. Guilty or innocent he can do no other than tactfully evade the question and defend the queen's name by presenting some sort of excuse. But interestingly, he chooses to do so with a defence of chivalry which amounts to a denial of love. The lady makes no comment, but one suspects that she could not believe what she was hearing. What Lancelot is saying scarcely makes sense in a world of romance, where ladies are supposedly the inspiration of knightly exploit. Malory's notion of love seems to go against everything the romance world stands for, and is decidedly his own. Love may be splendid in its own way, but for a knight who wants to achieve true worship, it is something of a burden. Of course the service of ladies is an essential part of a knight's duty, but in the *Morte Darthur* the emphasis falls on adventure.

In Malory, ladies are important but their charm and personalities are not. They are the distressed creatures who create the need and opportunity for adventure for good knights, or are the objects of lustful desire by bad knights. Most of them remain nameless, even the married lady who is exceptional enough to capture the heart of both her king (Mark) and the finest knight of his realm (Tristram). But desirable as she clearly is, her status as a married woman is what is crucial to the story, which is about the conflict of social relationships. She is the wife of Sir Segwarides; his name is far more important than hers.

Remnants of the Courtly Tradition

The reader cannot fail to notice this reticence to develop the love interest, as though Malory in his concern for action and adventure begrudged it space. And yet at the same time, the spirit of medieval romantic love remains present and some of its basic assumptions are taken for granted. Love is an aristocratic ideal, reserved exclusively for the nobility. It seems no reproach to King Pellinor that he takes advantage of the willingness of Torre's peasant mother, and there is no question of making an honest woman out of her (62.18 ff.; III.3).

Love when it arrives is love at first sight; there is no steady getting to know the loved one. Some couples even seem to be or to fall in love on principle. Gareth and his lady are exclusively devoted to each other before they meet, as though his exploits in her service are expressions of a love relationship which was part of the bargain when he took up the adventure. Most characters whose love entanglements are mentioned enter the narrative with their hearts already engaged. When Malory mentions the beginnings of a passion, he does so without any attempt to analyse the feelings involved: the relationship is a given element in his story. 'And there had Arthure the firste syght of queene Gwenyvere, the kyngis doughter of the londe of Camylarde, and ever afftir he loved hir' (26.28–30; I.18).

Instant love is possible, not because Malory's knights are easily satisfied, but because his ladies are all equally and exceptionally beautiful. Guenevere, is the loveliest of them all, a touchstone for the beauty of others, who are judged in relation to her: 'sir Launcelot thought she was the fayryst lady that ever he saw but yf hit were quene Gwenyver' (478.24–26; XI.1). Something of an exception is made for Elaine the mother of Galahad, who is not only described without reference to Guenevere, but is, quite frankly, for Lancelot 'the fayrest woman that ever he sye in his lyeff dayes' (486.2–3; XI.7).

Malory has no degrees of beauty. Guenevere and Elaine are above the norm, but no one is below – except perhaps the lady Ettard who has the distinction of being the only lady to be judged from the feminine point of view. In Malory's eyes all his ladies are equally lovely, but Ettard behaves so despicably towards Sir Pelleas that the other ladies protest. Many of them would have been only too glad to have his love; Ettard should consider herself lucky. And who is she to display such haughty indifference? After all, she is no oil painting herself (100.22 ff.; IV.22).

Love brings pain and suffering, and, at times, even death. Kayhadyns dies for love of Isolde and Palomides is convinced the same fate awaits him; Elayne of Astolat (in a reversal of the usual roles) dies of unrequited love for Lancelot. An element of secrecy is essential and this, too, can bring pain, After all, there can be no hope of relief if the lady remains ignorant of a knight's attachment. There is an interesting example of this in Malory. Meliagaunt, who in Book VII causes such havoc by kidnapping Guenevere, is in fact the typical lover who 'loved passyngly well quene Gwenyver, and so had he done longe and many yerys' (650.16–17; XIX.1), and we see him in Book V in his role as secret admirer of the queen, bemoaning his hopeless state and challenging Lamorak because he has denied the supremacy of Guenevere's beauty. Ironically, Lancelot separates them only to take over from Meliagaunt when he learns why they are fighting. Little did Lancelot realise that he would not always be fighting side by side with Meliagaunt for the sake of Guenevere (297–298; IX.13–14).

The sufferings of love are closely linked to the difficulties involved in courtship and, in the medieval tradition of love, the ladies in Malory who are the principal objects of love are unavailable. Lancelot, Tristram (twice), Mark, Palomides, Meliagaunt are all in love with married women, and although Lamorak's lady is a widow, her husband stands between them none the less. Only Gareth of Malory's major knights finds a lady who is free to love.

The lover is faithful, obedient and long-suffering. Service is its own reward and no joy is necessarily implied. Pelleas, degraded by the one he loves, is an extreme example, and the lady is clearly reprehensible here (100.32 ff.; IV.22), but Gareth gets little pleasure and no recognition (at first) for the deeds he accomplishes in the service of his lady. His sharp-tongued companion, the lady's sister, finally sees the light, but Gareth's long-suffering is seen as an essential part of his nobility. Most important of all is Lancelot, who constantly serves the queen and is rarely seen getting much joy for his pains. Guenevere is touchy, capricious, hot-tempered, illogical, and extremely difficult to please. She sends to Lancelot for help promptly enough when she is kidnapped by Meliagaunt, but when Lancelot finally arrives, having had his horse shot from beneath him and having had to suffer the ignominy of travelling by cart like a convict, the terrified Meliagaunt begs for mercy and Guenevere, preferring to settle the whole business out of court, cannot understand why Lancelot is itching for vengeance and making such a fuss (655–656; XIX.5). The scene is splendidly captured – Lancelot almost not managing to contain his irritation and Guenevere pettishly refusing to admit that she is being in any way unreasonable. For Lancelot, love is, in a real sense, a trial, and the question whether he is happy in the queen's service becomes an irrelevance. He is constant in her service: that is all that counts. He has been exclusively devoted to her for twenty-four years, ever since he started out as one of The Queen's Knights, a rank which in itself offers a fine example of chivalric devotion (see 650.22–35; XIX.1).

Malory is concerned with the details of active service, not the emotional justifications of that service, but his knights, none the less, descend in a direct line from the knights of courtly romance. For a lady they are even willing to endure shame, like the besotted Pelleas, or as when Lancelot rides in a cart, a proof of devotion which Guenevere, to her credit, is quick to acknowledge. There is a French version of this same event (the famous original story, the *Lancelot* of Chrétien de Troyes) in which Lancelot hesitates for a moment to enter the cart and the queen, rather than praise Lancelot's readiness to degrade himself for her, blames him for having hesitated at all. Malory will have nothing to do with excessive refinements of this sort. Of course he may well not have known this French version, but there is an incident elsewhere in the *Morte Darthur* where a similar reaction on the part of a lady does nothing to raise her in our esteem. That kind of woman is simply not worth serving and she is dismissed from the story. The lady is the wife of Sir Segwarides, who is having an affair with Tristram. A knight arrives in court, asks for a favour (which is granted) and says that he wants to take away with him the woman who pleases him most. The wife of Sir Segwarides is the lucky lady and off they go. Tristram cannot leave things like that, but since the lady is married he can scarcely rush off to rescue her himself. It is only when her husband fails that Tristram undertakes her rescue and rides after her. When the lady is given the choice between her lover, Tristram, and the knight who is leading her away, she refuses Tristram:

> Wete thou well, sir Trystrames de Lyones, that but late thou was the man in the worlde that I moste loved and trusted, and I wente ye had loved me agayne above all ladyes. But whan thou sawyste this knyght lede me away thou madist no chere to rescow me, but suffirdyst my lorde sir Segwarydes to ryde after me. But untyll that tyme I wente ye had loved me. And therefore now I forsake the and never to love the more.
>
> (250.30–36; VIII.18).

For Malory this is not justified indignation at a knight's failure in courtly service. The wife of Sir Segwarides is clearly not worth all this trouble and we are not surprised when the other knight is only too ready to let her go back to her husband. It is true that we must not draw too many conclusions from Tristram's early love intrigues since the morality is rather uncomfortably murky, but it is clear that the first object of his affections is unworthy of him and unjust towards him. Sir Segwarides' later comment 'I woll never hate a noble knyght for a lyght lady' (275.11; VIII.38) is a pretty fair assessment of his wife.

In the courtly tradition it is a knight's courage, worship, and prowess that are the masculine equivalents of a lady's beauty. The French romances give an important place to male beauty too – Gauvain admits to the demoiselle d'Escalot that Lancelot is more handsome than himself – but Malory will have nothing to do with this. Knights fall in love with ladies for their beauty, a lady chooses a man according to his deeds. Sir Segwarides' military incompetence – everybody seems to get the better of him – goes a long way to explaining why his wife sought comfort in the arms of another man. A fine record in arms makes a man attractive.

It is clear that Lancelot's extraordinary prowess is the basis of his sex appeal. Ladies are constantly in pursuit of him, vying for his affections or, more frankly, his body. He has done nothing to encourage their attentions or even cultivate this charm other than achieve the knightly preeminence that is sexually irresistible to a whole range of admirers, from the perverted to the perfect. There is the vampish lechery of Morgan le Fay and the necrophiliac urges of the sorceress Hellawes, who, if she cannot have Lancelot alive, knows how to enjoy him dead. There is the somewhat pitiful case of the guardian of his prison cell in Book VII, who resorts to blackmail as her only hope of having Lancelot: she will set him free from

Meliagaunt's castle if he sleeps with her. But Lancelot is a finer man even than she realises, and he refuses, although he feels morally free to grant a single kiss when she lowers her terms. Since she still sets Lancelot free, we can only presume that the kiss was worth having. And then there are Lancelot's other two Elaines – the mother of Galahad and the Maiden of Astolat – both pure and innocent and both determined to have him. One succeeds, though only with supernatural aid and against Lancelot's will; the other dies for him.

All of these are examples of the reversal of the usual courtly roles of amorous pursuit and service. It is the knight who tradionally makes advances and, therefore, in their different ways, all of these ladies are shocking. But then such is the power of Lancelot's appeal that they lay themselves open to blame. Elaine, the mother of Galahad, is excused because the end – the conception of the perfect knight – justifies the means, but the Maid of Astolat, however appealing we feel she is, is not justified. There is no place for this kind of love in the *Morte Darthur* and the Maid is – willy-nilly – a little forward. But then the whole point of her story is her innocent naturalness. She belongs to another world of everyday feelings and commitments, a world of pathos and natural love.

Love as a Knightly Privilege

Love, faithful love, is a proper motivating force for a knight, because it is one facet of that loyal service which is so important for Malory. But more attention is given to the practical manifestations of that loyal service than to its motives. Malory has little time for all the fuss.

In the *Morte Darthur* there is no 'luf talkyng', no dallying with sentiment. Women are not present for the emotional refinement or courtly manners they bring, but to bear offspring or to further the intrigue in the social and sexual context of a clear hierarchy. Or, more simply, they arrive in distress to provide the pretext for yet another adventure. Women serve a purpose in Malory's world, otherwise he shows little interest in them, and at one point – splendidly – betrays his irritation:

> So with thys there com a knyght rydyng all armed on a grete horse, and toke the lady away with forse wyth hym, and ever she cryed and made grete dole. So whan she was gone the kynge was gladde, for she made such a noyse
>
> (63.38–41; III.5)

Arthur, of course, is a gentleman and says nothing to the lady, but

Malory reveals (because, we feel, he shares) the king's lack of patience with a somewhat hysterical woman.

Relationships between the sexes are not Malory's central concern and he shows a soldierly lack of fuss about sex, which is, after all, perfectly natural. Sexual encounter is an accepted part of a knight's life, a normal and just reward for a fighting man. Morals are barely, if at all, involved, and there is none of the modern obsession with physical contact (its skills, fears, and fetishes) as a revelation of inner states. If Malory tells us that a man and a woman are in bed, what is there to add? When Lancelot finds himself in the bed of Elaine, the mother of Galahad, Malory's comment speaks for itself: 'Now leve we them kyssynge and clyppynge, as was a kyndely thynge' (487.6–7; XI.8). The word *kyndely* means 'natural' and the sentence could almost be Malory's motto.

This down-to-earth attitude to sexual encounter and relationships between the sexes is seen throughout the *Morte Darthur*. When Uther sees Igrayne he makes no bones about it: whether or not she is married, he wants to go to bed with her. When his desire is thwarted, he takes to his bed alone not because of the slow languishing of the heart, but out of sexual frustration. The sentiments are basic, and yet it is these sentiments which, as it turns out, are at the foundation of what appears to be a perfectly sound royal marriage. Uther and Igrayne marry because they are both young, both healthy, and both unattached. The political stability their union will bring counts for far more than any questions of personal preference or liking – especially, it would seem, on the part of Igrayne. Theirs is a relationship based on mutual comfort and political alliance, but there are clear signs of a genuine mutual concern which show that the marriage worked. There is much that is reasonable here, and though the relationship is a minor one on the overall scheme of things, it sets the tone for the rest of the book. Malory betrays no desire to go into detail, he refuses to consider the awakening of affections and the complexities of emotional response, but he shows great understanding. If his book is unromantic, it is so as the Church of England wedding service is unromantic. It recognises needs and affections, but when events are being recorded and celebrated in public, there is no call for effusion or excess.

It is taken for granted in the *Morte Darthur* that sexual encounters will exist and that this is only natural. No one raises an eyebrow at the sexual initiation of the young King Arthur, despite an outcome that could, in theory, have caused dynastic trouble: before he was well out of his boyhood, Arthur was a father.

Than in the meanewhyle there com a damesell that was an erlis doughter; hys name was Sanam and hir name was Lyonors, a passyng fayre damesell. And so she cam thider for to do omage as

other lordis ded aftir that grete batayle. And kynge Arthure sette hys
love gretly on hir, and so ded she uppon hym, and so the kynge had
ado with hir and gate on hir a chylde. And hys name was Borre, that
was aftir a good knyght and of the Table Rounde.

(26.6–12; I.17).

There was no more to it than that. No doubt the lady and her child
were well provided for, and the whole business handled with discretion,
but that is not Malory's subject. Nor is the nature of the affections, if any,
that brought the young people together. And certainly not the morals of
the affair. Was Arthur right or wrong is an irrelevant question. He was
young, healthy, unattached – and the lady was willing enough – that is all.

This total disregard for questions of sexual morality, this healthy acceptance of physical contact, can be found frequently. When a 'sterne
knyght' rides through the countryside and sees a comely wench on her
way to milk the cows it is not unnatural that he should show an interest in
her. Of course she will put up a certain amount of resistance, but it is not
every day that a peasant girl has to do with a fine knight. She was probably a little afraid, but also flattered by his attentions, and perhaps, good-
naturedly, of course, he led her on a little. It is almost certain that she
exaggerated the amount of resistance she put up when she had to explain
the event later, for she was left in such a condition that an explanation was
unavoidable:

Anone the wyff was fette forth, which was a fayre houswyff. And
there she answerde Merlion full womanly, and there she tolde the
kynge and Merlion that whan she was a mayde and wente to mylke
hir kyne, 'there mette with me a sterne knyght, and half be force he
had my maydynhode. And at that tyme he begate my sonne Torre,
and he toke away fro me my grayhounde that I had that tyme with
me, and seyde he wolde kepe the grayhounde for my love.'

(62.18–24; III.3)

It is an agreeable scene and there is world of meaning in that phrase
'half be force' – Malory sums up the circumstances of the seduction and
the virtue of the victim in a single word – but it is the lack of fuss with
which the events are described which brings the scene alive and makes us
want to embroider. The moral implications of seduction are the last thing
Malory has in mind and the sexual activities of knights is something he
takes entirely for granted. The right and wrong of the circumstances never
flashes through Malory's mind, any more than when he mentions that a
certain knight fathered a child with such and such a lady does he take
time off to worry whether the conception had been legalised or not.

The dismissive attitude towards emotional entanglement and sexual morality characterises the whole of the early part of the *Morte Darthur*. It is only towards the end, with the Grail book, that morality enters, and by then Malory has encouraged too much tolerance for us to accept the change. There, chastity is the essence of a knight's worship, and of the three who succeed in the quest two are virgins and the other lives a life of chastity and repentance after having known the pleasures of the flesh once. His single error makes him inevitably more worldly than the other two, and he, therefore, is the one who returns to tell the tale. In this scheme of things, Lancelot, as we have seen, is imperfect. He has lived wantonly in sin for twenty-four years. And yet Guenevere is his only sin; his persistence in error is another statement – in corrupt form perhaps – of his fidelity. Other knights, however, are castigated for the life of careless promiscuity that until Book VI had gone unnoticed.

Entirely unnoticed, for nothing in the early books suggests that casual sexual activity, though perfectly natural, ought to be discouraged. It is true that no one openly preaches dissipation, but the Arthurian world is sophisticated enough to take sexual liberty in its stride.

When Gareth has completed his adventures, Arthur himself asks whether the young man wishes to wed his lady or have her as his paramour. Gareth chooses marriage and we are pleased, but there is no evidence to suggest that he would have committed a *faux pas* if he had preferred to remain single. His reply would have been no more shocking in itself than the king's offer; he would merely have chosen an alternative life style. We are glad he chooses to marry not because our Victorian morality is rearing its head, but because it is a measure of his devotion to his lady which rounds the story off nicely. His total commitment to her makes the story complete. It is artistically, not morally, satisfying.

It is not often in the *Morte Darthur* that the sexual behaviour of knights is particularly shoddy, but there is an interesting example in Book I. When Gawain goes to bed with the lady Ettard he proves himself to be a cad not because he has taken advantage of a lady (for not everyone would agree that Ettard is one) but because he has double-crossed a fellow knight. Gawain, supposedly helping Pelleas to win the lady's affections, should not have been savouring those affections himself. But the sexual misdemeanour is of no importance in itself, except as a sign of a more fundamental corruption in Gawain.

There is something finely aristocratic, perhaps, in this disregard for conventional morality that we find in Malory. The working classes are not less immoral (as Torre's mother proves), but they are less openly so. In Malory's world, small-minded morality plays no part. It is no slur on Sir Torre that he is a bastard, and no one criticises Arthur for his wild youth, and not even, really, for fathering Mordred. In the overall scheme of things Arthur will be punished for his incestuous relations with his half-sister. To us, this seems rather unfair since Arthur did not know who she was when he slept with her, but ultimately it must be seen as an inevitable part of the story, not part of the morality. And as far as Mordred himself is concerned, until he becomes the positive villain of the piece, he is not a social outcast. This is not because a veil of discretion is thrown over the circumstances of his birth, but simply because the subject is never broached. Sexual matters count for little in Malory. King Pellinor is a man of such honour that being related to him – in whatever way – can only be an advantage. Torre should be proud who his father was, not embarrassed at his mother's somewhat easy virtue. Kinship not the rights and wrongs of amorous entanglements is what concerns Malory, and in the *Morte Darthur* nobility is the virtue that cancels a multitude of sins.

The circumstances of Torre's conception make this abundantly clear; not merely because when Pellinor came along Torre's mother was unmarried (although this assures us that Torre is not the child of some sordid adulterous encounter with ill-matched parents like figures from a fabliau), but because being fathered by a king defies all logic. It is something you just cannot hide. You only have to look at Torre, a fine strapping youth with a talent for knightly pursuits, beside his rustic brothers to see whom he takes after. A blood test of course – if you insist – would confirm paternity, but there is surely no need: not only does Aries' blood belong to the wrong group, it is also the wrong colour.

The Limits of Libertinism

Malory's knights (and ladies) may seem untroubled by the interdictions of conventional morality, but there are limits to the sexual freedom they enjoy. First of all, a certain strictness is observed in questions of inheritance and succession. Arthur is conceived out of wedlock (but not in adultery) and well before his birth, his parents are duly married. And even then, Uther was not making an honest woman out of Igrayne since she had been that all along. When Arthur was conceived she believed she was being a chaste wife.

There is no question of a bastard inheriting a title, and the ambiguous circumstances surrounding Arthur's infancy are, at first, an impediment to his being declared king. Arthur's own first-born son, Sir Borre le Cure Hardy, is never more than name because he is not a legitimate heir: in the list of knights – arranged in order of social importance – who try to heal Sir Urry he comes towards the bottom. Mordred, the other bastard son, comes near the top only because he is also Arthur's nephew.

It is in order not to complicate questions of inheritance that the married ladies of the *Morte Darthur* who take lovers appear to be barren. When knights meet ladies, desire to lie with them, and do so, the ladies regularly conceive. But that is because they are free to do so. It would be innappropriate however for Isolde or Guenevere to conceive. This is not because pregnancy or motherhood could tarnish their image as the heroines of famous love stories. The idea of Guenevere walking the halls of Camelot in the latter stages of pregnancy or with a flock of children pulling at her skirts is perhaps distasteful to our romantic imagination, but not all Malorian knights seem to have looked on life in the same way: Lamorak idolises Morgause because she is 'modir unto sir Gawayne and to sir Gaherys, and modir to many other' (354.32–33; X.8). Rather, it would be improper for the sordid business of paternity, inheritance and bastardy to come along and taint the splendour of these love affairs. It is of course part of the tragedy of the *Morte Darthur* that Guenevere is implicitly barren (both Arthur and Lancelot father children easily enough), that the kingdom has no heir, but for the emotional level of the story to have any power, it is essential that she should be so.

There is a second restriction to sexual liberty in Malory: casual sexual encounter is not acceptable in the clear context of a social setting. With reference to a family, questions of duty, loyalty, and allegiance arise to complicate matters. The sort of girl a knight comes across in a forest, on a mountain, or while out riding in search of adventure is one thing, but ladies who have fathers and brothers are quite another. It is at this point, of course, that Malory's morality comes closer to something resembling reality. It is hard to imagine all those unattached ladies who copulate, conceive, and give birth without meeting the slightest opprobrium in the *Morte Darthur* having such an easy time in fifteenth century England. A young woman, after all, could be important for the financial interests of her family. As a possession she was not to be devalued thoughtlessly since, through marriage, alliances could be made that would be beneficial to all. And at the very least her own welfare as well as family honour depended on her untarnished reputation. This very practical attitude is frequently overlooked in the *Morte Darthur*, but not always. The reader must be prepared for both.

When Gareth is being entertained by Sir Persaunt, he is offered the bedtime services of a young lady – none other than Sir Persaunt's own daughter. Gareth refuses the lady with polite firmness: 'God deffende me ... than that ever I sholde defoyle you to do sir Persaunte such a shame! Therefore I pray you, fayre damesell, aryse oute of this bedde, other ellys I woll' (192.40–42; VII.12). It is a puzzling incident, for although Gareth passes this test of his nobility we are – inevitably – left wondering about the wisdom of the father's methods. (It is a stroke of luck that he was not testing Gawain!). But Malory's moral position is made perfectly clear.

There may be occasions when a knight can take up life's little offers as they come, but when one owes a duty to a host, a modicum of self discipline is in order.

This incident is not the only one in which Gareth's moral rectitude is tested. When the first stage of his adventures is complete and he has won his lady, the two of them decide to anticipate the wedding ceremony. Neither of them is particularly experienced in the required duplicities of sexual encounter, and the lady's sister, finding out about their projects, decides to put a stop to them. The methods she uses involve supernatural skills but her motives show a natural concern for family honour. Gareth and Lyonesse see no shame in their love. Lyonesse has told her brother 'I shame nat to be with hym nor to do hym all the plesure that I can' (206.19–20; VII.22), but her sister is determined to hold them back from impropriety. The honour of the family is at stake, after all, and she has no regrets about interfering: 'all that I have done I woll avowe hit, and all shall be for your worshyp and us all' (206.37–38; VII.22).

A totally different aspect of family honour is seen in the story of Lamorak, in love with Queen Morgause of Orkney, the widow of King Lott, and mother to Gawain and many others. The lady is unattached, her sons are grown up, and since she has not lost her looks – Lamorak thinks she is lovelier than Guenevere; he is wrong of course, as Lancelot points out, but no one ever says the claim is ridiculous – she is surely allowed one final fling with a younger man. In itself there is nothing wrong with the affair. Unfortunately, her wanton boys are convinced that Lamorak's father killed theirs, and they see their mother's liaison therefore not as an unobjectionable Indian summer of a romance to beguile her solitude, but as an insult against their family name. And the insult is such that Gaherys, finding his mother in bed with Lamorak, strikes off her head in a fury of obsessive tribal honour. There is something almost Sicilian in the spirit of this honour, in which the sons gang up on their mother's lover to avenge their father's name. It is a primitive code and yet at the same time has a logic of its own. Gaherys has no qualms about beheading his mother, but refuses to fight with Lamorak because of an unfair advantage: Lamorak, rising from a bed of passion, is unarmed.

Perhaps the clearest – certainly the most central – example of the social context placing a restraint in affairs of love and sexual activity is the story of the Maid of Astolat. It is important because Malory handles the story in such a way that this restraint is made abundantly clear. When the maid makes her declaration of love, she does so not in private – this is not a courtly affair that concerns only Lancelot and herself – but specifically in front of her father and her brothers. When Lancelot declares that he has no intention of marrying, she asks – with her family as witnesses – to become his mistress, and Lancelot is able to refuse both firmly and honourably

with reference to those witnesses: ' "Jesu deffende me!" seyde sir Launcelot. "For than I rewarded youre fadir and youre brothir full evyll for their
grete goodnesse!" ' (638.22–23; XVIII.19)

The personal feelings of Elayne are ignored entirely. And when Lancelot makes a counter proposition to comfort Elayne, he does so within the
social context of her own future life: he offers to settle a fine sum of money
on her for her husband and her heirs. Some critics attack Lancelot for
trying to buy Elayne off, but this is not how Malory sees it. The Maid of
Astolat has approached Lancelot with a very personal and pointed request and he is forced to reply more directly than he would have wished.
He cannot rely on the rules of a courtly love game – no non-committal gallantry will suffice now – because she herself has broken the rules by being
so forthright. Instead, Lancelot shifts the emphasis most properly by referring to the very social context in which she has knowingly placed herself
to make her request. She is so enamoured that she declares, in front of her
family, that she is ready to sacrifice her honour for him: he is so enamoured (of Guenevere) that he turns to Elayne's family and refuses with
politeness, honour, and consideration not the maid herself, but her sacrifice.

In a clearly defined social setting – when a girl has a father and brothers
– the amorous conventions of romantic love can cause harm, and those
elegant literary manipulations of sentiment frequently gloss over the
moral issue. Malory is not always at ease here, and there is much ambiguity. Basically his story forces it all upon him. But when greater moral issues are concerned sexual encounter can be whitewashed. No one
criticises Galahad's mother, but then, here, the family context works differently. Her father is a party to her visiting Lancelot's bed, not because
like Sir Persaunt he is using his daughter to test the young man's virtue,
but because he knows how the story will end (479.26–32; XI.2). In a literal
sense, the *issue* of this encounter is all important. The honour involved is
such that all stain is eradicated and even Guenevere shows understanding
(485.14–19; XI.6). And for Guenevere to understand, something important
must be involved. Indeed, Elaine, albeit to puritan eyes an unmarried
mother, had such moral weight that she can even lecture the queen for her
morals:

> Madame, ye ar gretly to blame for sir Launcelot, for now have ye
> loste hym, for I saw and harde by his countenaunce that he ys
> madde for ever. And therefore, alas! madame, ye have done grete
> synne and youreselff grete dyshonoure, for ye have a lorde royall of
> youre owne, and therefore hit were youre parte for to love hym; for
> there ys no quene in this worlde that hath suche another kynge as ye
> have. And yf ye were nat, I myght have getyn the love of my lorde

sir Launcelot; and grete cause I have to love hym, for he hadde my maydynhode and by hym I have borne a fayre sonne whose name ys sir Galahad. And he shall be in hys tyme the beste knyght of the worlde.

(487.43–488.8; XI.9)

This is moral problem which in real life terms is inevitable, but within the conventions of his historical romance it is one Malory chooses to ignore not develop. The famous May passage – which we shall turn to in a moment – ignores this aspect of Guenevere's situation altogether.

Towards an Ideal

When higher motives are not involved and when Malory's material forces him to handle questions of amorous intrigue he begins to flounder. The material puts him in deep water, especially, perhaps, in the Tristram story, where much is – frankly – sordid. Although Tristram is repeatedly praised for his nobility and excellence, and although the Tristram and Isolde theme looks like a prelude to the later material, there is little in the amorous encounters of the book to win our wholehearted approval. Tristram's affair with the wife of Sir Segwarides, as we have seen, does nothing to enhance his reputation for clean living, and virtue does not seem to be the strong point of ladies in Cornwall. Of a hundred who, with Isolde, took the test of the horn sent by Morgan le Fay only four proved chaste, and even the queen failed the test. Inevitably, because there is no discreet ambiguity surrounding the love of Tristram and Isolde. It is true that compared with the sins of an evil and incompetent king, their misdemeanours seem trivial, but their moral excellence is undermined none the less. There are even tones of brazenness in their relationship which are hard to reconcile with the measured diplomacy of Lancelot and Guenevere. The idea that there should be only four true lovers in the world is moving in itself, but Isolde's declaration to Palomides is essentially tactless:

> Than take thy way . . . unto the courte of kynge Arthure, and there recommaunde me unto quene Gwenyvere and tell her that I sende her worde that there be within this londe but four lovers, and that is sir Launcelot and dame Gwenyver, and sir Trystrames and quene Isode.

(267.20–24; VIII.31)

Lancelot and Guenevere have had a hard time concealing their love from the ill-intentioned, prying eyes of trouble-makers, and Morgan with

her shields and horns is all out to cause trouble; it is consequently hard to
imagine Guenevere receiving Isolde's message with any degree of compo-
sure.

All this is no doubt intended to be lofty sentiment, but the reader is uneasy. Since the morality of Tristram's early amorous adventures is dubious and since his relationship with Isolde quickly goes beyond the pure
and platonic stage, it is hard for us to be convinced when an attempt is
made to restore the reputation of the lovers:

> 'A, fy for shame!' seyde sir Percivale. 'sey ye never so more! For ar
> nat ye uncle unto sir Trystram? And by youre neveaw ye sholde
> never thynke that so noble a knyght as sir Trystram is, that he wolde
> do hymselff so grete vylany to holde his unclys wyff. Howbehit,'
> seyde sir Percivale, 'he may love youre quene synles, because she is
> called one of the fayryst ladyes of the worlde.'
>
> (414.13–18; X.51).

To the pure, apparently, all things are pure, and this speech is indeed a
fine reflexion of the integrity of its speaker. But we have seen too much
and we know that this is no more than a lie. Later Lancelot will declare in
a similar way that Guenevere is true to her lord, King Arthur, but Lancelot's equivocation is designed to convey the essential truth of the queen's
irreproachable conduct as queen. What he says is not just sheer hypocrisy;
if you like, he avoids the precise question altogether. Perceval makes no
attempt to avoid the precise question at all, and tries hard to redeem Tristram. Unfortunately, he is defending a lost cause.

Malory may be fumbling with the moral implications of the Tristram
book, and yet we do get a clear statement of the key virtue that will gov-
ern the action later: fidelity. Tristram is forced to leave Cornwall for Brit-
tany, where he meets and marries another Isolde (Le Blanche Maynes).
Queen Isolde complains to Guenevere, who comforts Isolde with the reminder that good-for-nothing man-stealers (Tristram's legal wife, that is!)
will not have the last laugh:

> So quene Gwenyver sente hir another letter and bade her be of
> goode comforte, for she sholde have joy aftir sorow: for sir Trys-
> trames was so noble a knyght called that by craftes of sorsery ladyes
> wolde make suche noble men to wedde them. 'But the ende,' quene
> Gwenyver seyde, 'shulde be thus, that he shall hate her and love you
> bettir than ever he dud.'
>
> (274.9–14; VIII.37).

Lancelot, moreover, is equally shocked: 'Fye uppon hym, untrew knyght
to his lady! That so noble a knyght as sir Trystrames is sholde by founde
to his fyrst lady and love untrew, that is the quene of Cornwayle!' (273.32–

34; VIII.36). Tristram happily remembers himself in the nick of time and his marriage is never consummated; indeed, his wife never suspects that marital affection goes beyond kissing and cuddling.

This final aspect of the story raises a smile, of course, but it should not blind us to the fact that the notion of fidelity being offered here is distinctly awkward. First of all because it runs counter to legal marriage: Tristram must refuse his wife affection and remain faithful to his mistress, because she is his first love. And secondly, it is hard to accept for the simple reason that we know that this first love Tristram must remain faithful to is not his first love at all. Tristram has a past.

It may well be that Malory accepts the Tristram material too unquestioningly for him to sort out the moral issues. He tries to make what was originally separate material a part of and parallel to the central story of Arthur, but the whole thing fits uncomfortably. And yet however much Malory fumbles with the moral issues, it is clear that he is working towards the notion of perfect fidelity and service, a notion he concentrates on in the final books of the *Morte Darthur*, and one which forms the theme of his only comment on contemporary morals, the famous May passage.

Virtuous Love

At the opening of the Knight of the Cart episode of Book VII, Malory comments at length on fifteenth century morals in relation to ideals in Arthur's day (648.37–649.35; XVIII.25). It is an important passage and the first thing we should point out about it is its position in the *Morte Darthur*. Just at the point at which the *sexual* nature of the affair between Lancelot and Guenevere is to be the subject of a direct accusation, complete with proof, Malory chooses to lecture us on love in order to justify his lovers. The May passage is a strange introduction to the Knight of the Cart section unless we realise what Malory is preparing us for.

Having rescued the queen, Lancelot injures himself gaining access to the queen's chamber and her bed. Bloodstains on the sheets the following morning are evidence to the perfidious Meliagaunt – eager to distract attention from his own crimes – that Guenevere has taken to her bed one of the knight's who were wounded trying to prevent her from being kidnapped (Lancelot is careful to conceal his wound of course). The queen is accused of committing a 'shamefull dede' and we, who know the truth of the situation, might be tempted to believe that the accusation is only technically wrong.

Malory has made it clear that the charge is totally wrong: the queen committed no deed of any kind with one of her knights (the queen, of all people), and how can we imagine that there was any shame involved in what she did with Lancelot: their love was not shameful it was virtuous.

On a later occasion Malory again comes to the rescue when the sexual aspect of their relationship is about to cause trouble. Agravain, Mordred, and a gang of ill-wishers, eager to prove the infidelity of Guenevere, trap the lovers in the queen's chamber. They are unable to force their way in and find the indisputable evidence they want – Lancelot and Guenevere 'nakyd a-bed' together – and must make do with finding Lancelot, at night, in the queen's chamber at all. For them, it is obvious what the lovers were doing till they were disturbed, but Malory refuses to say: 'and whether they were abed other at other maner of disportis, me lyste nat thereof make no mencion, for love that tyme was nat as love ys nowadayes' (676.2–4; XX.3). By withholding information, he provides enough uncertainty to argue in favour of the lovers, and by situating the events once again in the month of May, he not only provides an ironic contrast – 'angur and unhappe' come at a period of rebirth – but also gives us a reminder of the theme of his first May passage, where virtue not guilt was brought to the fore.

May brings a revival of the courtly traditions and virtues of gentleness and service, which have been neglected because love these days is without stability. This is to be regretted, because stability in love is the virtue which covers a multitude of sins, and the virtue consists in getting one's priorities right. Knightly service is motivated first of all by devotion to God, and secondly by devotion to a lady. Love is selfless, and each lover will think of the beloved first – as Lancelot and Guenevere do (see 677.5–12; XX.3).

Nowadays, of course, love soon flares up and dies down because sex is all that counts. In the old days, love was often platonic, its essentials were truth and fidelity, and not merely hopping into bed on the first occasion. Such was the situation in King Arthur's days.

The problem with Malory's defence of love is that little in the *Morte Darthur* corroborates what is being claimed here. Who in Arthur's kingdom loves like this? Certainly not Tristram, and apparently only four out of one hundred ladies in Cornwall. Arthur himself was only too ready to get satisfaction from the ladies he loved, as was his father, and even Gareth, one of Malory's favourite knights, was unable to wait for his wedding night, let alone seven years. The amorous adventures portrayed in the *Morte Darthur* lead to the inevitable conclusion that only Lancelot and Guenevere experienced love of the old kind. Theirs was true, stable service and Lancelot was therefore 'the trewest lover, of a synful man, that ever loved woman' (725.20–21; XXI.13). He was not sinless, but this truth compensated for his sin, just as Guenevere was 'a trew lover, and therefor she had a good ende' (649.34–35; XVIII.25). Her love for Lancelot, that is, brought her to find another love, because, as Malory tells us 'all maner of good love comyth of God' (639.34–35; not in Caxton).

There is, however, one problem with Malory's defence of Lancelot and Guenevere: their love was not entirely platonic, not entirely without 'ly-coures lustis'; Lancelot did not, as Perceval would have said 'love [the] quene synles'. After the return from the Grail quest, their love grows 'hot-ter' and their 'prevy draughtis' (611.16–17; XVIII.1) set the court talking. The self-declared sexual motive of Lancelot's ostentatious boast 'Than shall I prove my myght . . . for youre love' (657.25; XIX.6), as he prepares to break the bars of a window to gain access to Guenevere's bed, is a pa-rody of courtly service, and the hermit's accusation that Lancelot was 'de-fouled with lechory' (540.9; XIII.20) does little to convice us of the virtue of his 'vertuouse love'. Worse than this is Lancelot's own confession – in total contradition to Malory's definition of the ideal love:

> And all my grete dedis of armys that I have done for the moste party was for the quenys sake, and for hir sake wolde I do batayle were hit ryght other wronge. And never dud I batayle all only for Goddis sake, but for to wynne worship and to cause me the bettir to be beloved, and litill or nought I thanked never God of hit.
>
> (539.7–11; XIII.6)

In the May passage Malory does his best to enhance the reputation of Lancelot in preparation for events where his virtue will be questioned, but the confessions of Lancelot's own lips make the task a difficult one.

We can, of course, argue that the contradiction was forced upon Malory by his source material and that the passage from the Grail book should not be given too much importance. Malory retold the Grail story with great fidelity to his source and cannot be held responsible – as he can in the May passage, where he speaks in his own voice – for everything an old French book makes his hero say. What is more, there is even evidence to suggest that Malory wrote his Grail book long before turning to the Knight of the Cart episode, in which case Lancelot's confession may have slipped his mind entirely. What remains essential, however, is that despite the moral error, Lancelot's love for the queen was stable, and that con-stitutes its greatness. He was unfailingly loyal in her service and – in spite of countless opportunities to profit from the amorous attentions of his all too willing and all too numerous admirers – he remained constant in his love. His love was sinful, if you must, but the very persistence in error is an expression of fidelity to the queen.

For Malory, the loyalty expressed in Lancelot's love for Guenevere is parallel to that perfect fidelity and allegiance a man owes to his lord. Love and loyalty are not opposite poles for Lancelot, are not different senti-ments he feels for Guenevere on the one hand and for Arthur on the other.

They are entirely confused. Hence, when it is all over, Lancelot bewails both the king and the queen as he weeps beside their tomb (723.21–32; XXI.11). In the same way, one knight can say of another 'he was the knight I loved best in the world' without any of the ambiguity there would be in modern English. And the clearest example of the confusion of love and loyalty is the relationship between Lancelot and the brother and sister of Astolat. Elayne is struck by love, Lavaine by loyalty at first sight. As he tells his father:

> she doth as I do, for sythen I saw first my lorde sir Launcelot I cowde never departe frome hym, nother nought I woll, and I may folow hym.
>
> (639.13–15; XVIII.19)

Lavaine is a happy figure because love like his can find its full and proper expression in knightly service; Elayne must die because her love can find no outlet at all.

It is as Lancelot realises that his allegiances to his lord and his lady are at cross-purposes that he recalls the importance of stability, and sees that, despite what his fellows believe, 'in me was nat all the stabilite of thys realme' (699.8; XX.18). And we recall the final words of Galahad before he dies; the son, the image of the father's perfection says:

> My fayre lorde, salew me unto my lorde sir Launcelot, my fadir, and as sone as ye se hym bydde hym remembir of this worlde unstable.
>
> (607.3–4; XVII.22)

For it is the clash of allegiances which is the only inherent drawback in the relationship of Lancelot and the queen. Their failure to control their private sentiments, their allowing these sentiments to conflict with public duty, means that things get out of hand, as they have been threatening to all along.

Lancelot and Guenevere have lived with the fear of revelation for some time. Morgan le Fay has been racking her brains to find new gadgets to betray the wicked secret of the lovers she is jealous of: the shield (340.10 ff.; IX.41 ff.) proved too cryptic and the horn never reached its destination. Rumours have been going around but usually from such untrustworthy sources that they are discredited. After all, in the face of loyal and open service something more solid than rumour is called for. Arthur, it is true, has his doubts, but prefers to dismiss them, not because it is less painful to suffer ignominy in private than to make a fuss and have it published abroad, but because indisputable public honour counts for more than hypothetical private shame. Everyone knows of Lancelot's devotion in the service of the queen; it is a relationship which brings honour to all concerned. It is no cheap adulterous affair, a source of shame and disruption.

That the queen should send for Lancelot and that, therefore, he should be found one evening in her chamber is not surprising. He had frequently served her and she, no doubt, had call to thank him yet again. Gawain explains matters clearly. For those who have the unity and well-being of the fellowship at heart all this is perfectly obvious.

The only people who give credence to the sordid interpretation are troublemakers whose minds are warped by private hatred and jealousy: Agravain, Mordred, and, earlier, Morgan le Fay analyse the relationship in the lowest possible terms for their own ends. While the private nature of the relationship remains unspoken, there are no public ill effects, only honour. And when the relationship is voiced and made public, it appears sordid and disruptive merely because there is disruption in the voice of Mordred and Agravain.

The lovers have managed to ward off danger so far, but from the very beginning of the final tales their private affairs start to dominate the action and the results are inevitably disastrous. The 'prevy thoughtes' that had hampered Lancelot during the Grail quest are given such free rein that the lovers' renewed 'prevy draughtis' set the court talking. Lancelot is not deaf to what is being said and although he sees the folly and boldness of their behaviour, he is still not ready to reform. He decides merely to divert attention by showing a gallant interest in other ladies: private concerns are governing his public behaviour.

Lancelot is obviously a gifted actor since Guenevere is the first to misconstrue his motives, and when, in a jealous rage, she sends him away from court, she, too, begins to be ruled by private issues. Her display of public indifference to Lancelot is designed merely to veil her inner thoughts. The 'pryvy dynere' she organises 'in a prevy place by themselff' is a direct result of private feelings she seeks to misrepresent publicly. Guenevere plans to 'shew outwarde that she had as grete joy in all other knyghtes of the Rounde Table as she had in sir Launcelot' (613.15–17; XVIII.3). These, of course, are perfectly proper sentiments for a queen, but the motives are improper, and far from saving her good name she puts it in jeopardy. She has created a situation which is eminently convenient as an outlet for other private motives – here, Pynel's envy and hatred of Gawain – and the queen has brought disaster on herself. Private sentiments are having distressing public repercussions. Their love is causing trouble; indirectly as yet, but it is becoming a source of disharmony. Significantly, Lancelot is privately glad that things have turned out as they have (616.37; XVIII.5), glad that he will be able to justify publicly, and earn public gratitude from, the lady who has wronged him in private.

As the adventures proceed, the conflicting claims of the public and the private worlds become increasingly clear, and private motives regularly lead to trouble. Lancelot's urgent desire to go to the queen makes him deaf to the warnings of Bors, who knows that Agravain is ready to pounce, and the lovers play into the hands of trouble-makers and are caught together. This is their crime, and one they realise only too bitterly. Their relationship has not been a sin so much as a security risk. Their lack of prudence has provided the excuse Agravain and Mordred have been looking for to cause trouble. The brothers cannot stop themselves, they declare with (feigned) abhorrence from calling for action.

There is, however, nothing sordid in the love of Lancelot and the queen, and even when it is made public Malory will not condemn it. Indeed, when accusations are finally brought, Malory refuses to let witnesses into the chamber and robs Agravain and Mordred of their evidence. And he refuses to tell us what the lovers were doing either. For Malory, their only crime is providing others with the opportunity to destroy the realm. Lancelot and Guenevere express no guilt for any sexual sin. They take to a life of contrition because they see themselves as destroyers of good knights not as adulterers. Their error is not sexual; rather they are guilty of provoking disharmony when the private roles implicit in their relationship take on such importance that the public roles can be misrepresented.

They can be blamed for a lack of moderation, a failure to keep personal sentiment under control. Trouble comes because Lancelot, as he confesses, 'had loved a quene unmesurabely and oute of mesure longe' (539.5–6; XIII.20) and has ignored the injunction 'loke that your harte and youre mowth accorde' (539.18; XIII.20). There is an immoderate gap between his feelings in private and his public declarations of fidelity.

Tragic Love   fail to keep personal sentim. under control.

This same lack of moderation is the great drawback, too, in Malory's only portrait of wholesome love, that of the Maid of Astolat, who, Lancelot declares: 'loved me oute of mesure' (641.28; XVIII.20). It is a love which, in Malory's world, stands clearly apart in that it is not formal, patterned, or courtly, but intensely real and natural, and far too unsophisticated for the sophisticated world of Camelot. The relationship between the Maid and Lancelot is a reversal of the courtly tradition. She does all the courting and serving and the obstacle to their union is not her being married but the fact that Lancelot's heart is engaged elsewhere. The reversal brings pathos and Elayne's love is more tenderly real than the loves of other knights and ladies. She is the only lady in the *Morte Darthur* whose heart Malory gives us a glimpse of. We see Guenevere's temper and her emotive reactions but never, or rarely (cf. 620.35–37; XVIII.7) her deepest sentiments.

Malory offers an unusually rich portrait of Elayne of Astolat. She is un-
assuming, natural, almost tomboyish, and quite unlike her counterparts in
the two other versions of the story, which Malory knew and adapted. In
one she is a weepy, sentimental lass, in the other she is artful, pushy, vin-
dictive and even worldly-wise: to approach Lancelot she puts on her pret-
tiest dress! Malory's Elayne is the infatuated young girl who hovers
around Lancelot. Her love is immediate and her request that he should
wear the token is frank. Lancelot has no desire to encourage her, but then
thinks of his own plan to fight in disguise and accepts her sleeve. Inevitably, both the token and the Maid are being used.

The Maid is totally without guile – so much so that she is ready to take
a knight to her bedroom until her father stops her. She is a young lady of
active spirit ready to ride after Lancelot and entirely devoted to his service. But she goes too far in her 'diligence' and Lancelot is somewhat
troubled. For the danger is that there is no place in the courtly world for
this real-life kind of love. Elayne serves Lancelot as a wife would serve a
husband and little by little she lays claim to him. This becomes explicit
when she threatens to 'appele' her brother and Bors if anything happens
to the wounded Lancelot (636.17; XVIII.17), threatens, that is, to take the
legal proceedings a wife could take if her husband died in her arms. But
although she claims Lancelot is "my lorde', in the strictest terms he is not.

Elayne is a young lady more aware of legal and social claims than of
courtly codes. As we have already seen, she makes her declaration of love
to Lancelot in a social context, in the presence of her father and brothers,
and Lancelot refuses to take advantage of her offer by drawing attention
to his own duty to the same father and brothers. To console her, he makes
the Maid an offer of more general friendship and of a considerable
amount of money.

It has been suggested that Lancelot's offer of money is an insult and
that his readiness to serve her as her knight is a tactless travesty of all her
hopes. Lancelot, apparently, even doubts the Maid's sincerity: 'ye love me
as ye *sey* ye do' he says (638.27–28; XVIII.19). This, it seems to me, is entirely wrong. Lancelot is indeed off balance faced with such feminine direct-
ness, but there is nothing in the text – or in the concepts of Malory's world
– to suggest that Lancelot's behaviour is anything but laudable. Indeed, although we could argue that Lancelot has at least thoughtlessly encouraged Elayne, Malory regularly excuses him. No one criticises Lancelot and
on two occasions Elayne's own brother speaks up in Lancelot's defence.
Lancelot's reply to the Maid is meant to be firm but kind. He offers
brotherly protection in place of love, and the (enormous) sum of money is
a measure of Lancelot's enormous generosity and concern.

The Maid's dying defence is a splendid piece of characterisation and
her 'earthliness' is clearly evident. God will not be offended by her love

since 'He fourmed me thereto, and all maner of good love comyth of God' (639.34–35; not in Caxton). Her only sin is that she has loved Lancelot 'oute of mesure'. Strangely enough it is only in death that she becomes a formal, courtly, ceremonial figure – the 'ceremony' of her death contrasting with the intense reality of her life. And in the end – unlike the Maid in the source versions – she makes no attack on Lancelot. Significantly, and splendidly, the only person to accuse Lancelot is the queen, an accusation which amounts to a total acquittal, of course: 'ye myght have shewed hir som bownté and jantilnes whych myght have preserved hir lyff' (641.29–30; XVIII.20). It is not difficult to imagine the scene Guenevere would have made if Lancelot had so much as thought of anticipating this advice.

The forthright naturalness of Elayne's love provides a striking contrast to the formal, courtly, public world of Camelot but, in the end, proves incompatible with it. The Maid is a young lady who, in a way, refuses to play the role attributed to her. Malory calls her 'the Fayre Maydyn off Astolat', the characters call her 'the Fayre Maydyn off Astolat', but she refuses, as it were, to be reduced to a title and asserts her individuality. In his portrait of her Malory emphasises her humanity and reality, but there is little place for personal response in the courtly setting. Love like the Maiden's cannot survive in a world of public, ceremonial loyalty, and the only loves that Lancelot knows, his love for the queen and the king, are part of his love for the realm, the realm he bemoans so bitterly when he is forced to abandon the court (697.8; XX.17).

Malory's emphasis on the importance of loyalty and service in love helps to show that his portraits of Arthur, Lancelot and Guenevere do not constitute an eternal triangle – as they do perhaps in the French versions where the king is more intensely aware of his private dishonour. We must not claim that Guenevere finds comfort in the arms of Lancelot because Arthur neglects her, because we simply do not know. Malory in Book I tells us 'And there had Arthure the firste syght of queene Gwenyvere . . . and ever afftir he loved hir' (26.28-30; I.18), and, as modern readers, we take that 'ever afftir' with the inevitable pinch of literary salt. But we must, I would suggest, take Malory's words at face value; it is not for us to ask indiscreet questions about the private lives of a king and a queen. It is true that we get the occasional glimpse of Arthur and Guenevere together. We know, for example, that Guenevere was planning to be back with Arthur by 10 o'clock on the fateful day she went Maying (650.10; XIX.1), and when Lancelot suggests that Arthur might have drawn the curtains of the queen's bed if he had wanted to sleep with her, the possibility of his doing so sounds perfectly natural (658.36; XIX.7). If the royal marriage was loveless, the reaction of the king and queen after the trial at the poisoned apple incident would not give that impression – 'aythir kyssed othir hartely' (620.11; XVIII.7) – unless we argue that on such occasions the sense of relief is so intense that an unburnt queen would be ready to kiss the most neglectful of husbands heartily. But apart from these occasions, Malory rarely shows us the king and queen in private. Instead, he constantly places the emphasis on their public roles, and there is every reason to believe Guenevere was as fine a *queen* as Bors claims (617.15 ff.; XVIII.5). Malory (and the Arthurian story) gives Guenevere a dual role – that of queen and mistress – and these she fulfilled properly. But, of course, these different roles are at odds, and the pull of loyalties destroys the land. None the less, loyalty, fidelity, and stability are what Malory admires.

In the courtly tradition it was permissable for a woman to have two men – a husband and a lover (Andreas Capellanus says all women should have a lover and argues that their husbands will understand!) – but a man cannot serve two mistresses, since active service must be exclusive. Nor can a man serve two masters, and the irony of Lancelot's wholehearted devotion to chivalry is that his exclusive devotion to his lord clashes with his exclusive devotion to his lady. That is, Lancelot, the perfect embodiment of both love and loyalty, is ultimately the most eloquent statement of the impossibility of divided service.

CHIVALRY AND SHAME   really

Chivalry is, first of all, an attitude to war. A knight may have amorous conquests and fight spiritual battles, but his proper occupation, for Malory, is adventure, combat, and war. The *Morte Darthur* concentrates on the martial aspects of the chivalric code and the structure of the book reveals the different stages of a basically military ideal.

As we have seen, in the early pages, Arthur consolidates his kingdom with the help of his loyal knights and, like a feudal lord, distributes lands as a reward. It is the role of the knightly class to guarantee peace, unity and a stable government, and to defend the lands and authority of the king, who, in turn, bestows land and authority upon his men in gratitude. Once the kingdom is established, we are shown the values and conventions of the system, chivalry in action: how a knight should behave to friends and foes. We see the workings of what is also a legal system, to which they are all fully committed: 'for the knights are indebted to maintain and defend justice', in the words of another fifteenth century writer, Sir Gilbert Hay. In their pursuit of adventure, knights are constantly taking arms for a cause, and by defeating the opponents they encounter they prove the justice of that cause. According to Professor Vinaver, Malory sees knighthood as 'the principal function of . . . a well-established order with its headquarters fixed in the household of a great prince'. The final tales show the breakdown of this order when the legal system that upheld the realm – might is right – becomes an apparent travesty of justice, and when the ties of allegiance that bound the fellowship together – reward for service – become a source of blackmail and division.

The Arthurian Code

At the beginning of his reign, Arthur makes his knights swear an oath which they are to renew annually. It is a statement of Round Table beliefs, in political terms a summary of Arthurian domestic policy:

> than the kynge stablysshed all the knyghtes and gaff them rychesse and londys; and charged them never to do outerage nothir mourthir, and allwayes to fle treson, and to gyff mercy unto hym that askith mercy, uppon payne of forfiture of their worship and lordship of kynge Arthure for evirmore; and allwayes to do ladyes, damesels, and jantilwomen and wydowes socour: strengthe hem in hir ryght-es, and never to enforce them, uppon payne of dethe. Also, that no man take no batayles in a wrongefull quarell for no love ne for no worldis goodis. So unto thys were all knyghtis sworne of the Table Rounde, both olde and younge, and every yere so were they sworne at the hyghe feste of Pentecoste.

> (75.36–76.2; III.15)

A number if points should be noted. First, the ideal of knighthood expressed here is not some vague code of gallant patriotism, but a social system with a clear financial and political bond. Malory takes this for granted. There is no need to elaborate nor to repeat the point. But generosity like Arthur's is always fitting in a great lord, and at the end of the *Morte Darthur*, Lancelot distributes lands and titles to the knights who have unfailingly served him (699.25 ff.; XX.18)

Secondly, the knightly code demands obedience to a number of precise do's and don't's, from among which violence, murder and treason are singled out first. Failure to follow the code results in the loss of one's honour and, even worse, of one's membership of the group. In many ways these are the same thing, since the greatest testimony to a knight's honour is his election to the group.

Thirdly, the Biblical tone of the injunction that a knight should always accord mercy reminds us that chivalry is anchored in religion. 'First and foremost,' Sir Gilbert Hay writes, 'knighthood was ordained to maintain and defend holy church and the faith', and the dubbing rituals of knighthood consisted in a serious of religious ceremonies which at times

get away from this

achieved almost the status of a sacrament. On the whole, Malory rejects or side-steps the religious vocation of chivalry – knights crusading for religious ideals – but this does not mean that Malory's knights are irreligious or that their ethic is entirely secular. Simply, heavenly values are not more important than earthly values. The Grail quest is one more adventure in an earthly career, and what upsets Lancelot after his return is not so much his spiritual failure in the quest but his failure in earthly achievement:

> For in the queste of the Sankgreall I had that tyme forsakyn the va-
> nytees of the worlde, had nat youre love bene. And if I had done so
> at that tyme with my harte, wylle, and thought, I had passed all the
> knyghtes that ever were in the Sankgreall excepte syr Galahad, my
> sone.
>
> (721.1–5; XXI.9).

When one's soul is in danger one should not be worrying about doing better than others. If Lancelot regrets not having outstripped his fellows, it is because earthly achievement is what was at stake.

Malory rejects the lesson of the Grail book though he cannot reject the religious content of chivalry. His knights are Christians and they do not forget to say their prayers, even if, like Lancelot, they pray for the oddest things. 'Jesu Cryste, be Thou my shylde and myne armoure!' he says, fighting his way out of a married woman's bedroom (677.13; XX.3).

We should not go too far, of course, in claiming that Malory secularises his source material (although he does), since the division religious/secular is inappropriately modern. His knights are believers but they are not enthusiastic evangelicals. Malory's brand of Christianity is, in fact, a trifle worldly. His hermits, for example, are rich gentlemen in retirement who enjoy nostalgic reminiscences with their knightly visitors, and it is not often that we see in them any genuine rejection of the chivalric ideal. When Lavaine asks a hermit to lodge the wounded Lancelot he is told 'sometyme I was one of the felyship, but now I thanke God I am othirwyse disposed' (628.29–31; XVIII.12). Not many of his fellow hermits take this line, and when the Bishop of Canterbury takes to a life of poverty and holy prayers he is careful to take 'parte of hys good with hym' (708.15; XXI.1). In Malory's world, there is obviously poverty and poverty.

It is only when everything is over that Malory allows his knights a real religious vocation. Till then, there is no question of denying the values of Camelot. When those values are annihilated, Malory's knights, properly, turn to God, but even then it is important to notice that the religious devotion they take to implies no criticism of their former, earthly ideals. They are as wholeheartedly committed to the religious life as they were to Camelot, because their religious life is a development of their allegiance to Camelot, not a denial of it.

Guenevere does not take to a life of devotion because she finally sees
herself as the woman taken in adultery; she is not rejecting an earthly for a
heavenly ideal. Rather, her spiritual vocation is a penance for having
helped to destroy the earthly ideal. In the same way, Lancelot enters the
church not because he is aware that he has blackened his soul, but to emulate his lady: it is the only way of following her to the end. And Lancelot's
knights, in turn, follow him. This, for us, may appear a rather empty faith,
in which imitation is the sincerest form of piety, but for Malory it is not
improper that one should enter the service of one's heavenly lord as a
final mark of fidelity to one's earthly lord. The closing pages of the *Morte
Darthur* are not a denial of the values of earthly chivalry: on the contrary,
they reaffirm those values. Now that Malory's knights have witnessed the
destruction of the Round Table community, what on earth could keep
them from heaven? We will need to return to this.

[handwritten margin note: yes they are!]

The next point to notice is the place given to women in Malory's
knighthood oath: it is a knight's duty to offer help and support. The tone
is clearly gentlemanly, but it is nowhere suggested that ladies are a
knight's main concern, nor that the endeavour to serve them can override
other moral issues. A knight should not take advantage of a lady; his service should be disinterested. It is not because he has been kind to her that
she should be kind to him. Sir Gilbert Hay writes that 'Office of knighthood is to maintain and defend widows, maidens, fatherless and mother-
less bairns, and poor miserable persons and piteable, and to help the weak
against the stark and the poor against the rich.' Malory shows little interest in the poor classes, but it is perfectly clear that he agrees with Hay that
it is the weakness and vulnerability of women that merit a knight's attention. A knight should serve ladies not so much because they can inspire
great deeds, but because they are weaker vessels who need their great
deeds doing for them.

It is for this reason that although Malory's knights frequently serve
ladies they are rarely, if ever, seen as ladies' men. Malory confiscates the
amorous reputations they have in certain French versions of the stories: it
is not in Malory that we hear a lady predict that Gawain's death will be a
great blow to womankind. Most obviously, Malory removes Lancelot's
reputation – or, at least, though certain people have heard of Lancelot's
reputation, he will have nothing to do with it himself. He is undeniably
ready to serve them, but it is essential for a knight to put women in their
proper place. They are, in a way, a threat to knighthood. Married knights
become uxorious, and those who resort to paramours not only offend
God, their energy is sapped and they set themselves on the road to misfortune. It is, of course, one of the ironies of the *Morte Darthur* that Lancelot
himself proves the truth of his own words. It is his own relationship with
a married woman that leads to the greatest misfortune of all.

A knight must not be led astray by love or avarice, the oath goes on to recommend. In the Arthurian world physical amd moral superiority go hand in hand. The best man always wins. Take Lancelot, for example, whose preeminence in battle is an outward expression of his inner worth. When a knight takes arms for a just cause, since right is on his side he will succeed. He will have no difficulty proving that his cause is just, because it is – precisely – just. Might is right is the theory, and it is one to which the community is entirely committed.

But it is a theory which must not be turned upside down: military success reveals the justice of a cause; a knight must not set out to prove the justice of a cause through brute force. And he must not be lured into defending a wrong cause for the sake of love or financial gain. It is, of course, one of the ironies of the *Morte Darthur* that Lancelot should, for the sake of love, take up arms to fight for a cause which at least *appears* morally dubious. The accusations of Mordred and his band concerning the queen's adultery would appear to be wrong, since Lancelot has no difficulty withstanding fourteen knights singlehanded. Disruption comes to the Arthurian world when might and right seem to part company, when Arthur feels that Lancelot is just a little too ready to rely on brute force 'for he trustyth so much uppon hys hondis and hys myght that he doutyth no man' (682.43–44; XX.7). Love leads Lancelot to fight for a cause that *seems* to be wrong, but I believe Malory never quite allows his favourite knight to be guilty of this particularly heinous crime. We shall come back to this too.

Nor are Malory's knights guilty of avarice; they are above base mercantile interests. They are professional soldiers not mercenaries; their service may bring them reward, but they fight for justice not money. Consequently, Mordred's villainy is finely characterised when, at the end, Arthur has to *buy* a truce with him (712.21; XXI.3), and we see the extent to which values have collapsed when there is nothing to keep even a faithful soldier from sinking (for an instant) into greed. As Bedevere carries Excalibur to the water's edge, he has an eye on its price but not on its value, on what it must have cost not on what it represents and why, therefore, it must be returned to the waves.

The knighthood oath, then, is a formal statement of certain essential Arthurian values, and one of the most basic values of all is the unity that comes from allegiance to a group, all sharing the same code. It is because fellowship itself is such a great virtue that Arthur is led to bewail the breakdown of his realm as he does:

And much more I am soryar for my good knyghtes losse than for the

losse of my fayre quene; for quenys I myght have inow, but such a
felyship of good knyghtes shall never be togydirs in no company
(685.29–32; XX.9)

Many critics have taken this to be a slight on Guenevere, an eloquent if
unintentional statement of how unimportant the king's marriage was to
him. Surely not: Arthur is not expressing his indifference to Guenevere,
but his unconsolable grief at the loss of his fellowship. That loss is so terrible that even his exceptional and dearly loved queen takes second place
in his thoughts. If the loss of Guenevere had brought little pain to Arthur,
it could be no point of reference here. Those who underestimate Arthur's
affection for the queen, underestimate his affection for the Round Table
too. It is only because Guenevere means all that she does to Arthur, that
this claim has any meaning at all. Malory makes no mention of the court's
reaction at Arthur's lament; it was no doubt a moment for silence. But if
any comment was whispered at all, it was surely 'The Round Table must
have meant a lot to him' not 'Wait till the queen hears that!' For there is
not the slightest evidence to suggest that Guenevere – never slow to take
umbrage – would have been shocked by Arthur's words. Her own expression of grief at the end (720.15 ff.; XXI.9) shows how clearly she
understood.

Knightly Virtues

Knighthood for Malory means first of all a bond between men. His
knights are courtly and refined but courtly refinement is a less important
part of their chivalry than the virtues of a fighting man. The military ideal
is one which has lost much of its prestige. The greatness of Othello, Mac-
beth, or Antony as soldiers is something we respond to half-heartedly, but
with the *Morte Darthur* we must make an effort to resurrect our enthusiasm for the soldier's profession, first, because it is the only one Malory is
interested in and secondly, because its moral connotations are, for Malory,
self-evident: a fine soldier is a fine man, and the virtues of a fine man are
the soldier's virtues – bravery, honour, truthfulness, loyalty, generosity,
prowess, in a word what Malory calls 'worship'.

A knight is a fighting man, always more than ready to take up arms for
a just cause and, it goes without saying, fight cleanly. Inevitably a number
of characteristics define all Malory's knights; it would be impossible to
think of them in other terms. They are big men, healthy and strong, who
can stand hours of mutual buffeting. They are fine horsemen – a *chevalier*
who could not handle a *cheval* would cut a poor figure – although, of

course, they need time to learn their trade. Young knights, it is admitted (Malory writes with the amused perception of an old soldier himself) may have more strength than old ones, but their horsemanship is less practised: quite simply, they keep falling off. There is nothing shameful in this: they all have to learn, even Lancelot, Malory tells us;

> for he that muste be a good horseman hit muste com of usage and excercise. But whan he commyth to the strokis of his swerde he is than noble and myghty. And that saw sir Bleoberys and sir Palomydes; for wete you well they were wyly men of warre, for they wolde know anone, when they sye a yonge knight, by his rydynge, how they were sure to gyffe hym a falle frome his horse othir a grete buffett. But for the moste party they wyll nat lyght on foote with yonge knyghtes, for they ar myghtyly and strongely armed.
> For in lyke wyse syr Launcelot du Lake, whan he was fyrst made knyght, he was oftyn put to the worse on horsebacke . . .
>
> (287.6–15; IX.4)

This leads us to another point: the best knights are not exactly young. A reputation is won with deeds, and deeds take time. Malory turns a blind eye to questions of age, but it is clear that the Malorian knight is a mature man. Chivalry is not a teenage sport.

Interestingly enough, Malory's knights have survived into twentieth century popular culture: American cowboys are direct descendants, and have all the same virtues. They too are gallant men who fight to defend women and children, but who are ill at ease in feminine company. They are not without sexual experience, but they are not philanderers. They are fine looking men, but they have nothing of the overgroomed elegance of the playboy. They are not talkers; if anything they act first and think later. Their reactions are felt not reasoned; they settle matters with their fists. They do not sit down and talk things over calmly or work out a compromise. If they are hot-headed it is because they are big-hearted. There is something boyish about them and their ready enthusiasm to help. The best of them can defend the community against enemies of extraordinary villainy, and even infidels (though this happens more frequently in the West than in Malory; there are always more Red Indians around than Saracens). It would be unthinkable for a cowboy to be asthmatic, verbose and lecherous, an incompetent gunman who rode a buggy and relied on ruse to get him through. He is a strong, silent man of moral fibre, a skilled horseman and a crack shot who is not afraid, if need be, to fight his way out of any situation. My comparison is cheap, perhaps. I hope, at least, it is clear. In their day Malory's knights were the same, men devoted to a just cause and proud to earn a reputation for being so.

A knight's worship is his honour, his reputation, his good name. A true knight should be 'besy and aboute to wyn worshyp' (695.18–19; XX.15). This is his duty, and the worship he wins is part of his own individual reputation, but it is also shared by the group, an aspect of their together-ness, for they are fighting for a joint cause. Consequently, Lancelot is not only the man with the most worship, he has brought more worship to the group than anyone else, and this is why Bors upbraids the queen when she sends Lancelot away. Lancelot is the one 'by whom ye and all we were dayly worshipped by' (616.5–6; XVIII.5). Similarly, of course, one knight's shame taints the whole group, as Guenevere, this time, is only too ready to see: 'Thou shamyst all knyghthode and thyselffe and me' she tells Me-liagaunt as he kidnaps her (651.7–8; XIX.2). Comradeship for a knight, that is, is not a vague notion of benevolence and fellow feeling towards one's peers, it has precise manifestations. A knight may fight as an individual, but he is first of all part of a group.

Knightly Vice

Proper chivalric behaviour implies not only an attitude to one's fellows but also to the enemy. The notion that all's fair in love and war is a reflex-ion of modern cynicism, for although a good knight cannot be expected to love his enemy, he will certainly respect him, admire his skill and never resort to underhand methods. Combat is not a free-for-all; there are rules to obey. It may be dangerous – chivalry is a professional not an amateur sport – but one can fight in earnest without being guilty of barbarism. Pa-lomides at times tends to forget the rules of the game and fights in single combat as though he were fighting a real war. No one approves, but then Palomides is a fierce man and not (for most of the time) a Christian. At the height of his enmity with Lancelot in Book VIII, Gawain behaves in a simi-lar way; he fight by the rules of war while Lancelot follows those of a tour-nament. Gawain wants to fight to the death (his own if need be); Lancelot is only too ready to spare the life of the vanquished Gawain.

We are frequently reminded that it is inadmissable to defeat a knight by outnumbering him (which says little for the honour of the fourteen knights, all armed, who lay in wait for Lancelot outside the queen's cham-ber), as it is unthinkable to wait till a knight is tired before attacking him. Tristram even refuses to obey a royal command when Mark tells him to challenge Lamorak, weary from defeating thirty others (268.30 ff.; VIII.33). It is a measure of Tristram's integrity that he should refuse, and of Mark's caddishness that he should give the order at all. Such a disreputable idea would never have crossed anyone else's mind; but then, throughout the book King Mark is a byword for villainy. The occasionally tarnished

knighthood of Gawain in the central books pales into insignificance
beside the persistent shoddiness of Mark, whose only fellow among
Round Table knights is Meliagaunt.

Meliagaunt is an interesting figure. He enters the *Morte Darthur* as a
love-lorn knight languishing in his unrequited passion for Guenevere,
and ready to challenge even Lamorak (in the early days Guenevere inspired him to mad feats of courage!) to prove the unparallelled beauty of
his queen. He leaves the *Morte Darthur* in ignominy and death, an object
lesson in all that the chivalric knight is not

His craven fear of Lancelot is unworthy of a knight: he dares to abduct
Guenevere only when Lancelot is away, and when Lancelot rides to the
rescue, Meliagaunt is quaking with fear and begging for mercy before the
combat begins. To capture Guenevere he vastly outnumbers her bodyguard. This is not military common sense, nor is it merely a reflexion of
how desperate Meliagaunt is to succeed. It expresses his basic lack of chivalry: he finds courage only in the safety of numbers. And when he orders
Lancelot's horse to be killed we see how shabby his conduct is. Once his
villainous behaviour proves ineffective, he resorts to craft, wheedling
Guenevere into sticking up for him, till the bloodstained sheets come as a
God-send to his sordid mind. It is a measure of Meliagaunt's baseness that
he can accuse the women he loves of treason to hide his own treachery.

Fortunately for Guenevere his accusation is outrageously wrong, but
unfortunately for her it is too near the truth for comfort, and Lancelot is
reluctant to grant the mercy Meliagaunt inevitably begs for. Lancelot
would prefer to silence the blackguard for good and offers him very ad-
vantageous conditions to tempt him into continuing the fight. Lancelot's
offer is extraordinarily generous (662.31 ff.; XIX.9), recklessly so, we
would say if we did not know Lancelot's strength and the fact that right is
on his side because the queen is innocent of the precise charge. Meliagaunt is only too ready to leap at the opportunity. For him, any kind of
cheap victory over Lancelot is better than defeat and exposure, and his
baseness in accepting the terms goes a long way to justifying Lancelot's
reluctance to grant him mercy. Lancelot has been accused by critics of devious behaviour, enticing Meliagaunt to his death to disguise a vengeance
that dare not speak its name. But the alacrity with which Meliagaunt rises
to the bait does nothing to raise him in our esteem. The Arthurian world
will be a better place without him.

Chivalric Practice

The virtues of a soldier, of course, find expression in war and (since Arthur's authority is unquestioned and peace reigns) in war games. The tournaments of the *Morte Darthur* are organised with greater frequency and on a larger scale than has ever been historically the case, but it goes without saying that Arthurian days were a golden age when traditions of this sort were lavishly kept up. And if we refer to the tournaments as war games we must not forget that Malory's knights enter them in earnest not for fun. When we read that 'the kyng was wrothe oute of mesure that he and hys knyghtes myght nat prevayle that day' (647.11–12; XVIII.24) we realise to what extent Arthur has entered into the spirit of the tournament; we should not accuse him of getting carried away while playing at soldiers.

Malory writes, of course, for an audience familiar with the conventions of knighthood, and so we should not look to the *Morte Darthur* for precise details of chivalric procedure or documentary descriptions of the typical tournament. Malory takes all this for granted, as he takes it for granted that a certain amount of licence is permitted concerning rules, customs, and, even, equipment. Armour in the *Morte Darthur* is a good example: it is a mixture of thirteenth century, fifteenth century, and fictitious armour which never hinders a man until it has to. Knights leap on and off horses with greater agility than any fifteenth century fighter did, and Lancelot, fully armed, has no difficulty climbing out of a window down a sheet, nor swimming the Thames. A reader would appreciate that in Arthur's days conditions were a little different and knights more hardy. On the other hand, having had his horse injured beneath him, Lancelot feels the weight of his armour and equipment only too heavily when faced with a two mile walk to his destination, and, there, the reader would understand the situation only too well.

This mixture of documentary accuracy and total disregard for known historical conditions is, in itself, no problem. The reader recognises similarities or admits differences willingly. The *Morte Darthur* is not a textbook of chivalric practice but a record of great deeds, capturing the spirit of an age. In certain points, that age resembles Malory's own, as his readers would recognise at once, and thus require no elaboration; in others, that age had standards and practices of its own. In that case, 'custom was those days' is explanation enough.

The tournaments of real life, of course, could be dangerous for political reasons. They could get out of hand and turn into miniature wars, so that in stead of providing activity for restless soldiers, they masked genuine hostilities. Scores could be settled and feuds carried on under cover of official army entertainment, and in times of weak central government they could be a serious political threat. It was only as techniques of war developed that tournaments became less dangerous: when they encouraged skills that were obsolete in actual warfare they became sport again and lost all connexion with the tactics of war. They were pageants to embellish

great occasions, as much of a real threat as the sword a modern naval officer wears with his dress uniform.

In Malory, tournaments are the events of great occasions, but the encounters involved are the same as those a knight has as he rides in search
of adventure. His everyday life and the sport of great occasions coincide.
Malory shows us nothing of the political intrigue of tournaments, but the
dangerous side is visible none the less. Knights frequently take advantage
of tournaments to settle a private score. They all take part in earnest, but
some are more earnest than others. A good example of this is Palomides'
attempt to harm Tristram at the tournament at Lonezep, while the Orkney
brothers keep a sharp eye out for Lamorak at all times.

As tournaments became more expensive, individual jousting became
more popular and although the Arthurian world was never reduced to
abandoning full-scale tournaments in favour of one-against-one combat in
the lists, duelling (outside the lists) always appears important in the *Morte
Darthur* because Malory tends to reduce joint action to individual encounter anyway; the mêlée is described as though it were a series of jousts.
Moreover, one particular kind of individual encounter, the duel of chivalry, is intimately connected to Malory's moral view of chivalry as a legal
system.

The duel of chivalry is a development of the earlier duel of law, which
was fought on foot with blunted weapons till one knight yielded. It was
not a fight to the death and was used when murder or land trials were at
stake. The logic is simple: victory in combat is the proof of innocence. This
is the principle too for the duel of chivalry, which was used in cases of
treason (Guenevere, represented on the battlefield by Lancelot, is accused
of treason not adultery). The duel was presided over by marshals and con-
stables (618.5; XVIII.6) and was fought on horseback, with armour, sword,
and spear. There was a clearly defined procedure with a written accusation (659.17; XIX.7) and precise calls to begin and to halt (662.1–2; XIX.9).
Malory never explains all the details since his audience would be familiar
with the system, but the details are occasionally important for the
meaning of his book.

The central passage concerns Agravain and Mordred's accusation that
Lancelot is the queen's lover. Arthur is reluctant to listen to rumour; he
wants proof. More than that, he wants the lovers to be caught *en flagrant
délit*:

> I wolde be lothe to begyn such a thynge but I myght have prevys of
> hit, for sir Launcelot ys an hardy knyght, and all ye know that he ys
> the beste knyght amonge us all, and but if he be takyn with the dede
> he woll fyght with hym that bryngith up the noyse, and I know no

knyght that ys able to macch hym. Therefore, and hit be sothe as ye
say, I wolde that he were takyn with the dede.

                                                        (674.31–36; XX.2)

The reason is simple: a man caught in the act could be sentenced forth-
with, and did not have the right to fight a duel of chivalry. We might think
that Arthur is being ungenerous here, expressing reluctance to allow his
finest knight a chance to justify himself. In fact, what Arthur realises is
that if Lancelot is not 'takyn with the dede' he will claim his right to prove
his innocence in a duel and nothing will be proved at all: Lancelot is so
strong, innocent or guilty he will be victorious. As it turns out, fighting his
way from the queen's chamber, Lancelot kills thirteen men singlehanded,
which (by the logic of the law) he would not be able to do if he were
guilty. This is either the final breakdown of the system – might is no
longer right – or else it eloquently expresses the moral ambiguity which it
is essential to recognise for an understanding of the final tales.

Might and Right

In Malory, the idea that might is right, that proof is to be had with the
sword, is not limited to the duel of chivalry, it runs throughout the book.
The *reductio ad absurdum* is combat to prove that one knight's lady is more
beautiful than another's. We might be tempted to dismiss this as idiocy,
but we must remember that even Lancelot is ready to fight to prove that
Guenevere is fairer than Queen Morgause. Lamorak sums up the situation
most reasonably, but it is hard to believe he is convinced by what he is
saying, since he was quite ready to champion Morgause himself:

> every man thynkith hys owne lady fayryste, and thoughe I prayse
> the lady that I love moste, ye sholde nat be wrothe. For thoughe my
> lady quene Gwenyver by fayryst in youre eye, wyte you well quene
> Morgause of Orkeney ys fayryst in myne eye, and so every knyght
> thynkith hys own lady fayryste.

                                                        (298.33–37; IX.14)

Behind the faith in the law is the idea that physical strength and success
are God given, just as Lancelot's knightly preeminence, we are told, is a
direct gift of God. The sword can be the agent of truth because God speeds
the right or, as Meliagaunt claims, 'God woll have a stroke in every batayle' (659.6–7; XIX.7). This is the theory, and in its perfect state there can
be no corruption and no string-pulling: strength will always be accorded
to the just. Hence Meliagaunt has absolute faith in the logic of the law be-

cause he believes that, for once, he is in the right – even though this does not stop him from tricking Lancelot and having him locked up. Meliagaunt is too much of a bounder to turn virtuous now, and with Lancelot one can never be too sure anyway.

Lancelot's victory over Meliagaunt suggests to some readers that God does not speed the right nor have a stroke in every battle. The queen is guilty of adultery after all, and yet Lancelot wins the day. The victory is another example of the moral ambiguity which dominates the final tales. Books VII and VIII describe the disruption of the chivalric ideal, and Lancelot's three rescues of the queen are clearly seen as important stages in the decline of the kingdom. The duel of chivalry, which was at the basis of the legal system, seems to be going all wrong. At the first rescue, when Guenevere was accused of poisoning Sir Mador, she is totally innocent; at the second she is technically innocent – she has slept with a wounded knight, but not one of those in her retinue who are accused with her; and in the third incident she is apparently guilty: she and Lancelot have been trapped together in extremely compromising circumstances. And yet on all three occasions, Lancelot's sword asserts the queen's innocence, and where she is most guilty he has the greatest success, killing thirteen knights singlehanded.

The irony of events, of course, is that the greatest knight, the one who can prove everything, is now proving more or less anything. As he takes up a quarrel for causes which are progressively less right, so he undermines the law and the realm. The system is getting out of hand. And Malory makes this clear when he adds the evidence of the Lady of the Lake after Lancelot has proved Guenevere's innocence over the poisoned apple affair. The queen has been acquitted; why does Malory need to bring in extra proof? It has been suggested that he obviously felt that judicial combat was insufficient to establish innocence, but I think not. I would suggest that by adding corroborative evidence after the first incident, Malory emphasises that none can be added later. There can be no Lady of the Lake to tell us all about the bloodstained sheets or to explain why Lancelot suddenly starts wearing a glove in Meliagaunt's castle. Corroborative evidence could only establish guilt not innocence. The duel of chivalry from now on must stand alone. Nothing else can offer proof and protection at the same time. When Lancelot is on his way to rescue the kidnapped Guenevere he says to Meliagaunt's archers:

> 'What commaundemente have ye,' seyde sir Launcelot, 'to cause me,
> that am a knyght of the Rounde Table, to leve my ryght way?'
>   (653.27–28; XIX.4)

It is worth recalling that, from one point of view, this is the last time Lancelot is on the 'ryght way'.

Inevitably, as we read the final tales, we see Lancelot taking up arms
for a cause which is only arguably right, and yet the very ambiguity of his
position reveals with great clarity what is essential to the code of chivalry
he embodies. Malory refuses to say what Lancelot and Guenevere were
doing together in the queen's chamber – he refuses to pander to the demands of Agravain and Mordred by providing the sordid evidence they
were after – but we know that they are lovers. The sin they are guilty of,
however, is a minor matter compared with the profound evil of Avravain,
Mordred, and, later, for a while, Gawain. The behaviour of the lovers implicitly calls to question the allegiance they owe to Arthur, but the offence
remains personal and private; Mordred and Agravain want to make a
public issue of the matter and proclaim openly the shame the lovers, they
feel, have deserved. And as the final tales show the balance of public and
private error, we begin to see clearly one of the central issues of the *Morte
Darthur*. It had been formulated long before the final incidents, in the early
pages of the Tristram story. Sir Segwarides is forced to admit the infidelity
of his wife and come to terms with it, Malory tells us, 'for he that hath a
prevy hurte is loth to have a shame outewarde' (246.32–33; VIII.14). This is
not the *raison d'être* of a lily-livered cuckold; it is profound wisdom. Shame
not private wrongs is the greatest threat to the Arthurian world.

only half allegiance to themselves no longer Art, & never god in any substantial way.

Shame

All men are, inevitably, sinners. Although a knight should, no dount,
strive to attain perfection, sin is part of his human condition. But a knight
must not tolerate shame. It contradicts his whole existence as a knight; it
contradicts knighthood itself. Sin can blacken the soul, but the blackest
soul can find forgiveness; shame can destroy the realm for a knight and
knighthood without honour cease to exist. Malory, of course, never ex-
pounds this theory in so many words, but he writes constantly on these
assumptions. When told that there is a knight who 'dystressis all ladyes
and jantylwomen, and at the leste he robbyth them other lyeth by hem'
Lancelot replies:

> What? . . . is he a theff and a knyght? And a ravyssher of women? He
> doth shame unto the Order of Knyghthode, and contrary unto his
> oth. Hit is pyte that he lyvyth!
>
> (160.10–12; VI.10)

These are famous words. They are most often quoted in comic contrast to
the supposed life of the rapist, thief Sir Thomas Malory. But they are elo-

quent testimony to the *Morte Darthur*'s basic position. Such an accumulation of shame is in total contradiction to the chivalric ideal.

From a strict moral point of view, Lancelot's relationship to the queen is reprehensible, but from a chivalric point of view it is a source of honour not shame. Lancelot's achievements in the queen's name have increased the glory of the realm as a whole, and it is this public honour and service that Lancelot asserts before the court as he tries to draw attention away from the private relationship. He is playing with words, if you like, but his endeavour is not merely to avoid a scandal but to hold the realm together. Of course, Agravain and Mordred have the letter of the truth on their side, but Lancelot has the spirit. They, not he, are demanding destruction. However much Lancelot has threatened existing loyalties at a private level, it is he who is now wholeheartedly devoted to saving the state; they are motivated by nothing higher than private spite. Lancelot is not merely out to save his own skin or the threadbare reputation of an adulterous queen; the cause he is defending is the survival of the Arthurian world itself. Consequently, according to the logic of the Arthurian system, he is able to defeat thirteen knights and rob them of evidence they will put to evil use, just as later he can resist the 'grace and gyffte' of Gawain's miraculous strength. Because there is justice in their cause, he can call Guenevere 'Moste nobelest Crysten quene' at the very moment we (wrongly) suspect her behaviour of being the least noble and the least Christian, and without a hint of hypocrisy he can invoke the aid of Jesus as he fights his way from her chamber. Before he does so Guenevere assures him:

> I woll take my dethe as mekely as ever ded marter take hys dethe for
> Jesu Crystes sake

> (677.1–2; XX.3)

Modern readers may be shocked that an adulteress should compare her death to a martyr's (the editor of the Caxton edition may have been shocked too, since he replaces the offending word by 'queen'), but not Malory. Without a trace of blasphemy we are asked to accept the words as they stand, for in his world the great chivalric virtues of stability, unity, and fellowship are what Lancelot is fighting for. He repeatedly asserts (and represents) the honour that binds the community together, while Agravain and Mordred assert (because they represent) the shame that tears it apart.

The tragedy of the *Morte Darthur* is centred clearly on the notions of chivalry and the pull of allegiances. Lancelot has a duty to serve Arthur and Guenevere, as he rightly says:

> My lorde . . . wytte you well y ought of ryght ever to be in youre
> quarell and in my ladyes the quenys quarell to do batayle, for ye ar

the man that gaff me the hygh Order of Knyghthode, and that day
my lady, youre quene, ded me worshyp. And ellis had I bene
shamed, for that same day that ye made me knyght, thorow my has-
tynes I loste my swerde, and my lady, youre quene, founde hit, and
lapped hit in her trayne, and gave me my swerde whan I had nede
thereto; and ells had I bene shamed amonge all knyghtes. And therefore, my lorde Arthure, I promysed her at that day ever to be her
knyght in ryght othir in wronge.

(620.21–30; XVIII.7)

Those final words are, of course, fateful. They are, in a sense, a polite exaggeration – Lancelot will come whenever she needs him – but they become
reality, and since Lancelot is the one who puts the queen in the wrong, his
duty is his duty right or wrong. As Bors says later: 'whether ye ded ryght
othir wronge hit is now youre parte to holde wyth the quene' (680.21–22;
XX.6). Wrongness and rightness, that is, are less important than loyalty,
less important than the need to preserve honour by remaining faithful to
one's promise to serve. Lancelot's men join him not because they are convinced of his innocence in his affair with the queen (because it is highly
unlikely that they are), but bacause of the ties of allegiance.

And yet these ties of allegiance are precisely what provokes division in
that they force Lancelot into action. He is so reluctant to defend himself
against Arthur that he holds back and refuses to attack fully. Inevitably
his own men suffer. They have been provoked and are itching for action.
What is more, Lancelot owes it to them; as they say, 'wherefore we pray
you and charge you as ye woll have oure servyse, kepe us no lenger wy-
thin thys wallis' (690.10–12; XX.12). The attitude is perfectly logical, of
course, but they are fighting against their own king. Their devotion to
Lancelot and the queen is a splendid act of fidelity, but at the same time it
is an act of betrayal because these same men owe allegiance first of all to
Arthur. On the other hand, Gawain's allegiance to Arthur becomes suspect because he forgets the duty he owes to Lancelot. 'I woll never be
ayenste sir Launcelot for one dayes dede, that was whan he rescowed me
frome kynge Carados of the Dolorous Towre and slew hym and saved my
lyff' (673.40–674.2; XX.1), says Gawain, but Lancelot is forced to remind
him of this later, when Gawain has taken on narrower notions of loyalty.
By then, allegiance has become a way of exerting pressure (Gawain will
help Arthur only if Arthur refuses a reconciliation with Lancelot); the ties
which held the realm together are now tearing it apart as the bonds of allegiance are reduced to their most primitive and destructive.

The shame which destroys knighthood is not Arthur's (supposed) cuc-
koldry; this 'prevy hurte' is a mere excuse to plaster over the more profound shame at the heart of the kingdom: when knights put personal

enmity before public allegiance, they forsake their roles as guardians of the common weal and become political agitators. Arthur, the prince whose interests Mordred and Agravain are defending, is not fooled. He knows who is in fact responsible for the destruction that lies ahead:

> A, Aggravayne, Aggravayne! . . . Jesu forgyff hit thy soule, for thyne evyll wyll that thou haddist and sir Mordred, thy brothir unto sir Launcelot hath caused all this sorow.

> (685.35–37; XX.9)

One of the fundamental assumptions of feudal chivalry was that the preservation of the state and the welfare of society depended on the virtues of the governing class. It is an assumption that has not become entirely obsolete, of course. Even today, politicians whose private lives will not bear close scrutiny are promised to an uncertain career. In the medieval period the Church felt that the great danger to chivalry was not any external force, but the failure within of the Christian virtues. And one sin which the Church singled out was the betrayal of a lord by sexual transgression with his wife. This is, of course, Lancelot's sin, and yet for Malory Lancelot's wholehearted devotion to the group, and so to knighthood, becomes the virtue to cover a multitude of such sins. Arthurian society collapses but Lancelot remains the perfect picture of chivalry.

Malory is not fond of giving definitions, although the knighthood oath helps to isolate his notion of chivalry with clarity. But there are two other passages which add to our understanding of what chivalry meant to Malory. There is the description of Gareth:

> 'Be my hede,' seyde sir Launcelot, 'he ys a noble knyght and a myghty man and well-brethed; and yf he were assayed,' seyd sir Launcelot, 'I wolde deme he were good inow for ony knyght that beryth the lyff. And he ys jantill, curteyse and ryght bownteuous, meke and mylde, and in hym ys no maner of male engynne, but playne, faythfull an trew.'

> (638.1–6; XVIII.18)

With this passage, we should also read the famous threnody spoken by Ector, which constitutes almost the final words of summary:

> 'A, Launcelot!' he seyd, 'thou were hede of al Crysten knyghtes! And now I dare say,' sayd syr Ector, 'thou sir Launcelot, there thou lyest, that thou were never matched of erthely knyghtes hande. And thou were the curtest knyght that ever bare shelde! And thou were the trueste frende to thy lovar that ever bestrade hors, and thou were the trewest lover, of a synful man, that ever loved woman, and thou were the kyndest man that ever strake wyth swerde. And thou were

the godelyest persone that ever cam emonge prees of knyghtes, and
thou was the mekest man and the jentyllest that ever ete in halle
emonge ladyes, and thou were the sternest knyght to thy mortal foo
that ever put spere in the reeste.'

(725.16–26; XXI.13)

It is, of course, a measure of the tragedy and a terrible irony that it is the
subject of the second passage, Lancelot, who pays tribute to Gareth since
he both knights and kills him. It is a most unhappy accident, but Lancelot
has told us himself that those who take paramours will be unhapy. It may
not always be true that each man kills the thing he loves, but when Lancelot kills Gareth and contributes to the disruption of the state, it certainly is.

Public Virtue

If we wish to read the *Morte Darthur* correctly it is essential to grasp the
importance of the concepts of honour and shame. As modern readers, we
are more trained to consider questions of innocence and guilt, and we run
the risk of turning Malory's book upside down.

One of the great themes of the novel is the problem of personal integrity, the difficulty of remaining upright in a corrupt world. Worldly success means the compromise of one's inner convictions: the wicked or the
clever flourish, but the honest are trodden under. The unscrupulous make
a fortune, get elected, or get their man; the scrupulous win the world's
scorn. This is all part, of course, of a Christian tradition. We must not compromise our souls for earthly glory because we will be justified in the end.
In the Christian tradition, virtue is rewarded.

So too in the literary code, in which the themes of justification and exposure are central. Those whose hearts are pure will be rewarded (by marriage with the hero or heroine), while those whose hearts are corrupt will
be banished. The hero will not risk his integrity for mere show; rather he
will risk a bad reputation for the honesty of his heart. Although the two
can go together, being upright is better than seeming upright. A very
straightforward example of this in nineteenth century fiction is *Mansfield
Park*: Fanny Price appears ungrateful by refusing a dubious proposal,
however dazzling it is socially. She prefers to *seem* ungrateful than to *be*
immoral, because private, inner virtue counts for more than social ad-
vancement without moral fibre, counts for more than 'dropsied honour'.

We are accustomed to this scheme of things, but Malory is totally different. In the *Morte Darthur* all the virtues are public not private. No one
rides through the streets of Camelot with head held high convinced of his

own inner integrity and oblivious to ill-willed gossip, because what you are and what people say you are are the same thing. There is no distinction between being and seeming honest because all the virtues of the Arthurian world are evident for all to see.

A knight is in search of worship and a reputation; what men will say about him is all that counts. In Jane Austen's world, what people will say is less important than the verdict of one's own heart. So, her Mr Knightley (an eloquent name) is a gallant man, a benefactor who helps the poor and the weak. But his virtue is unspoken; there can be no vulgar show. In Camelot, Mr Knightley could not have survived. He would be a dreary, faceless non-entity unable to handle his own personal publicity campaign, while in Highbury, on the other hand, Lancelot would appear a show-off, flashy, slick and somewhat tasteless. No gentleman would treat the Maid of Astolat as he does; only Mrs Elton would have been impressed! I labour the comparison, perhaps, because I believe we must at all points resist the temptation to judge Camelot by the standards of Highbury. Malory's characters worry about public opinion because it is only in public opinion that they exist. It is for this reason that we never see their inner hearts or any of their personal qualities. All the virtues for which Lancelot is praised in the threnody are public virtues. No one in the *Morte Darthur* is thoughful, tolerant, understanding, tender, or kind. Make a list of private virtues and you will have a hard time finding any of them in Malory. Lancelot, of course, accuses himself of unkindness towards Arthur and Guenevere (723.30; XXI.11), but even this is not a private failing. He is upbraiding himself for his lack of the proper, natural behaviour to his lord and lady.

What is good, honourable and fine in Malory is proper behaviour in a public context. A nineteenth century hero must not sacrifice his integrity for worldly success; in Malory worldly success is a knight's highest aim, and the only way he can compromise his honour is by winning worship cheaply. The word 'worship' these days has predominantly religious overtones; for Malory it is an essential part of this world. He is not interested in the contrast innocence/guilt in reference to another world, but in the contrast honour/shame in reference to this world. Virtue and vice are not rewarded in an after life, accounts are settled here and now.

Malory's shame culture was first investigated by Derek Brewer, and the concept is one which has proved extremely useful for understanding the *Morte Darthur*. Moreover, some very influential (if unexpected) people in Malory's world offer interesting confirmation that shame matters more than guilt. When the Pope sends word that Arthur and Lancelot should be reconciled, he does so because of their great prowess not because the evidence for the queen's guilt is insufficient. He has nothing to say about the legal and moral question involved; quite simply – as we say even now – it is a shame to see two such fine men at odds.

The great evils of the Arthurian world are not sins which imperil one's place in another world, but those which imperil one's place in *this* world. And the greatest sins are those which imperil the world itself. Sexual error, which has so obsessed Christian teaching, as a danger to the soul, is less important for Malory than social anarchy as a danger to the chivalric fellowship. And for the individual in a shame culture, public opinion counts for more than conscience, because one *is* what the world says one is. As the world recognises you, so it identifies you.

Private Sin

There is never a total division between shame and guilt cultures and it would not do to oversimplify. Our own society is guilt orientated but we have not lost all notions of shame. Even today, young couples 'have to get married' and we are reluctant to speak openly about what the French eloquently call *les maladies honteuses*. Nor is guilt absent from Malory as Lancelot makes clear when he claims that Elayne of Astolat is, as far as he is concerned, pure 'bothe for dede and wylle' (639.9; XVIII.19). But most obviously and most awkwardly, there is the Grail book, in which sin not shame is the guiding spirit and which therefore seems to run counter to the rest of the *Morte Darthur*.

It would be convenient to dismiss the Grail book as an exception. It has been suggested that it was the earliest book that Malory wrote, that he translated it hastily, and that he only half-understood its implications. It is certainly true that Malory forgets certain aspects, as, for example, the impressive attack by Elaine, the mother of Galahad, on Guenevere (not in the Grail book but part of the Grail story) quoted earlier (see page 65 above). Not many people speak to Guenevere in this way. No one else tells her she should be ashamed of herself for behaving disgracefully to that lovely husband of hers. But Malory drops the idea altogether and Guenevere's sin is entirely forgotten.

Any discussion of shame and honour must face the Grail book squarely however. We cannot claim that it is an early work that has slipped Malory's mind because he chooses to open Book VII in reference to it. Not merely with a time reference – the sort of thing he might have hastily added in revision to bind his tales together: 'So aftir the quest of the Sankgreall was fulfylled . . .' – but he integrates it into his story. It is Lancelot's regrets over his part in the Grail quest that cause him to put on a show of gallantry for other ladies in order to conceal his relationship with Guenevere. In the Grail quest he had promised to forsake sin; back in the shame orientated world of Camelot it is enough to hide his sin. Lancelot carries out his plan so successfully that even Guenevere misunderstands, she send him away in a fury, and the plot gets under way – all because of Lancelot's reaction to the Grail quest.

In the French Grail book that Malory used, Lancelot is regularly and relentlessly attacked. He fails totally in the quest and the failure of Camelot's finest knight reveals the failure of earthly chivalry as a whole. In its place another kind of chivalry is put forward, with another kind of hero: the virgin, celibate knight fighting for heavenly glory. Lancelot, defouled with lechery, is made to grovel for his sexual sin. Now, although Malory cannot change the material of his story, he can and does alter its meaning. At the opening of Book VII we read:

> Than, as the booke seyth, sir Launcelot began to resorte unto quene Gwenivere agayne and forgate the promyse and the perfeccion that he made in the queste; for, as the booke seyth, had nat sir Launcelot bene in his prevy thoughtes and hys myndis so sette inwardly to the quene as he was in semynge outewarde to God, there had no knyght passed hym in the queste of the Sankgreall.
>
> (611.10–15; XVIII.1)

But Malory's French book does not say this; indeed it runs counter to everything the French book does say. And yet Lancelot is obsessed with the idea and even tries to explain it to Guenevere, the tortuous syntax of his speech revealing that he has not worked it all out logically in his mind, and even if he had, this is not the sort of thing one can say blandly to one's mistress, especially, no doubt, when she is a queen:

> 'A, madame,' seyde sir Launcelot, 'in thys ye muste holde me excused for dyvers causis: one ys, I was but late in the quest of the Sankgreall, and I thanke God of Hys grete mercy, and never of my deservynge, that I saw in that my queste as much as ever saw ony synfull man lyvynge, and so was hit tolde me. And if that I had nat had my prevy thoughtis to returne to youre love agayne as I do, I had sene as grete mysteryes as ever saw my sonne sir Galahad, Percivale, other Sir Bors. And therefore, madam, I was but late in that queste, and wyte you well, madam, hit may nat be yet lyghtly forgotyn, the hyghe servyse in whom I dud my dyligente laboure.
>
> (611.32–41; XVIII.1)

In Malory's account of the Grail quest, the attacks on Lancelot are softened, often abbreviated, or omitted altogether. Where this is not possible his earthly prowess is emphasised and justified. For Malory, Lancelot's sin exists as a handicap to his achieving further glory, not as a way of rejecting earthly glory altogether. What rankles with Lancelot is not the blackness of his sin but his lack of success in arms:

> For in the queste of the Sankgreall I had that tyme forsakyn the vanytees of the worlde, had nat youre love bene. And if I had done so at that tyme with my harte, wylle, and thought, I had passed all the knyghtes that ever were in the Sankgreall excepte syr Galahad, by sone.
>
> (721.1–5; XXI.9)

No one engaged in a spiritual quest worries about doing better than the other competitors. The French Grail story shows the debilitating power of sin and the vanity of earthly glory. For Malory too the sin is to be regretted, but because it hinders earthly glory. Lancelot rejects sin because of its results, not as sin *per se*, and this is the spirit of Books VII and VIII too. The lovers come to renounce their love not because it is sinful but because of its social consequences. Their adulterous passion leads them to hazard a kingdom; it is only proper that in the end they should do penance, because hazarding kingdoms is a heinous crime.

In other words, Malory puts the Grail story into an earthly context. Lancelot is not the figure to be rejected in favour of the pure Galahad, for he is the best of earthly knights. Malory shows little interest in perfection. His subject is the best we have on earth and hence Lancelot's important phrase: 'I saw in that my queste as much as ever saw ony synfull man lyvynge.' We find similar words in Ector's lament: Lancelot is the 'trewest lover, of a synful man', and Guenevere, too, is seen in these terms: 'and grete penaunce she toke uppon her, as ever ded synfull woman' (717.43–718.1; XXI.7). For Malory, 'synfull' equals 'earthly', and because he is entirely concerned with things earthly, the best is, inevitably, the best of the sinful. Sin is an unavoidable part of our human condition, and sin is therefore no cause for rejection in itself. Consequently, in the Grail quest Lancelot obtains a partial vision of the Grail. This is totally alien to the spirit of the French story, and especially the way the adventures are put on record:

> So whan sir Bors had tolde hym of the hyghe aventures of the Sankgreall such as had befalle hym and his three felowes, which were sir Launcelot, Percivale and sir Galahad and hymselff, than sir Launcelot tolde the adventures of the Sangreall that he had sene. And all thys was made in grete bookes and put up in almeryes at Salysbury.
>
> (607.33–38; XVII.23)

In the French story, three knights succeed, in Malory there are four. Lancelot's achievement is incomplete, but anyone reading these words alone could easily misconstrue.

The arrival of Galahad signals the demotion of Lancelot in the French story, but Malory, while admitting Galahad's moral superiority, cannot resist asserting Lancelot's greatness:

> '. . . I make unto you a remembraunce that ye shall nat wene frome hensforthe that ye be the best knyght of the worlde.'
> 'As towchyng unto that,' seyde sir Launcelot, 'I know well I was never none of the beste.'
> 'Yes,' seyde the damesell, 'that were ye, and ar yet, of ony synfull man of the worlde . . .'
>
> (520.28–33; XIII.5)

Lancelot's modest admission of inferiority and the maid's disagreement are Malory's own addition to the scene, and at the same time his comment on it.

Malory's Grail quest does not undermine the basic ethic of the whole book, however much notions of sin may, temporarily, come to the fore. There is no rejection of earthly chivalry or of Lancelot. The Grail quest is seen as another adventure appropriate for an earthly knight. Even Bors, one of the successful three (or four) declares that 'he shall have much erthly worship that may bryng hit to an ende', and the hermit who hears his words does no more than shift the emphasis a little, he does not hold up his hands in horror:

> 'Sertes,' seyde the good man, 'that ys sothe withoute fayle, for he shall be the beste knyght of the worlde and the fayryst of the felyship. But wyte you welle there shall none attayne hit but by clennes, that ys pure confession.'
>
> (564.10–13; XVI.6)

The French Bors had said nothing of the sort, but for Malory there can be nothing wrong with earthly endeavour and success.

Lancelot's Finest Hour

That Malory refuses to reject Lancelot is made clear in a part of his book which is almost entirely his own invention: the healing of Sir Urry. It is an odd incident, which consists, for a large part, of a long list of all the knights who try and fail to heal the chronic wounds of the Hungarian knight, Sir Urry. In many ways, the list itself is the most obvious justification of the incident. It is a reminder of the knights we have met before, with occasional brief echoes of the glory they have achieved. By gathering them all together, it emphasises the unity of the Round Table on the brink of decay and disruption: the relentless naming of names is a final statement of fellowship. Here they are, wholly together, just before being wholly destroyed.

But more importantly, for Malory's favourite knight the incident is a statement of his finest hour just before the decline. The period following the queen's rescue from Meliagaunt is one of joy: 'than the kynge and the quene made more of sir Launcelot, and more was he cherysshed than ever he was aforehande.' (663.16–17; XIX.9), but the dubious moral overtones of that episode mean that the joy is vulnerable. Lancelot may be at the top of the wheel of fortune – an image he recalls later (697.12; XX.17) – but it is about to go down. Until now in earthly achievement he was invincible, but where spiritual matters were concerned he was found lacking. And yet here, although his virtue has long since been compromised, he succeeds: he is able to perform a miracle and heal Sir Urry.

The healing, therefore, would appear to be a total justification of Lancelot's perfect knighthood, and yet, at the same time, we become aware that for him failure is now a possibility. His reticence to attempt the healing is an expression of his humility – he does not wish to presume that he can succeed – but, above all, it betrays how afraid he is of failing, so afraid that he is ready to dissociate himself from the group. But Lancelot cannot cut himself off, and must make an attempt. To be genuinely unpresumptuous, he must face the possibility of failure (like theirs). As it turns out, it is by affirming his allegiance, by following the example of all the others, that he is able to succeed. And it is important to notice Lancelot's self-abnegation: he says 'secretely unto hymselff':

> Now, Blyssed Fadir and Son and Holy Goste, I beseche The of Thy mercy that my symple worshyp and honesté be saved, and Thou Blyssed Trynyté, Thou mayste yeff me power to hele thys syke knyght by the grete vertu and grace of The, but, Good Lorde, never of myselff.
>
> (668.22–26; XIX.12)

Appropriately, no one congratulates Lancelot; they all praise God.

For once Lancelot has undertaken an adventure for God not for Guenevere (cf. 539.7; XIII.20), and when he realises the success he can achieve in this way all he can do is weep 'as he had bene a chylde that had bene beatyn'. Those tears are tears of relief that his 'symple worshyp and honesté' have been saved and that his sinful state has not been exposed by failure. They are tears of humility, for Lancelot is aware of his unworthiness, but they are also tears of recognition of what might have been if he had always put God first. It is a moving scene, and one which heightens the tragedy. For we realise that Lancelot's greatest achievement, which could have been one of may others 'had nat [Guenevere's] love bene' (721.2 3; XXI.9), will be the last, because, as Malory tells us:

Thus they lyved in all that courte wyth grete nobeles and joy longe tymes.

But every nyght and day sir Aggravayne, sir Gawaynes brother, awayted quene Gwenyver and sir Launcelot to put hem bothe to a rebuke and a shame.

(669.17–21; XIX.13)

That 'but' is a terrible word. It marks the change which is to come. Shame is a possibility because Lancelot's sin exists, and in this context, sin made public becomes shame.

The theme of the final tales is the public consequences of the private transgression of Lancelot and the queen. Their relationship becomes a source of shame, and shame is what shakes the foundations of the chivalric structure. And as disruption sets in and Malory portrays the anarchy and disorder which invade the realm, so he begins to lay the blame precisely where it is due. Lancelot and Guenevere accuse themselves of destroying the fellowship, but we begin to see how little they are in fact responsible. Malory shifts the blame from the lovers because he changes the charges. They have been accused of adultery, but no one is really interested in that offence in the light of the disorder which is being caused. The lovers, if pushed, might ask for a count of adultery to be taken into consideration, but that is not what they are pleading guilty over. And it is this shift in emphasis that explains Malory's attitude to honour and lying in the final books. *adultery subsumed in categ of all earthly vice,*

Trouthe is the Hyeste Thyng that Man May Kepe

Lancelot's devotion to the queen is an aspect of his loyalty to Arthur and the realm. The relationship is (sinful, if you insist, but) stable and brings glory that binds the fellowship together. French versions of the story describe the lovers' first meeting, their first kiss, etc., but Malory constantly turns away from the private side of their affair and, as an important result, keeps our minds off its sinful nature. All we ever see, the public devotion of a knight to his lady, is perfectly above board.

It is only when there is any danger of discovery that the exact nature of the relationship is brought to our attention, and even then it is clear that it is those who are seeking to reveal things who are at fault; exposure is entirely connected with the villains whose credibility is undermined by their love of strife and debate, the greatest sin in the Arthurian world, the one that attacks the very heart of the chivalric community.

In Books VII and VIII, the work of exposure begun by Morgan le Fay is taken over by Agravain and Mordred who are more redoutable figures since they have greater credibility: Agravain, we remember, was one of the ten Maying knights who so gallantly defended the queen against Meliagaunt. Moreover, as the king's nephews, they have greater sway in the balance of allegiances. Both of the brothers, however, are trouble-makers motivated by hatred, and Agravain, we recall, is open-mouthed (611.19; XVIII.1), a dangerous quality where there are revelations to be made.

On the other hand, all the characters who refuse to speak of the affair are noble. They are not naively unaware of what is going on, nor are they condoning a sordid affair and helping to smother the rumours simply because they are afraid to take their responsibilities and tell Arthur. They are diplomats firmly convinced that the welfare of the state must come first. In this context, Gawain's defence of the lovers is important:

> 'My lorde Arthure, I wolde counceyle you nat to be over hasty, but that ye wolde put hit in respite, thys jougemente of my lady the quene, for many causis. One ys thys, thoughe hyt were so that sir Launcelot were founde in the quenys chambir, yet hit myght be so that he cam thydir for none evyll. For ye know, my lorde, ' seyde sir Gawayne, 'that my lady the quene hath oftyntymes ben gretely beholdyn unto sir Launcelot, more than to ony othir knyght; for oftyntymes he hath saved her lyff and done batayle for her whan all the courte refused the quene. And peraventure she sente for hym for goodnes and for none evyll, to rewarde hym for his good dedys that he had done to her in tymes past. And peraventure my lady the quene sente for hym to that entente, that sir Launcelot sholde a com prevaly to her, wenyng that hyt had be beste in eschewyng and dredyng of slaundir; for oftyntymys we do many thynges that we wene for the beste be, and yet peradventure hit turnyth to the warste.'
>
> (682.23–37; XX.7)

This speech is, of course, important dramatically in the subsequent structure of the narrative, when Gawain turns against Lancelot, but first of all, it is the perfect defence of the lovers from the point of view of a shame culture. It refuses anything but the official, public interpretation of their deeds, and the only private sin it takes into account (cleverly) is the private ill-will and desire for disruption of those who are seeking to make a public issue out of the business at all. Gawain puts his finger on the real crime – the desire to cause trouble – as he bends over backwards to defend not Lancelot and the queen merely, but the realm. He is not being naive, but higher things are at stake than private passions, and he remains stoically noble, totally able to subjugate his personal feelings.

Agravain and Mordred, on the other hand, exploit personal feelings and in a speech which cleverly captures the modulations of their hypocrisy, they feign injured innocence as a cover up for their love of strife. They too refer to the concepts of a shame culture, to the loyalties and allegiances of Lancelot, Arthur, and themselves – they even remind Arthur he is their uncle – but they do so as a way of putting their private rancour into action. They protest their devotion to the king's authority, when the king's authority counts for less than their own private grudge against Lancelot (674.22–29; XX.2)

After the death of Gareth, Lancelot speaks in his own defence. He does so at length and in terms which are a close parallel to those used by Gawain earlier. He asserts his public devotion to the queen and refuses to consider anything else. By this time, of course, Gawain no longer believes. The speeches are long and important. Lancelot, like all of Malory's knights, is not given to verbalising and the fact that he speaks at such length is important in itself. But for the modern reader there is one main problem: Lancelot says the sort of thing that Gawain has already said, only Lancelot must know that what he is saying is a pack of lies. For Malory, I would suggest, this problem does not exist:

'My moste noble lorde and kynge,' seyde sir Launcelot, . . . 'as for my lady quene Gwenyver, excepte youre person of your hyghnes and my lorde sir Gawayne, there nys no knyght undir hevyn that dare make hit good uppon me that ever I was traytour unto youre person. And where hit please you to say that I have holdyn my lady, youre quene, yerys and wynters, unto that I shall ever make a large answere, and prove hit uppon ony knyght that beryth the lyff, excepte your person and sir Gawayne, that my lady, quene Gwenyver, ys as trew a lady unto youre person as ys ony lady lyvynge unto her lorde, and that woll I make good with my hondis. Howbehyt hit hath lyked her good grace to have me in favoure and cherysh me more than ony other knyght; and unto my power agayne I have deserved her love, for oftyntymes, my lorde, ye have concented that she sholde have be brente and destroyed in youre hete, and than hit fortuned me to do batayle for her, and or I departed from her adversary they confessed there untrouthe, and she full worsshypfully excused. And at suche tymes, my lorde Arthur,' seyde sir Launcelot, 'ye loved me and thanked me whan I saved your quene frome the fyre, and than ye promysed me for ever to be my good lorde. And now methynkith ye rewarde me evyll for my good servyse. And, my lorde, mesemyth I had loste a grete parte of my worshyp in my knyghthod and I suffird my lady, youre quene, to have ben brente, and insomuche as she shulde have bene brente for my sake; for sytthyn I have done batayles for youre quene in other quarels than in myne owne quarell, mesemyth now I had more ryght to do batayle

for her in her ryght quarell. And therefore, my good and gracious
lorde, 'seyde sir Launcelot, 'take your quene unto youre good grace,
for she ys both tru and good.'

$$(688.13\text{–}44; XX.11)$$

If we see Lancelot as a liar (and this is no longer the gentlemanly sort of
lie that we excused him for in Book III), Malory, it is clear, does not. When
Lancelot presents the same sort of public defence later (694.20 ff.; XX.15),
Malory comments: 'thus he seyde full knyghtly'. It is true that Lancelot is
avoiding a direct answer. He is, if you insist, equivocating, but at the same
time he is asserting all the eternal verities of the Arthurian world. He
speaks of service, of honour, of glory; he speaks of the perfection of Guenevere as a queen who never failed in her duty. And this is no lie; in the
Arthurian world it is the truth, the whole truth, and nothing but the truth,
so help me God – and God did help Lancelot: 'had nat the myght of God
bene with me, I myght never have endured with fourtene knyghtes'
(694.35–36; XX.15). The truth of all Lancelot asserts has been proved with
the sword. His love for Guenevere is not contrary to the chivalric code because that code has justified him. His defence is both logical and truthful
viewed from within the system. If we find it less than convincing, it is simply because we are outside that system. We are waiting for Lancelot to say
yes or no to a simple question – Are you and the queen lovers? – but when
the life of the realm is at stake, there are no simple questions.

For Lancelot, it is his accusers who are liars; if they had been telling the
truth he could never have killed thirteen of them, unarmed and unpre-
pared as he was (694.34–37; XX.15). If we have already decided that
Lancelot's defence is simple perjury, this accusation will seem to us merely to confirm the fact that he has taken a turn for the worse. But this is
surely not what Malory believes. Within the logic of the knightly code, a
liar is a man who cannot prove the truth of his words with his sword. The
death of the thirteen knights is eloquent proof of their perfidy, and Lancelot's success shows the queen is, indeed, true to her lord. There is, I believe, no boubt as to where Malory stands. In a world where unity and
fellowship are the highest good, disruption is the greatest sin. Ultimately,
Agravain and Mordred are the real sinners. Lancelot can call for and receive the aid of Jesu in his plight; it is they whose souls are in danger
(685.35–37; XX.9). Malory is not shifting the blame from Lancelot out of
his commitment to his favourite knight, he is laying the blame precisely
where it should be laid.

Our society sees public exposure and private error in a different light.
Judging by our standards, Lancelot is a man with his back against the
wall, forced, out of gallantry then out of bravado, to utter untruths, till
there is no going back. We forgive – or understand – him because he has

always had our admiration, but for once he has been caught out and he is guilty. But we must try to suspend our moral disbelief and put ourselves within the Arthurian code. Then, with Malory, we will see Lancelot avoiding a certain line of enquiry but uttering the truth which is the highest thing that a man can keep. He is not dodging the issue to save his own skin and the tawdry name of a royal adulteress, he is sacrificing everything to remain true to his knighthood oath of wholehearted devotion and allegiance to the realm.

It is difficult for us to imagine a situation which in any way compares with this in our modern world because of the basic change in outlook. Comparisons do, however, exist if we remember to look to the public sector. Important statesmen have been involved in political scandals in which the affairs of their private lives, or their interference in public matters in a private capacity, or their use of underhand methods, has finally been discovered. When the press reveals the facts, the statesman will use all the legal loopholes he can find before finally lying. He will protest his innocence till journalists or a legal commission prove his guilt. Since we tend to be disillusioned with politicians, we will see those lies merely as a desperate attempt to salvage a shoddy career, but there can be other interpretations depending on our political affiliations.

The resignation of the American President over the Watergate scandal was inevitable. He should not have done what he did, and his lies in public simply aggravated the situation. Everyone would agree to this except, perhaps, committed Republicans. They will admit, reluctantly, that the President was wrong, but (especially among themselves) they will perhaps suggest that – after all – it is not a bad idea to be able to keep an eye (or rather an ear) on one's opponents. You never know what they are getting up to: they are becoming dangerously red, it seems. And what else could the President do but lie? He could scarcely play into their hands by admitting everything. There was not merely his own career to save; there was the good of the country to think of. All the extremist will admit is that the President should not have got caught. What he did privately was not wrong – if you are consolidating America against socialism what do a few microphones matter? – that he should let it become public knowledge was his real error.

The Language of Destruction

In a public world, where the welfare of the state is of prime importance, private misdemeanours matter only when, through carelessness, they rear their heads in public. Throughout the *Morte Darthur*, but particularly in the final tales, it is not adultery but speaking about adultery, not private sin but public shame, which matters, and its importance can be seen in the shift in emphasis given to language, noise, and the public word.

Malory's knights are taciturn men. One aspect of the poor repuation of Cornish knights is that they are all talk and no deed. Lancelot's long speeches in Book VIII, therefore, are both unusual and important, a final attempt to avoid conflict by bringing reason through the power of words. Till now, speech has been important as the basis of a reputation. Actions speak louder than words, and actions are the only fit subjects for words. A knight seeks not only to *be* the best, but to be *called* the best, and phrases of the type 'he is called the best knight in the world' occur often. In the context of honour, knights want to be talked about; what becomes clear in the final books is that in the context of error silence is best: 'he that hath a prevy hurte is loth to have a shame outewarde.'

Even before any real trouble begins, Guenevere is aware that 'the lesse noyse the more ys my worshyp' (655.22; XIX.5) and Lancelot grudgingly agrees that he 'was never wyllynge nor glad of shamefull sclaundir nor noyse' (656.4–5; XIX.5). When the queen is later returned to Arthur, Lancelot makes it clear that she 'shulde nat be seyde unto of the kynge nother of none other for nothynge done of tyme paste' (692.43–44; XX.14). Camelot, that is, has implicit faith in the proverb 'least said soonest mended' and we can be sure that trouble is brewing when many in the court spoke of Lancelot's relationship with the queen. Lancelot sees the danger and in order to 'eschew the sclaundir and noyse' (611.25; XVIII.1) devotes his attention to other ladies. Guenevere misunderstands and Lancelot has to remind her how vulnerable she is in the face of slander: 'ye muste abyde all that woll be seyde unto you' (612.6: XVIII.1). Later, having become recently wise, she refuses to let Lancelot stay with her because 'what woll youre enemyes and myne sey' (622.13; XVIII.8), and trouble finally comes to Camelot when Arthur who was deaf to rumour and 'wold nat here thereoff' (674.39; XX.2) is forced to listen because Agravain and Mordred claim they can remain silent no longer. This is what they claim; we know quite simply that Agravain is 'opynne-mowthed' (611.19; XVIII.1).

Because Malory's knights are men of action, any attempt to present a reasonable verbal defence inevitably seems superfluous and unknightly. Arthur dismisses Lancelot's reluctance to fight with 'Fye uppon thy fayre langayge' (688.7; XX.11) and Gawain goads Lancelot into action with 'and thou darste do batayle, leve thy babelynge' (703.32; XX.20). Meliagaunt fobs off Guenevere's attempt to reason him into gallantry with 'As for all thys langayge' (651.11; XIX.2) and silences her bodyguard's later protests with 'away with youre proude langayge' (658.22; XX.6). The feeling of the destructive power of words is perhaps best expressed when Gawain attacks Lancelot, who has no desire to be provoked and can only listen: 'All thys langayge sir Launcelot harde' (705.28; XX.22), and even Lancelot's own men feel that his attempt to talk his way to peace is utterly vain: 'for all your fayre speche hit woll nat avayle you' (690.13–14; XX.12).

Words in Malory should properly be used to speak of fine deeds; deeds which are not fine should be shrouded in silence. The clearest statement of both of these points is Lancelot's anger when he is trapped without his armour in the queen's chamber. He wants men to 'speke of my dedys or ever I were slayne' (677.8–9; XX.3), forgetting that the predicament he is in has arisen bacause men have indeed been speaking about his deeds. He is thinking of honour, they of guilt. They think he has offended the king, he is afraid of offending reputation. He is worried that the rest will be silence in a context in which, quite frankly, the best would be silence.

3

Against Interpretation

REALISM

On the occasion of his wedding to Guenevere, Arthur declares that he will grant the reasonable request of any of his subjects. To take up this offer, a poor man comes to court with his eighteen year old son, a handsome youth riding – appropriately for their condition – an undernourished horse. The old man is not a habitué of court circles and, somewhat out of place, has to keep asking his way to King Arthur. He is admitted and asks the king to knight his son – no small request, the king points out, given their social status. The old man is called Aries and explains that the idea of knighthood is his son's. He goes on:

> I have thirtene sonnes, and all they woll falle to what laboure I putte them and woll be ryght glad to do laboure; but thys chylde woll nat laboure for nothynge that my wyff and I may do, but allwey he woll be shotynge, or castynge dartes, and glad for to se batayles and to boholde knyghtes. And allwayes day and nyght he desyrith of me to be made knyght.
>
> (61.24–29; III.3)

Arthur asks to see the other sons and when they arrive he understands the situation clearly, for they 'all were shapyn muche lyke the poore man, but Torre was nat lyke hym nother in shappe ne in countenaunce, for he was muche more than ony of them.' Arthur knights Torre and Merlin predicts that he will turn out to be a fine soldier, explaining why: King Pellinor is Torre's father; Aries is no relation at all. The family group is completed by the arrival of the wife, summoned to tell her version of the tale.

It is an amusing scene, finely handled by Malory. His account is brief – no attempt is made to suggest the time gap necessary for the sons and then the mother to arrive – but it contains all the elements we need to be able to visualise it clearly. We have no difficulty picturing the rather awkward eldest son, a bit of a handful with his ideas above his station, but warmhearted and courageous enough to defend his mother's good name by contradicting the king's counsellor, even though he is just a country boy. There is the buxom mother with her rustic forthrightness, and the dominated father, who admits the paternity of Pellinor with all the resignation of a man who has probably been out of his depth for some time and who is only too relieved to discover that this spoilt, stuck up boy is not one of his own sons, but a royal cuckoo. There might even be something in it for him, too – but, here, we are perhaps taking our elaboration a bit too far, although the desire to elaborate testifies to Malory's skill as a writer: the scene is presented so convincingly that we readily respond.

Now, the *Morte Darthur* is full of pleasant, convincingly presented scenes of this sort and these are often picked out to illistrate Malory's talent for realism. Once we make allowances for the medieval settings and conventions, the details and particularly the dialogues have an immediate appeal. There is only one problem: although the *Morte Darthur* is full of scenes that are as realistic as this, it is also full of scenes which are definitely not. If we want to put forward Malory as a master of convincing presentation then we must be willing to face the objection that the *Morte Darthur* is a very uneven book, that Malory's talent for realistic description is only occasional, and that much of the time he is not very good at it at all. There are situations that will never come alive to the reader's imagination, for they are peopled with cardboard characters whose language is stiff with formality. Parts of the *Morte Darthur* are – given the settings and conventions – presented quite like the books we are used to reading, but other parts are resolutely not.

But to see the *Morte Darthur* as an uneven book and Malory as an occasionally talented writer is, I believe, an error, and the passage concerning the arrival of Sir Torre can, perhaps, lead us to a more reasonable appreciation of the book. It is true that Malory pays perceptive – if dismissively brief – attention to the details of convincing presentation, and that we have no difficulty in dramatising the scene for ourselves, but at the heart of the passage there is a glaring detail which defies all notions of realism. Since it is the key feature of the passage – the reason why the story has been chosen – it would suggest that realism as such is not what Malory is aiming for.

Malory is asking us to believe that Torre's tastes and character have been untouched and unpolluted by his modest rustic surroundings and that his noble tastes are a matter of instinct to him. Without any prompting from those of his milieu, and positive encouragement in the opposite direction, he has acquired a love of the knightly arts. That he should not resemble Aries physically is not in itself unbelievable, but that he should take after Pellinor spiritually is a total sacrifice of verisimilitude for the sake of a moral stance: in matters of nobility, truth will out; the flower of chivalry cannot be born to waste its fragrance in the desert air of rural England.

I am not suggesting that the situation is in itself unbelievable if an attempt were made to explain it. Torre is a fine-looking lad. Perhaps some of the knights of a neighbouring castle took an interest in him and encouraged his admiration of the knightly skills. So much so, that they gave him ideas, and his parents could do nothing with him. It would not be difficult to find some rationalisation of the situation, but Malory has none to offer. For him, quite simply, nobility has physical manifestations and Torre's finer stature reveals his relationship to Pellinor because knights are finer men. In simple terms of realism, the idea is preposterous. But in Malory's moral world there is nothing strange. For him, nobility is a visible characteristic; it has obvious physical manifestations. A knight is able to stand pain not because of his physical strength but his moral strength (86.13; IV.9). For Torre, in a literal sense, knighthood is in his blood, as it is for his half brothers Aglovayle and Perceval, who tell their mother when she wants them to stay with her:

> 'A, my swete modir,' seyde sir Percyvale, 'we may nat, for we be comyn of kynges bloode of bothe partis. And therefore, modir, hit ys oure kynde to haunte armys and noble dedys.'
>
> (490.22–24; XI.10).

Moral Realities

Malory's desire to present convincingly is part of his desire to reveal moral significances. His descriptions, that is, are not, first of all, presented with documentary realism, they set out to evaluate. For him the moral and the physical exist on a single plane of reality, and his interest in the physical is for what it can reveal.

This is not to suggest that Malory has a moral axe to grind, but that he is interested in highlighting the significance of an event rather than describing its strict reality. The world he describes is full of meaning but remains basically non-realistic. A clear example of this is the way in which all verisimilitude is sacrificed in the plot of the healing of Sir Urry. Urry has been wounded in Spain fighting a knight whom he kills, but whose sorceress mother casts a spell that makes Urry's wounds bleed and fester until he can be cured by the best knight in the world. Urry's mother takes him from realm to realm for seven years before he is finally healed by Lancelot. And yet throughout the *Morte Darthur* (and we are nearly at the end) it has been made plain that Arthur's kingdom is the finest on earth. His reputation and authority are international; everyone knows that the best knights are to be found in England; and of those knights Lancelot is unsurpassed. And yet the lady comes to England last. Indeed her trip is even perversely roundabout enough for her to reach England via Scotland. The structure of the story is totally illogical: if she had had any common sense she would have shipped her son from Spain to England straight away. The whole of the *Morte Darthur* so far has gone to justifying the reputation of Arthur's kingdom and we are now asked to believe that a woman desperately in need of help was so badly informed that it took her seven years to find a cure. Her only stroke of luck was, having arrived through Scotland, finding Arthur holding court up in Carlisle.

The answer of course is obvious. Malory had fashioned his story of Urry not to give us a moving little slice of life, but to emphasise Lancelot's moment of glory. If Urry had been healed easily and at once there would have been no miracle; it would have been mundane not adventurous. The nature and the logic of the story demand delay; the logic of reality has no importance. And just as in folktales lost princesses are found with great difficulty, not bumped into on the first day's search, so Lancelot must be the last to try to heal Urry. Given his rank, of course, he could not come last, and so he must be kept out of the way till everyone else tries, at which point in the story he must delay no longer. The totally unreal pattern of the Urry story is designed to underline one thing: the essential reality of Lancelot's untarnished preeminence.

Examples of this kind are found throughout the *Morte Darthur*. Trust the Lady of the Lake to turn up with all the inside information about the poisoned apple incident *after* Lancelot has cleared the queen's name. She would have saved a lot of fuss if her omniscience had included the fact that her presence was urgently needed at court. But Lancelot must defend the queen. The action and adventure involved are far more important than explanatory proof, which can arrive at any point to keep the records straight.

As we have already seen, the Arthurian world is one with a logic of its own, a world working with different principles and different assumptions. Adventure is so important that any excuse for action will suffice and regularly, throughout the book, everything is sacrificed to the needs of action not the needs of verisimilitude. When Lancelot finally arrives, fuming with rage at Meliagaunt's villainy, to defend Guenevere, the queen urges him to take things more calmly. Reluctantly he agrees and less reluctantly he spends the night with her, after wounding himself gaining access to her chamber. His blood stains the bedclothes and this gives Meliagaunt a brilliant idea to hide his own treachery. The queen is accused of betraying Arthur and once again Lancelot comes to her defence. In all probability, Lancelot must be infuriated with this villainous trouble-maker, and no doubt itching to get at him with his sword (as events prove). But until the day of combat arrives, Meliagaunt offers – of all things – to take Lancelot on a courtesy tour of his castle, and Lancelot accepts. Sheer madness, of course, if the author wants us to believe the strict reality of events, but absolutely essential if you want to have Lancelot drop through a trap door and be in prison on the day of the combat.

Strangely enough, although this detail is excessively contrived, Lancelot's absence is then explained in a perfectly natural way: no one wonders what has happened to him because he was in the habit of disappearing without warning. Even then, although the explanation is perfectly reasonable, this is the first we have ever heard of the habit, and it is mentioned only because it serves a purpose in the narrative. In a similar way we are given other realistic details: we learn that Lancelot talks in his sleep when Guenevere needs to find whose bed he is in, and that the queen has a distinctive cough, when Lancelot needs to be awoken to the reality that his lady is the one outside and not the one with him in bed. Otherwise, there is no reference at all to these traits. No cough echoing down the corridors of Camelot ever heralds the arrival of Guenevere on any other occasion.

Malory has the art of picking out details to present incidents in a convincing manner, but he shows no consistent interest in convincing presentation as such. Once a detail has served a purpose it is jettisoned and if there is no purpose to serve Malory is extremely thrifty with detail. An obvious example is, once again, the circumstances of the discovery of Guenevere's adultery in Meliagaunt's castle. Lancelot breaks the bars to the queen's chamber and cuts his hand badly. His rapture is such that he pays no heed to his wound until it is too late and the bed is stained with blood. He wears a glove to conceal his part in the business. Meliagaunt has all the clues he needs for his accusation. But although the presentation of the incident is realistic enough (it is hard perhaps to believe that a man who has cut himself to the bone would not notice immediately, but still, 'love that tyme was nat as love ys nowadayes'), once the events are under way all semblance of reality and logic is dismissed. The essential thing is the ambiguity of the accusation. Meliagaunt has jumped to the wrong conclusions, and Lancelot will be able to defend the queen because she is innocent of the precise charge levelled at her. And because this is what Malory is interested in, he and his characters turn a blind eye to all the rest. No one wonders why Lancelot has suddenly taken to wearing a glove (no one seems even to notice it), and no one asks where the bloodstains did come from if the queen is innocent. No one even notices the bars of the window, hastily reconstructed by Lancelot on his way out. All these things are there for the reader, symbols not of Lancelot and Guenevere's guilt, for what is at stake is their reputation not their conscience.

Lancelot is ready to face the world; Malory never makes him face himself. The unnoticed clues are rather a token of the vulnerability of the situation. Will anyone notice, we wonder? But no one does notice, and the preposterous accusation follows its due legal course without even the most summary supplementary investigation.

There is a veneer of realistic presentation is the *Morte Darthur*, and although this has a genuine appeal which I would not seek to minimise, on the whole, Malory has less physical awareness than moral awareness. He is interested not in the size, colour or appearance of an object, character or incident, but in its value. We know that Lancelot is the best knight in the world and that Guenevere is the 'moste nobelest Crysten quene', but we do not know what either of them looked like. Arthur, we are told, had grey eyes, but if we complained that this is the only clue we have for recognising the king, Malory would no doubt register surprise. Do we honestly mean to say that if the greatest Christian king in the world walked into the room, we might mistake him for someone else? For Malory, the moral excellence of his characters makes them immediately recognisable. When Sir Urry saw Lancelot approach he knew at once that this was the best knight in the world. He started to feel better right away.

Malory's eye is so regularly on the moral realities of the Arthurian world that his physical descriptions constantly slide into moral evaluations. We become so used to this that we begin not to notice. As Lancelot leaves for Guenevere's chamber on the night they are trapped together, Malory writes:

> So sir Launcelot departed and toke hys swerde undir hys arme, and so he walked in hys mantell, *that noble knyght*, and put hymselff in grete jouparté.
>
> (675.41–43; XX.3 italics mine).

No modern author could get away with such an overtly biased narrative. We are not invited to assess Lancelot's nobility, we are simply told that he is noble. But for Malory, his nobility is an essential part of him, as plain to see as the mantle he is wearing. Malory is not invoking the ironic contrast between Lancelot's apparent integrity and the fact that he is on his way to an illicit rendez-vous with a married woman. He is stating a fact. 'That noble knyght' is no more biased than *that tall knight* would be; the moral world has an objective existence of its own.

A clearer and rather bizarre example of the same thing can be seen at the death of Morgause, Arthur's sister. Her son Gaherys finds her in bed with her young lover, Lamorak, and to save the family honour he strikes off her head. Malory describes the scene as follows:

> So whan sir Gaherys sawe his tyme he cam to there beddis syde all

armed, wyth his swerde naked, and suddaynly he gate his modir by the heyre and strake of her hede. Whan sir Lameroke sawe the blood daysshe uppon hym all hote, whyche was the bloode that he loved passyng well, wyte you well he was sore abaysshed and dismayed of that dolerous syght.

(377.41–378.2; X.24).

We are tempted to smile. It is a somewhat gory notion of love when a knight can take time to register the affection he feels for the blood that is splashing over him. But there is, of course, quite simply a gap in the thought. The blood is Morgause's and Lamorak loves Morgause. But conflations of the moral and physical along these lines are found throughout the *Morte Darthur*; it is a feature of style we shall come back to.

The Superlative Mode

Drawing attention to the realism of the *Morte Darthur* is, for twentieth century readers, a reasonable way of approaching Malory, and yet, however much Malory convinces us that the Arthurian world was as real as our own, we are forced to admit that it exists on an entirely different plane of reality. Arthurian society was a superlative world. Of course it bore resemblances to ours, but it was much better, less impoverished. We will naturally recognise features as similar to those in the world we know, but more often than not, everything is larger than life. Like life of course, but simply built on a larger scale.

There are, it is true, glimpses of a world we recognise very much as our own, reminders of the humdrum existence, the decay and corruption that will take over when Arthurian society finally decays:

And so as he yode he saw and harkened by the moonelyght how that pyllours and robbers were com into the fylde to pylle and to robbe many a full noble knyght of brochys and bees and of many a good rygne and many a ryche juell. And who that were nat dede all oute, there they slewe them for their harneys and their ryches.

(714.23–27; XXI.4)

This sudden glimpse of scavengers is all the more shocking in that we rarely ever see anything but the exclusive world of noble chivalry. Lancelot is shown to Gawain's tomb by certain townspeople, but there are not many townspeople in Malory. Arthurian society seems to be made up entirely of the knightly class, the kings, lords and ladies of the court. There is an occasional hermit (usually an ex-knight), and a dwarf or two, but not much more. Malory regularly identifies the places in which events occur, giving real, modern names for the cities of legend (Camelot is Winchester, Astolat is Guildford, and Lancelot's castle is probably at Bamborough or Alnwick), but although the names give a semblance of reality we have the feeling that nothing else exists. There is no bustling activity going on in the towns and villages of England; Arthurian society is somehow *in* the world but not *of* it.

It is also a world suspended in time, a world which, till the end, never changes. No one grows old in Malory; no one, indeed, has an age. Logically some of the characters at the end must be quite old (Guenevere in the French stories is around fifty) but we have no awareness of their age. Galahad comes to court at the age of fifteen, but we do not picture him as an awkward adolescent sporting his first, tentative moustache; he is a young man, that is all. In theory, of course, he is a generation younger than his father who is a generation younger than Arthur, but these are details we can calculate, not facts we appreciate. Age cannot wither Arthurian society, and though the passing of time is mentioned, it is not really felt. One tournament is presided over by Guenevere and a group of retired knights (644.35; XVIII.22), but otherwise there is rarely any feeling of knights moving through their careers to retirement, even if the company known as the Queen's knights inevitably reminds us of the passing of time (650.22–35; XIX.1).

Malory's is a formal, ordered world of ceremony and decorum, a public world where everything fits the proper hierarchy. When the group attempts to heal Sir Urry, Arthur tries first, to encourage the others of course, and 'as was kyndely', as was only proper because of his rank. Then the other kings try, then the dukes, then the earls, then the knights of the famous families (starting with Arthur's nephews) and finally the lesser knights. Even the one mistake in the list (Constantine is mentioned twice) shows Malory's concern for the hierarchy. He is mentioned with the knights, but also among the kings, foreshadowing his later status as Arthur's successor.

Even success in battle (especially in relation to Arthur) respects rank. On one occasion, Lancelot defeats Gawain, Agravain, Gaherys, and Mordred, but Lavaine and Arthur reach a stalemate. It would be improper for Arthur to be defeated by a young new-comer, though for the sake of events Lavaine is not beaten outright. Guenevere receives similar treatment: when, at the end, she retires to a nunnery, she is made abbess, not because of her piety or flair for religious administration, nor because of what she deserves, but because she is queen. 'She was abbas and rular, as reson wolde' (718.9; XXI.7). Even today, of course, rank remains a qualification in the same way: a royal princess will be awarded an honorary doc-

torate by a university, not an honorary B.A. In a patterned world of order
and ceremony this is all the more normal.

Malory's fine eye for convincing detail is often and deservedly mentioned, but it also needs pointing out that just as readily Malory turns his
back on realism and resorts to superlatives and even exaggeration to
measure the value of the world he describes. Part of Malory's task of do-
cumenting the Arthurian world is the need to give a proper evaluation of
what it was all worth. He cannot merely present the facts and let the
reader decide – which would perhaps be too modern an attitude to history
– for the world he is writing about is not subject to debate. It is Malory's
job not merely to chart out the Arthurian world with fidelity, but to give
us a proper awareness of the scale to which it is drawn.

The scale is, of course, larger than life. Everything is the biggest and the
best of its kind. A knight will serve his king till the end:

> Than sir Lucan toke up the kynge the tone party and sir Bedwere the
> othir parté, and in the lyfftyng up the kynge sowned, and in the
> lyfftynge sir Lucan felle in a sowne, that parte of hys guttis felle oute
> of hys body, and therewith the noble knyght hys harte braste. And
> whan the kynge awoke he behylde sir Lucan how he lay fomyng at
> the mowth and parte of his guttes lay at hys fyete.

> (714.37–42; XXI.5)

This description is probably not a strict physical reality any more than all
those battlefields swimming in blood or the casualty figures recorded
after the final disaster: there are 100,000 dead; only two remain alive. The
figures are exact only as an assessment of the tragedy.

Everything in Malory's world appears to us heightened and overstated,
but that is because nothing nowadays can have anything like the same importance or worth. In repentance for his part in Gareth's death, Lancelot
says:

> I shall firste begyn at Sandwyche, and there I shall go in my shearte,
> barefoote; and at every ten myles ende I shall founde and gar make
> an house of relygious, of what order that ye woll assygne me, with
> an holé covente, to synge and rede day and nyght in especiall for sir
> Gareth sake and sir Gaherys. And thys shall I perfourme from
> Sandwyche unto Carlyle; and every house shall have suffycyent
> lyvelod. And thys shall I perfourme whyle that I have ony lyvelod in
> Crystyndom, and there ys none of all thes religious placis but they
> shall be perfourmed, furnysshed and garnysshed with all thyngis as
> an holy place ought to be.

> (696.13–22; XX.16).

The physical effort involved in walking barefoot from Sandwich to Car-

lisle is hard for us to conceive these days, though in terms of fifteenth century penance it was perhaps not such an overstatement of contrition, but
the financial expense involved is enormous. Lancelot is offering to finance
some twenty ot twenty-five religious houses. For Malory this is not an ex-
travagant expression of grief but a just assessment of what Gareth's death
means.

It is only as we realise that Malory heightens reality to express the
deeper reality of his material that we can understand much of his book. A
clear example is the reaction of Arthur and Gawain on the death of
Gareth:

> 'Alas,' seyde sir Gawayne, 'now ys my joy gone!'
> And than he felle downe and sowned, and longe he lay there as he
> had bene dede. And whan he arose oute of hys swoughe he cryed
> oute sorowfully and seyde,
> 'Alas!'
> And forthwith he ran unto the kynge, criyng and wepyng, and
> seyde, 'A, myne uncle kynge Arthur! My good brothir sir Gareth ys
> slayne, and so ys my brothir sir Gaherys, whych were two noble
> knyghtes.'
> Than the kynge wepte and he bothe, and so they felle on sownynge.
>
> (686.20–28; XX.20)

This is not an example of Malory's incompetant attempt at realism, nor is
it an isolated example. Arthurian knights regularly dissolve into tears as
readily as any nineteenth century heroine. Malory's narrative could not be
taken as stage directions for a dramatisation of the *Morte Darthur*; it is a
formal, heightened expression of superlative grief. Even when we make
allowances for changes of custom – we now feel it more appropriate to re-
strain our emotions, not give vent to them; earlier reactions to grief were
obviously more Mediterranean – it is hard to see the reality of 'than the
kynge wepte and he bothe, and so they felle on sownynge'. Pamela yes,
King Arthur no. But Malory is measuring the size and impact of a moment
of profound emotion; the actual physical manifestations are a metaphor. It
is true that a stiff upper lip is occasionally fitting, like the contained sor-
row of Gawain when his brother Agravain and two of his sons are killed
by Lancelot. But ultimately, Gawain did not approve of their behaviour:
they were not worth crying over anyway. The (modern?) realism of
Lancelot's restraint on seeing the dead Guenevere is, of course, shattering.
But then this is a moment when even tears can express nothing: 'he wepte
not gretelye, but syghed.' (723.1–2; XXI.11).

Formality and ceremony have a limited appeal for modern readers, but
we must never underestimate their importance in Malory. Take for
example:

Then sir Launcelot purveyed hym an hondred knyghtes, and all well clothed in grene velvet, and their horsis trapped in the same to the heelys, and every knyght hylde a braunche of olyff in hys honde in tokenyng of pees. And the quene had four-and-twenty jantillwomen folowyng her in the same wyse. And sir Launcelot had twelve coursers folowyng hym, and on every courser sate a yonge jantylman; and all they were arayed in whyght velvet with sarpis of golde aboute their quarters, and the horse trapped in the same wyse downe to the helys, wyth many owchys, isette with stonys and perelys in golde, to the numbir of a thousande. And on the same wyse was the quene arayed, and sir Launcelot in the same, of whyght clothe of golde tyssew.

(693.37–694.4; XX.14).

The description of the procession is Malory's own addition to the story, and for him it is both unusual (since he rarely troubles to give descriptions of the sort) and unusually long. But at an emotional high point in his narrative he perhaps unconsciously shows an interest not in the personal emotions of the characters involved, but in proper, ritual behaviour. The circumstances of Guenevere's abduction were exceptional – she had been publicly humiliated, stripped, and led forward to be burnt – it is only fitting that the circumstances of her return should be exceptional too: she will be accorded the honour and pageantry that become the 'moste nobelest Crysten quene'.

Perhaps a clearer illustration of Malory's love of pattern and ceremony as opposed to naturalistic behaviour is Lancelot's distribution of lands and titles to his men when they return to France (699.24–700.8; XX.18). A great lord must reward his loyal supporters and Lancelot is the perfect leader whose generolity must be recorded by the historian. But the rewards are symbolic of the outstanding fidelity of Lancelot's knights and of his own greatness; the list is totally out of keeping with any notion of political reality – as the last words of embarrassed haste perhaps suggest: 'Thus sir Launcelot rewarded hys noble knyghtes, and many mo that mesemyth hit were to longe to rehers.' Lancelot and his followers have spent most of their life in England. Imagine the feelings of the local rulers of these lands having new kings foisted upon them by someone for whom, till now, France was obviously not good enough. There are grounds enough for a Barons' Revolt at least, I wager. But of course no logic, no realism exists here. These countries, however real their names may be, do not exist until Lancelot touches and enlivens them. Modern historians might quibble about the historical accuracy of the titles distributed; what Malory is taking pains to put on record is Lancelot's exemplary largesse and the great deserving of his men. The spiritual values involved need a physical manifestation and this is it.

Malory concentrates on this superlative world and focuses on the evaluative not the pictorial. It is for this reason that his characters have an extraordinary emotional impact. We never see what they look like, but we are made to feel what they are worth. Before turning to characterisation in Malory, to see how his realistic presentation of a non-realistic world continues there, a few remarks should be made on one final aspect of Malory's realism: magic.

A Further Note on Magic

Critics who draw attention to Malory's fine eye for realistic detail usually hasten to point out, as corroborative evidence, the way he reduces the quantity of magic in his story. Many magical elements remain of course, and some of them are among the most haunting aspects of the book, but the number has been reduced considerably. Malory's French source books are far more magical. What is more, as his book goes on, Malory shows less and less interest in the supernatural. It never disappears entirely, but he does dispense with wizardry of the cheaper kind, like Morgan changing herself into stone to avoid being captured (92.11 ff.; IV.14).

The meaning of this reduction has been disputed. Many believe it shows Malory's more realistic outlook – although, as we have seen, Malory's interest in realism is only a passing one. Moreover, if he were so interested in verisimilitude, there is much more that Malory could have easily cut out. It has also been argued that the reduction in the magical elements is a sign of Malory's fondness for magic, which he wanted to put to fullest effect by paring away the excess. This is certainly a convincing point of view: one ghost is indeed more eerie than a legion of them popping up all over the place. And yet Malory rarely seems to use the magical elements fully; he takes them for granted somewhat, and I think we could suggest that they are, for Malory, another aspect of the superlative world he was describing. Although he is presenting a historical record, he can include supernatural elements because things in those days were not what they are now. Magic is an integral part of the world of heightened significance, and Malory can take it in his stride not because he is a simpleton (forced into a corner he might well admit that kings or holy knights do not pull swords from stones and that these revelatory devices do not float down rivers), but because it helps to express the superior worth of the Arthurian world. Life was like that in those days. Our world has gone downhill since, and supernatural revelation and election have been replaced by political scheming and brute force. If swords in stones floated down rivers these days or if magic horns were sent to court to test feminine chastity, they would make the headlines of every broadsheet or billboard in town. But they do not. In Arthur's days life was lived on a different level. Some things, admittedly, were strange for the people even then, and they express their wonder, but most of the time they do not even bat an eyelid. When Morgan's magic horn comes to Mark's court, not a single voice is heard asking for a closer look, no one ever wonders how it works, and not the slightest surprise is registered. The magic in Malory is further evidence of the importance, the moral weight of the Arthurian world. It does not indermine its reality, but shows how real its superiority is.

CHARACTERISATION

Malory is interested in the formal and ceremonial as much as in the natural and lifelike. He may offer naturalistic dialogue to render a scene lively, but he invariably does so with brevity because the presentation and analysis of character through speech is not one of his aims. When our imagination is roused by what we read, we naturally embroider, we wish to interpret and make explicit the features Malory has chosen to leave unspoken. We want to explore character by considering in greater depth the hints Malory has given us. This tendancy is only natural and Malory at times seems to encourage it positively, but I would suggest that he was not very interested in characterisation and we should resist the temptation to read between the lines too much.

We, today, are interested in the private man behind the public figure. Witness all those magazines and newspaper articles devoted to members of the Royal Family or film stars off duty. The question we are likely to ask about the *Morte Darthur* is 'What kind of a man was Arthur?' Malory sees himself as a historian and is totally concerned with public figures. The question he asks is 'What kind of a king was Arthur?' Malory's characters are public figures in a superlative world. There are many points of similarity between Lancelot and ourselves, but it is going perhaps too far to say that Lancelot is merely a man like any of us. If he is, in his private moments of doubt and regret, we never see him, for Malory is not interested in private behaviour. He shows us not what men feel in their hearts but how (and how well) they behave in public; not what they think (for they seem almost entirely untroubled by thought) but what they do.

A knight's individual character is of little interest to Malory, who is concerned far more with what makes a man knightly, what makes him, that is, like other knights. The qualities that Malory concentrates on – courage, honour, fidelity, worship, etc. – do not identify knights as individuals, but identify them as knights. And strangely enough, even when they are singled out for their knightly excellence, it is a singularity they share with all their fellows.

Everyone agrees that Lancelot is the best knight in the world. When someone else is given the same distinction, it is taken for granted, we suppose, that Lancelot has not been taken into consideration; he is in a class apart. After Lancelot, Tristram is the best knight in the world, and after Tristram, Lamorak. These three form a triumvirate of reference and the other best knights in the world are given the status of *proxime accessit*. The number of runners up is large, but then Malory's knights are all outstanding men. What is more, as we are introduced to a new best knight in the world, his preeminence is vouchsafed in that he is unbeatable in battle. Gareth, for instance, is not quite one of the three, but he is a remarkable knight who, in the book devoted to him, remains invincible. Once Malory takes the spotlight off these runners-up, they resume a more vulnerable excellence: Gareth, for example, is beaten in Book V by, among others, Sir Segwarides, who enters the *Morte Darthur* as a fighter of rare incompetence.

What looks, therefore, like an individual assessment – this knight at least stands out from the others; he is on a par with the top three – is in fact no more than a measure of their shared excellence. Malory's knights are distinguished from their fellows for only a moment – at most for the length of the book or section recounting their adventures – before being allowed to retire to the common background where they are all equally outstanding, all head and shoulders above the rest, except for Lamorak, Tristram, and Lancelot. In Malory's very hierarchical kingdom, his notion of knightly achievement is extremely democratic. Their superiority characterises his knights with perfect equality.

Character and Role

We seek the individual, Malory the ideal representative. We wish to see the real man behind the public image, whereas for Malory one's real image and one's public image are the same thing. We want to strip away the mask, but Malory's knights are not themselves or have no existence until they put on the mask. There is perhaps a Lancelot who, stripped of his armour, off duty and away from the tinselled existence of Camelot, speaks from the heart – to Guenevere perhaps – of his secret doubts, of his fears, of his plans for the future, and of the things that touch him most deeply. But if there is, there is not the slightest trace of him in Malory.

A knight has his whole existence in public and that, for Malory, is how it should be. If he removes his public identity (his armour) there is nothing left to give him away. When Lancelot fights in disguise before all the men who know him best, although his skill in fighting and style of riding (both public, military traits) set people guessing, not a soul recognises him. Although his accent was apparently distinctive, no one even recognises his voice. In Malory's world, the kind of individual characteristics which betray identity do not exist.

Malory is not interested in the idiosyncracies which define an individual but in the shared virtues that make a knight a member of the group. He rarely shows any concern for what sets a man apart from others, only what makes him one of them. Hence, apart from the occasional scar (mentioned to serve the purposes of the plot) we have no idea of what Malory's knights looked like. Inevitably, once they disguise their armour, there is nothing of the real man to reveal who they are.

Malory writes the official history of Arthur's kingdom and individual affairs are of no importance. He takes us on a guided tour round Camelot but the doors marked private remain shut. Indeed, it is probably best that way. Things that are private in the *Morte Darthur* are frequently suspect. The sentiment that leads Agravain and Mordred to stir up trouble is a 'prevy hate', what sets the court talking are Lancelot and Guenevere's 'prevy draughtis', and even the unfortunate dinner which the queen organised and during which she got herself accused of murder was a 'pryvy dynere' in 'a prevy place by themselff'. If a deed or a sentiment cannot face the light of day, it should perhaps not exist.

A clear sign of Malory's interest in the public side of his knights and ladies is that we rarely ever see them alone. Even Lancelot and the queen are rarely presented alone together, because Malory is interested in the public consequences of their affair not in the private details of it. He shows us everything from the outside. We see an individual's role not his personality. Indeed, the *Morte Darthur* reveals an almost theatrical sense of character: those with a role to play.

The Queen

Even the character we seem to know best in the *Morte Darthur*, Guenevere, is seen essentially as playing a role – that of queen, first of all, and it is for this reason that, except before her marriage to Arthur, when the title is not hers, she is never referred to without a title (queen, sometimes dame).

And her future role is so important that even before she marries the king she is twice called queen.

Guenevere plays another role of course, the duel role of mistress and wife, and this is emphasised by the fact that implicitly the story makes her barren. Conception is an easy thing in Camelot: Arthur fathers sons as a result of two brief encounters; it took only one half-forced seduction to produce Torre; Bors' virginity was blemished by the pleasures of the flesh only once and he became a father; and Lancelot only had to be enticed into Elaine's bed once for Galahad to be conceived. According to fertility rates of this order, in all probability Guenevere would have given birth, but probability cannot be taken into consideration at all. Guenevere has a suspended existence; no time span, no reproductive cycle is possible. She is; she does not develop. She has a role to play and her existence as a woman is sacrificed not only because a child would be a sign of shame and cast a shadow over the legitimacy of the succession, but because it is essential to the pull of loyalties and the tragedy that there should be no heir, that the disaster should be complete.

Malory, of course, inherits his story, but he pares away the private aspects of Guenevere to emphasise her role. She is a queen, not an experienced older woman who seems almost to be toying with the adolescent sentiments of a bashful Lancelot, as she is in one of the French versions. We see nothing of how she behaves with Lancelot in moments of intimacy and we have no access to her presence when she is alone with Arthur. What interests Malory is the relationship of conflicting loyalties – king, queen, knight – not the personal intrigues of Arthur, Guenevere, Lancelot. The *Morte Darthur* is not the story of a suburban *ménage à trois*, and it is for this reason that we are never given any sense of the nature of the relationship between the lovers. We are shown nothing of its developing stages; it exists merely as one of the data of the story. Above all, we see the labour of love, and its trials, for we are able to perceive, behind the role, a woman who is jealous, unreasonable, possessive, and headstrong.

This is, admittedly, the beginning of a personal portrait of Guenevere the woman, but it is to be noted that the only aspects of her personality that we see are those that influenced public events, those that stem directly from her role and position as queen. Malory, that is, offers details of characterisation to serve the plot, and until a personality influences events we remain largely unaware of it.

Malory's portrait of Guenevere is certainly brilliant and convincing (it is also possible to find her exasperating) but it is basically one-sided. We know no more about her than her part in certain events betrayed. All her great qualities, all those virtues that made her an exceptional woman, that captured the hearts of the greatest king and the greatest knight in Christendom remain untold. Because Malory is ready to show an interest in character when it impinges on the public sphere, we know more about Guenevere than anyone else in the *Morte Darthur*; but we know no more than events reveal. He certainly has little time for the exploration of personality for its own sake.

This, of course, is something we find unusual. We are used to the idea of characters in fiction with a developing personality. The reader gets a growing awareness of them as they reveal themselves progressively in action and thought. In Malory there is no developing characterisation as such. His characters enter the Arthurian world in their complete state. They do not evolve or improve or suffer influence any more than they are changed by the passage of time. All we know about them we know from the start. Events may provide further information, but when they do, our previous knowledge is confirmed. There is nothing to surprise us, no unexpectedly individualistic response to throw us off balance, just the perfect conformity to expectation of men who know how to play a proper role in society. And if there is ever any surprise, no psychological explanation is offered; merely the role they are required to play has changed.

While her personality dominates events, Malory is ready to take trouble with his characterisation of the queen. A man cannot win with this kind of woman; it is impossible for Lancelot to put a foot right. She is a law unto herself. Since Lancelot endangered his life by fighting in disguise with a maiden's token, Guenevere wants to be sure in future that Lancelot will not jeopardise his life again. He must take care to be clearly identifiable and to this end she gives him a sleeve of gold of her own to wear. Her fear for his safety is expressed as she jealously imposes herself by getting one step ahead of any future Maids of Astolat. She has had difficulties with Elaines before; she has obviously been too easy-going. There was King Pelles's daughter Elaine, the mother of Galahad. A lovely boy, so like his father, but Elaine was extremely sharp tongued. She forgave Lancelot for his infidelity then – it was not really his fault, he said – but look where her tolerance has brought her now: he is still favouring other Elaines.

Malory's attention to the personality of Guenevere has led critics to take this as an example of his interest and talent throughout. But this is not the case, for once the action is under way in the final books, Guenevere's character is entirely forgotten. The clearest example of this is when she is returned to Arthur. After all we have learnt about Guenevere – her possessiveness, her temper, her headstrong personality – we might have expected her to have her word to say on the issue. Perhaps she pleaded to be allowed to stay with Lancelot. Perhaps she suggested eloping to France. But we will never know. How Guenevere took the matter personally is of no interest to Malory. For the good of the political situation it was imperative that the queen return to the throne. Uncharacteristically, Guenevere therefore says nothing, and, indeed, is virtually absent from the *Morte Darthur* until the end, when the role she plays becomes totally dominant. Indeed, she takes on a new role as she assumes a life of penitence, devotion, and rejection of the world. Her religious habit is a further denial of her individual status as a woman.

It is true that at one point we read that Guenevere is a woman like any other, or rather Bors tries to assure Lancelot that the queen did not mean it when she banished him; it was merely a typical feminine reaction:

> Women in their hastynesse woll do oftyntymes that aftir hem sore repentith.
>
> (612.34–35; XVIII.2).

But ultimately, Guenevere is not like other women and the words that say she is are those of Bors speaking to Lancelot (and trying hard to convince him), not Malory speaking to us. We must not trivialise Guenevere and pretend we know her, for Malory never lets us become familiar with the 'moste nobelest Crysten quene'. Her personality in Book VII is the motivating force of the early action and Malory takes pains to present it convincingly so that we will see the issues involved. His portrait of Guenevere exists, that is, because of the purpose it serves; it is at the heart of the public/private clash which heralds and provokes the downfall of the realm.

Reading Between the Lines

Modern readers of the *Morte Darthur* are on the look-out for the human reactions behind the formal situation, but Malory's attention to individual behaviour is tantalisingly brief. Inevitably therefore we attempt to expand Malory's brevity, and in doing so we are, I believe, justified as long as we follow along the lines of the information he gives us. When we begin to fill in Malory's silences, however, when we follow what are no more than hints to say what Malory chooses not to say, we are on less solid ground. The characterisation for which we offer evidence might be psychologically convincing, but it will be our work more than Malory's. New readers will be thrown off balance somewhat when they find that they have to provide all the characterisation themselves by relentlessly reading between the lines. Let me give an example.

When Guenevere is accused of murder at the poisoned apple incident, there is no one to take her defence since she has banished Lancelot. Sir Bors says that he cannot help since he was present at the dinner and might therefore be accused of being in league with the queen. Much later, when

Gawain hints that Lancelot is fond of the Maid of Astolat, Bors says to the queen:

> Madam, . . . I may nat warne sir Gawayne to sey what hit pleasith hym, but I dare sey, as for my lorde sir Launcelot, that he lovith no lady, jantillwoman, nother mayden, but as he lovith all inlyke muche.
>
> (632.43–633.2; XVIII.15).

The reactions of Sir Bors, it has been suggested, show his latent dislike of the queen. P. J. C. Field writes: 'he first refuses to help her lest he should be suspected of complicity' and 'the strength of his dislike shows in the way he avoids saying a single word of comfort to her, and never mentions the possibility of her being innocent', and 'when he tells her that Lancelot loves no one lady more than any other, the fact that he makes no soothing exception for Guenevere herself is no doubt deliberate.' In many ways this is an excellent analysis, and Field is one of Malory's wisest critics (these remarks are taken from the commentary to his edition of the final tales), but perhaps too much of what he says here is an explanation of Malory's silences and, as it turns out, is in contradiction to what Malory does say.

After all, if Bors refuses to help Guenevere, so do all the others, even her husband's nephew, Gawain, who in his privileged position could have been expected to help, and especially since, as the intended victim, he could not be suspected of complicity. If Bors never asserts Guenevere's innocence, neither does anyone else, not even Arthur, not even Guenevere herself at first; and perhaps it shows far greater gallantry to take her innocence for granted. And yet in public, where it counts most, Bors does protest the queen's innocence (617.15–29; XVIII.5). The speech in which he does so is long and must surely have almost choked him if his dislike for Guenevere is so real. And when Bors mentions Lancelot's equal gallantry to all ladies without making any exception for Guenevere, he is not being deliberately spiteful. Everyone knows of Lancelot's special devotion to the queen. If Bors were pretending not to know, he would be making himself look ridiculous. But however much he is *au courant* it is hardly polite or gallant to speak so knowingly to a queen, to her face. Bor's silence reveals his discretion, not his dislike.

Ultimately the notion of Bors' latent dislike of the queen is unhelpful because in the *Morte Darthur* no one likes or dislikes anyone else. They love, hate, honour etc., they display all the public and superlative sentiments, but they do not *like*, not even in secret. The nuances of feeling appropriate to the author interested in psychological analysis, the various shades of liking that we know in private are unknown in Malory. His public sentiments are far more clear-cut; his characters are far more committed. Lancelot loves Tristram, Marhalt hates him. Palomides loves and hates him at the same time, but nobody quite likes Tristram.

If we wish to read between the lines in the *Morte Darthur* we should uncover the kind of information Malory himself is ready to give us on other occasions, not the sort of psychological interpretation familiar to us from more recent fiction. It is an unfashionable and unsubtle thing to say, but I believe that there are fewer insinuations in Malory than is sometimes thought. I would argue against interpretation because his characters speak their minds more than they hint. I admit that this is not always easy to assess. When Lancelot remarks that 'love muste only aryse of the harte selff, and nat by none constraynte' (641.37–38; XVIII.20), he is surely not merely summing up the Maid of Astolat affair, but reminding Guenevere to be a little less demanding in future. Other examples, however, are not so clear and I think that there are fewer than some critics pretend. We are all reluctant to appear naive, I know, but it is worth taking Malory and his characters at face value: they have a habit of saying what they mean.

The Sacrifice of Gawain

In the *Morte Darthur*, personality and the analysis of character always take second place to the definition of role. The attitude is visible throughout in tiny details: Malory's eye is on the formal situation not the individual reaction. When Lancelot rescues Guenevere from the stake, her position as queen is what occupies his thoughts. The first thing he does is to make sure she is fittingly clad. She had been stripped to her smock, and the public ignominy must be corrected at once, even before she is carried off to safety. It is only when she is (as near as possible) dressed according to her rank that Lancelot offers any words of comfort:

> than he rode streyt unto quene Gwenyver and made caste a kurdyll and a gown uppon her, and than he made her to be sette behynde hym and prayde her to be of good chere.
>
> (684.32–35; XX.8).

Not many modern writers would see the situation in these terms; the human aspect would predominate, and it would be unthinkable at such a moment of tension to report the words that Lancelot used in indirect speech and with such formality and imprecision. But for Malory what Lancelot said was no doubt fitting. The actual words are part of a private moment the court historian cannot know.

Gawain is a clear example of this interest in the formal rather than the personal position. We know little about him and most of the time his role seems enough. He may be Arthur's nephew, but there is something less than ideal about him. He enters the *Morte Darthur* seeking family vengeance and he dies as a result of the same obsession. He is a fine fighter who plays an important part in Arthur's victory over Lucius, but the flaw in his character and his failures in chivalry are not hidden. But in all this, Malory insists on Gawain's function not his nature. We do not have any feeling that we know him, merely we know in which category to place him. He is a figure of corruption in high places. He does not have the positive evil of a Morgan le Fay or, later a Mordred, but he is a constant reminder that even the most influential knights are far from perfect. Gawain can be a fine man but when we consider him closely we see full well that Malory is writing about the best of the sinful. Gawain is one of the best and undeniably (as the Grail book shows) one of the sinful.

There are however two scenes in the *Morte Darthur* where Malory presents far more than Gawain's function. His behaviour comes as a surprise and we are given the portrait of a man we have so far, perhaps, judged too hastily. Malory momentarily shows an interest in Gawain's character, though, needless to say, he does so for the narrative purposes of his book.

The first scene is when Gawain refuses to join his trouble-making brothers in picking a quarrel by denouncing Lancelot and Guenevere to Arthur. He shows himself to be a peacemaker, a stern, wise, and diplomatic adviser devoted to the unity of the realm. He is not blind to ill-will, corruption and intrigue. He is sober, spartan, and self-effacing. He warns his sons and brothers. They owe allegiance to Lancelot, but they refuse to listen. When they are killed, Gawain's personal grief is sacrificed to the good of the realm. For the first time we get a more intimate view of Gawain and it turns out that he is not quite the sinister figure we had imagined. The brief portrait here is essential for the plot, essential to clarify the moral questions involved, but it seems somewhat out of keeping with the Gawain we have seen so far.

And then Gareth is killed. Gawain the diplomatic peacemaker gives way to unreasonable, illogical, blind and frenzied revenge. He refuses to hear the logic he himself had put forward previously, just as he refuses to see Gareth's death as an accident. Malory's account of this mad thirst for vengeance with its rancour and its pettiness is entirely convincing: Lancelot, he claims, killed Gareth deliberately to spite Gawain (689.19–20; XX.11). He begins to blackmail Arthur into taking sides with him, and all logic disappears as he begins to contradict himself. His claim 'the beste of us all had bene full colde at the harte-roote had nat sir Launcelot bene bettir than we' (673.38–39; XX.1) becomes the accusation that Lancelot has 'many longe dayes overlad me and us all, and destroyed many of oure good knyghtes' (689.27–28; XX.11).

In the end, of course, Gawain sees his error and becomes the noble knight again who seeks Lancelot's forgiveness. What is interesting is that at each stage Gawain is presented in entirely convincing terms. His noble stoicism and diplomacy demand respect, and we have a clear picture of Gawain the elder statesman, while his vengeful hatred is extremely well presented and put into dialogue. But the characterisation as such is totally unconvincing because Malory is not interested in it; Gawain's behaviour dominates the action but no attempt is made to present a reasonable psychological development. It is simply that Gawain's role changes. His sudden rage is given no motivation, for there is little in the *Morte Darthur* to suggest that Gawain was so dearly attached to Gareth. It is true that he spoils the youth – without recognising him as his brother – when he comes to court, but the idea is soon dropped and we are reminded more often of the family rift than of the family attachment.

Malory's lack of interest in Gawain's personality is shown in that he is reluctant even to make moral judgments and decide whether Gawain is good or bad. When Lancelot is in combat with Gawain at the end, Malory talks of 'the batayle of thes two noble knyghtes' (706.2–3; XX.22); even when Gawain represents the force of destruction Malory refuses to abandon him. He is made, momentarily, to play the villain's role, although he is rehabilitated by the arrival of Mordred. Gawain then becomes a symptom of disruption more than its cause: such is the real corruption of the realm that even noble Gawain can appear shoddy.

Arthur and Lancelot

It is part of Malory's great art that, while concentrating on characters who play (or fail to play) their proper public roles, he presents them with flashes of such convincing insight that their emotional impact is extremely powerful. They are moving figures who represent values we all admire or (at least) know how to respect. Because their impact is strong, we feel that Malory's characters are real, whereas in fact it is their emotional impact that is real, while the characters themselves remain basically formal and ceremonial. They are not like the people we all know, however much we recognise traits of character; they are figures in a drama of vast importance. What we see are the occasional vivid details, sudden flashes that illuminate the whole *tableau vivant*.

When Guenevere expresses regret that Lancelot is not around to save her over the poisoned apple affair, she makes no reference to the fact that his absence is her fault. Arthur replies:

'What aylith you,'seyde the knyge, 'that ye can nat kepe sir Launce-

lot uppon youre syde? For wyte you well,' seyde the kynge, 'who
that hath sir Launcelot uppon his party hath the moste man of worship in thys worlde uppon hys syde. Now go youre way,' seyde the
kynge unto the quene, 'and requyre sir Bors to do batayle for you for
sir Launcelotis sake.'

Malory, it is pointed out, has finely captured the tetchiness of a middle
aged husband after a lifetime with a tiresome woman. For once her lover
could save the day and she is too much of a pain even to keep him around.
For a moment Arthur reveals his personal irritation and we see the man
behind the king, but it is unwise to take this example as an illustration of
Malory's art, for Arthur's speeches as a man are few and far between.

In the French versions of the legend, Arthur is a man eaten by suspicion
of his wife and ready to act. He will use his authority as king to wreak
vengeance so cruelly that future generations will speak of it, and he is
more than ready to encourage the plotters in their scheme to expose
Lancelot and the queen. Malory's Arthur hides the personal insult to himself as a man behind his conviction that Lancelot has served him well and
done his duty to his king. When the rot finally sets in, his famous speech
regretting the loss of his fellowship more than that of his queen is again
the formal, ceremonial complaint of a king. With all due respect to Guenevere, what Arthur says, *for a king*, is true.

Malory's portrait of Arthur is the portrait of a king, and there is little
concerted effort made to render the character psychologically convincing.
Once the final battle is under way we are shown no reasonable development of his personality. He begins by expressing reluctance for a show-
down. He does all he can to avoid an open conflict but then, suddenly,
gives way to 'hete and malice' and – uncharacteristically we would say if
Malory had troubled to give him a consistant character – he is driven to
desire a shameful death for Lancelot. But these sentiments are foisted
upon him by the needs of the action. It is true that the later portrait of Arthur is moving. He wants to take Guenevere back, he longs to make peace
with Lancelot, but the ties of allegiance mean he is forced to listen to Gawain. It is the portrait of a king who has become a prisoner of the system
and cannot escape. His personal position remains unspoken or at best unexplained. When Gareth is killed Arthur declares:

'I charge you that no man telle sir Gawayne of the deth of hys two
brethirne, for I am sure,' seyde the kynge, 'whan he hyryth telle that
sir Gareth ys dede, he wyll go nygh oute of hys mynde.'
(685.14–17; XX.9)

But as soon as Gawain enters, he is organising reprisals not advocating
silence or forgiveness. Each scene is moving in itself, but neither con-

tributes to the portrayal of a man with motives and sentiments like ones we know.

And with Lancelot the moments of perception are similarly rare. Rather, we see a greatly impressive, larger than life figure with the occasional touch of humanity. But we see little or nothing of Lancelot's personal feelings, not even for Guenevere. Is he weary of the strain of loving such a capricious woman? We would be. But we are never shown Lancelot's personal thoughts. Malory presents him in his role as official lover to the queen and asks no questions because the historian, unlike the *romancier*, cannot ask questions of the sort.

Of course Malory brings the picture of Lancelot's perfect allegiance alive with glimpses of the man. There are splendidly captured scenes in the knight of the cart episode. When Lancelot reaches Meliagaunt's castle, Malory portrays his fury and irritation – in front of Meliagaunt's treachery and Guenevere's sudden and unexplained easy-going readiness to overlook the matter – with great skill, and when Meliagaunt reveals the blood-stained bed, Lancelot swallows hard, collects his thoughts, and criticises Meliagaunt on a technical point of court etiquette while giving himself time to think. But Malory's eye never stays for long on details of this kind. He is sensitive to human reactions and has a talent for putting them into words, but he always gives pride of place to the formal aspect of a scene. Consider the passage where Lancelot and the queen are trapped together. It is an important event in the narrative and an emotional high point too, but Malory sees it entirely from the formal point of view. The lovers kiss, they exchange rings; but Lancelot is more concerned with vowing his service to Guenevere than expressing his affection. The characters are a queen and her husband's chief knight, not a man and a woman whose private affair has been discovered. Everything they say is eminently proper. Anyone who wanted to dramatise this passage for the modern theatre would have to rewrite the dialogue entirely if he wanted to give any semblance of reality. It would pass as it stands in an opera, where the formality of sentiment and lack of strict verisimilitude have never worried anyone.

Malory's knights have a name, a function and the occasional distinguishing characteristic (Kay is sharp-tongued; Dinadan is a japer) but all the individual qualities that make a person what he is and different from others are overlooked by Malory, who defines his characters exclusively through their knightly achievements. Except for war and combat, all the character building incidents of life are omitted, for it is war and combat that forge the only kind of character Malory is interested in. When a knight has won a reputation he has all the character he needs. We learn nothing of Arthur's formative years, the long period during which, while still a youth, he had to impose his authority and please his barons. In what

way, if at all, this made him the king he was Malory never says. We learn
nothing of the early stages of Lancelot's love for the queen, the suffering,
the intrigue, the guilt, the jealousy perhaps, which helped make him the
man he became. Rather, the public achievements of Malory's knights
define their identity entirely. An unknown knight is one whose achievement we have heard nothing about. Once his adventures are over and his
reputation is established, we know all there is to know.

The characterisation and psychological enquiry that we find at the end
of the *Morte Darthur* and that critics single out to illustrate Malory's art
give his book a deceptively modern, novelistic air. They certainly help
new readers approach the book, but we must be prudent. The interest in
character (and it is still only sporadic or incomplete) is not evident because the final books are the best of Malory (though they are), nor because
at the end of his career Malory took an increased interest in psychological
analysis. Rather, there is less characterisation in the early books because
there is less call for it in a largely episodic plot, whereas the closer chain of
cause and effect at the end of the *Morte Darthur* and the fact that character
is inextricably linked to action make the interest in characterisation more
essential.

There is, in the final books, one example, perhaps the clearest, of vivid
characterisation as opposed to the portrayal of role: Elayne, the Maid of
Astolat. She is, in a way, an exception to the rule that confirms Malory's
attention to public function rather than private existence. She is intensely
real. 'Am I nat an erthely woman?' she asks (639.31; XVIII.19), and she is
indeed. She is so real that her presence and her death come as so much
more of a shock. She refuses to play the part allotted to her by society and
demands a personal response from a man who lives entirely for his public
role. She represents the world of private people impinging on the formal
world of ceremonial order, and it is a world that must be rejected. They
are figures in a stately pageant, she has a life of her own.

STYLE

'Who the deuce would begin talking about the style' asked C. S. Lewis,
'till all else was given up?' He was referring in particular to the novel, but
many people would be ready to express more general agreement. With
Malory, however, it is impossible to consider style as a merely secondary
topic – one taken up to ensure an exhaustive survey – for the simple reason that Malory's style has been almost universally admired, whereas
there is little agreement about anything else in the *Morte Darthur*. It is a
powerful and intensely moving style and yet, apparently so simple; in-

deed, almost artless, unexpected. And just as the realism and characterisation of the *Morte Darthur* are not as 'modern' as some would have us believe – Malory does not really lead forward to the novel; its assumptions and interests are not his – so his style seems to look back rather than ahead. It is plain, formal, stately, and more akin to older, oral modes of narration; it is never learned, sophisticated or refined. Malory's turn of mind, as D. S. Brewer points out, is 'archaic', and the bases of his style are also those of the traditional writer; they have their roots in oral tradition.

Oral Tradition

Much emphasis has been placed in recent years on the impact of writing on culture and thought. Writing does not merely provide thought with a new mode of expression, it has totally transformed it. Literate and oral (pre-literate) cultures do not merely express themselves differently, their perception is not the same. The thought processes of literate cultures are those we take for granted, they are the assumptions we work with every day; but oral cultures function in other ways.

A useful definition of oral cultures can be found in W. J. Ong's *Orality and Literacy*, and although he has nothing to say about Malory, the relevance of his remarks to the style of the *Morte Darthur* is, I think, immediately evident.

The cultures of orality and literacy have an entirely different attitude to memory. We write something down in case we forget. If the spoken word is forgotten, it is lost. Writing replaces memory; oral cultures must, unless they are ready to accept oblivion, defend memory at all costs. They therefore devise all sorts of mnemonic aids: charms, lists, alliterations, formulae, devices which will stimulate recall. In this respect there are times when Malory writes as though he were not *writing* at all, writes not as though he were *recording* great deeds, but trying to anchor them in our minds.

Oral cultures are additive rather than subordinate; they rely on accumulation not a hierarchy of ideas. They prefer to organise items into appropriate groups rather than separate identity, and their expression tends to be repetitive, never too dense for the attention or the memory. What is presented often enough rather than what is presented persuasively carries weight. They prefer to concentrate on situation rather than on abstraction, and their point of view is not distanced, objective, or ironic, but participatory and committed. They see from within not from without.

This is a useful context in which to consider Malory's style. Malory is very much a traditional writer with his roots in an oral tradition. Indeed, it is more than likely that his first literary inspiration was the writings of the alliterative tradition, which look back to oral cultures, and there are still signs within his book that occasionally Malory is thinking in terms of a listening audience. His famous apostrophe on the state of the realm in his day – 'Lo ye all Englysshemen' (708.34; XXI.1) – is a collective address not a private aside to the reader. Malory's style has been analysed at length and very well by a number of eminent specialists; I merely wish to draw attention to certain (isolated) features of style which, like Malory's use of realism and characterisation, are indicative of his outlook. Style is not the icing on a cake, but an essential ingredient. To this extent, critics who fall back on Malory's style for want of something else to praise, have, in fact, singled out a vital aspect of his art.

Coordination

One thing which distinguishes Malory from the French prose romances he was working with is his attitude to subordination. It has been suggested that the structures of Malory's prose are based on French models, but this is probably wrong. French prose uses a highly developed system of subordination; Malory's sentences are almost exclusively coordinated: he rarely strays beyond 'and' and 'but'. The use of parataxis was a common feature of fifteenth century translation and was, perhaps, one aspect of its low level of competence, and yet in Malory it gives a deceptively simple appearance totally in keeping with the author's outlook and presentation.

Malory's prose is accumulative not causal; emphasis is clearly placed on events not the relationship between events. The important question is 'What happened?' not 'What happened next?' Malory's eye is on the act not on the interpretation, and he provides a kind of objectivity by letting everything speak for itself. He presents what happened, and then what, and then, without organising things into a pattern or analysis. He reports the news, as it were, without commentary and without organising the details in such a way that a point of view comes across. Subordination inevitably reveals the analytic mind of the narrator, who fits events into a hierarchy of importance and cause. Malory merely provides us with the facts; we are free to assess them as we read. His parataxis is not mere artlessness, it implies an outlook. It gives an appearance of objectivity, of historicity. Malory is a historian recording great deeds; he is not a journalist writing an editorial.

Malory's prose is not totally without subordination, but he tends to say what he has to say by piling one detail on top of another rather than with the aid of complex organisations of the thought. Cumulative weight not

logical force is the basis of his prose, and even when explanations are
being offered, Malory still uses a paratactic presentation. At times he appears to use subordinating conjunctions, but they turn out to be 'ands' in
disguise. The words suggesting logical analysis are mere sand in our eyes:
information is being added not sifted. Consider the sentences:

> wyte thou well I am sette in suche a plyght to gete my soule hele.
> And *yet* I truste, thorow Goddis grace and thorow Hys Passion of
> Hys woundis wyde, that aftir my deth I may have a syght of the
> blyssed face of Cryste Jesu . . .
>
> (720.18–21; XXI.9)

and:

> And if that I had nat had my prevy thoughtis to returne to youre
> love agayne as I do, I had sene as grete mysteryes as ever saw my
> sonne sir Galahad, Percivale, other sir Bors. And *therefore*, madam, I
> was but late in that queste . . .
>
> (611.36–41; XVIII.1)

The italicised 'yet' and 'therefore' are present under false pretences.

The use of parataxis gives a semblance of objectivity; it is also responsible for there being little or no simultaneity of action in Malory. We have
no sense of things going on at the same time: when Malory describes a
mêlée there is little to distinguish it from a series of individual encounters.
It is as though knights stand by inactive until the narrator can turn his attention to them. As Malory's sentences are sequential in structure, so are
the events he describes in time.

Repetition

Malory does not rely on the logical force of reasoned structures but the
emotional force of insistence. The accumulation and repetition of loaded
words arouse a massive response and achieve an effect logical structures
would miss. There are several kinds of repetition. First of all, at moments
of intensity, Malory repeats key words frequently in a very short space.
One eloquent example is from the Grail book, in a passage which is, uncharacteristically, a very free rendering of the French:

> 'Now,' seyde the kynge, 'I am sure at this quest of the Sankegreall
> shall all ye of the Rownde Table departe, and nevyr shall I se you
> agayne holé togydirs, therefore ones shall I se you togydir in the
> medow, all holé togydirs! Therefore I woll se you all holé togydir in

the medow of Camelot, to juste and to turney, that aftir youre dethe men may speke of hit that such good knyghtes were here, such a day, holé togydirs.'

(520.39–44; XIII.6)

It is Malory who chooses to load the force of this passage by repeating the key word. The effectiveness is perhaps a matter of opinion, and the editor of the version of the *Morte Darthur* published by Caxton clearly considered the passage to be a scribal error, and reduced it. But it is a feature of style Malory uses regularly and although it can appear artless, this is precisely how emotional speech works. In the heat of a moment of intense feeling we do repeat ourselves; it is only later that we are cool enough to vary our discourse.

I would not always want to defend Malory's use of repetition. At times the repeated words are too banal to suggest intended effects and he would have done well to revise. A good example of this poverty of expression is the very first page of the *Morte Darthur*: it is as though the challenge of actually getting started took the words from his mouth. When key words are concerned, however, their repetition is essential to the emotional impact. There are even passages where the power of the language resides entirely in the verbal repetition, for the syntax, less important, disintegrates. The famous May passage is a good example of this: it is worth examining its structure logically and then considering the impact of the words. Most obviously, in the dialogue of scenes of dramatic interest verbal repetition plays an important part. Consider the passage where Lancelot arrives at Meliagaunt's castle, for example (655.5–656.23; XIX.5). Repetition is still a forceful linguistic device, of course. It is one of the tricks of the advertiser's trade to repeat the name of the product as often as possible.

Not only does Malory repeat words over a brief passage, the descriptions he gives throughout the book rely heavily on the same limited set of adjectives and stock phrases time and again. To modern eyes this inevitably looks like poverty of expression; in fact it reveals a different outlook. A modern writer would look for variation; Malory relies entirely on conventional vocabulary. His knights are forever noble, his ladies all passing fair. Just as he never attempts to individualise his characters through any analysis of their personalities, so he never distinguishes them in description. They all belong to the appropriate category; they all conform to the pattern. The adjectives he singles out with which to describe them are, in a way, the ones which make them least singular, least worth the attribution of an adjective at all. Even when Malory seems to give an exceptional detail of information or an unusual comparison, we can be fairly sure it will crop up later. When knights come rushing together like two wild boars, we feel that the image is vivid and unusual, until it turns out to be a part of the standard vocabularly of combat. The image does not single out one battle from many, it links it to all the others. And so too with the vocabulary of warfare in general. Malory employs the same range of stock vocabulary each time he takes up the same kind of context. To some extent perhaps the repeated vocabularly reflects the repetitions of life – the number of actions in battle and the number of outcomes is limited – but it is also a way of relating each incident to its proper context. What some will see as a sign of Malory's lack of imagination is, for others, a legitimate aspect of his art. There are appropriate terms for each event. It is Malory's version of the proper word in the proper place. The right words are more important than mere embellishment. Malory's repetitions do not betray a pedestrian lack of verbal imagination; his traditional, normative language accords to everything its proper category or role. It is part of the decorum both of his style and his outlook.

There are repetitions within Malory's narrative and within the speech of his characters; at times they and their author share the same vocabulary, and in this way Malory introduces a sense of verbal inevitability. As the author confirms the choice of words of the characters, or as they speak as he does, so the words seem doubly appropriate to the situation. What we have is not merely one point of view (the author's or a character's), but the right words for the occasion. By disappearing behind his characters, the author gives weight to what they say. He is not analysing or suspecting their speech, he is – in a literal sense – taking their word for it. Consider the following extract, where the repetitions underline the support the author is giving his characters:

'. . . But I se well,' seyde sir Bors, 'by her *dyligence* aboute you that she lovith you intyerly.'
'That me repentis,' seyde sir Launcelot.
'Well,' seyde sir Bors, 'she ys nat the first that hath loste hir payne uppon you, and that ys the more pyté.'
And so they talked of many mo thynges.
And so within three or four dayes sir Launcelot wexed *bygge and lyght*. (*stronge*, Caxton)
. . .
'. . . I fele myself resonabely *bygge and stronge.*'
'Blessed be God!' seyde sir Bors.
Then they were there nyghe a moneth togydirs, and ever thys maydyn Elayne ded ever hir *dyligence* and labour both nyght and day unto sir Launcelot . . .

(635.12–28; XVIII.16–17)

Repetition always runs the risk of appearing artless, but the simple, emphatic style of Malory's prose owes a lot to it. What we are told three times is not necessarily true, but at least it sticks.

The Sliding Scale of Values

The coordinating structures, which present without analysis, help to give Malory's prose a veneer of objectivity, as does his readiness to insert detailed lists. What should also be noticed is the way in which Malory's extremely subjective glance parades as objectivity too. As we have seen, for him the moral and the physical exist on a single plane of perception, and he is constantly passing from one to the other. Where we would expect a physical description Malory gives a moral one, constantly offering value judgments and assuming our agreement. He takes the truth of a moral statement for granted and repeats it so regularly that our acquiescence is readily achieved. For Malory, to describe is to evaluate; a knight's moral worth is part of the only description Malory is interested in giving. And strangely enough, as we read, we begin to suspend our moral disbelief rather than scream out our indignation. It is as though in a prose narrative which appears so plain and in which no attempt is made to manipulate or embellish, the subjectivity goes unnoticed. Malory rigs out his prose with the trappings of an objectivity which disguises his total commitment. He is not consciously deluding us; the implication is that the nobility of a Lancelot is as patent for all to see as the colour of his eyes or hair, which, being so much less important, are not even mentioned.

All those lists which seem so drearily objective for our tastes, which link Malory to older, oral traditions and give a semblance of history, exist side by side with a subjective gaze of the most unashamed kind. Nor is this the only way in which Malory's objectivity is suspect. His use of the superlative mode is another. When a knight is the best of a category it suggests that an objective scale of evaluation exists and that an attempt at reasonable judgment is being made. In fact the assessments implicit in the use of superlatives are just a front. Since all the knights are the best in the world, all the ladies the fairest in the land, the scale of evaluation is without value, except in that it gives the impression that unbiased assessment itself is something which counts. But it is an impression only, for Malory is not the distant narrator scrutinising with cold irony the world he creates. Indeed, the word 'narrator' is itself inappropriate, with all that it suggests of detachment and criticism. Malory is part of the world he describes, the traditional writer who participates, and his moral judgments are inevitable because he is clearly on the side of the community he describes. Arthur's knights, we have seen, are our noble men of merry England.

Dialogue

Malory's use of dialogue also reveals his commitment to the Arthurian world. His voice is frequently confused with those of his characters: he slips in and out of dialogue in a way which is disconcerting for a modern reader and something of a headache for editors of the *Morte Darthur*, who have to take special care with the punctuation. When Malory seems to be describing events he suddenly withdraws to let the actors in those events speak for themselves: their voice is heard through his, or his through theirs. It is an important feature of his prose, and one which becomes more obvious towards the end of the *Morte Darthur* as the sheer mass of dialogue there makes clear. In the final tales, of course, speech and deeds go together: what certain characters say leads to further events. When Gareth refuses to be a party to Agravain and Mordred's plottings he says he 'woll nat be knowyn of your dedis' (673.25–26; XX.1), but the deed he will not 'be knowyn of' is the speech his brothers are about to make to Arthur.

Malory lets his characters speak, but makes no attempt to individualise them by their speech. Lancelot at one point is said to have a distinctive voice (154.11; VI.5), but the detail, once mentioned, is at once forgotten. No one in Malory can be recognised by the way they speak. This does not mean that Malory's dialogue does not ring true, for it often does, and superbly so. Quite simply, speech never identifies a character. For us it is one aspect of a man's individuality; for Malory, on the contrary, it is a way for a man to reveal his allegiance to a group. In the *Morte Darthur* speech is normative not particular, appropriate to a knight's role, never to his character. Malory shows us proper, fitting speech, not idiosyncratic discourse. 'That is knyghtly spokyn' is a compliment they all deserve.

The clearest example of normative discourse is one which is totally un-believable for twentieth century readers, but an example of the extremely formal, public, non-naturalistic attitude of Malory: his knights speak together with a collective voice, chorus-like, referring to themselves in the plural. In modern fiction the only equivalent is always expressed through indirect speech. No one could hope to make us believe that several charac-ters said exactly the same words, at the same time and speaking of them-selves in the plural as a group – except fans in a theatre chanting 'We want . . .' whoever it is.

Malory's collective discourse shows the abandonment of the individual for the group, and this, in the *Morte Darthur* is a healthy state of mind. For Malory, virtue and prowess involve living up to a standard, behaving in a fitting and characteristic manner, and in this Malory's style expresses his outlook well. He does not hesitate to make his knights speak with one voice because, ideally, this is how they should speak.

Malory's characters speak in a formal, ceremonial way. This aspect of Malory's dialogue style has often been overlooked since his talent for crisp idiom – often mixed with light comedy and understatement – is more immediately attractive for modern readers. The conversational ring is entirely convincing and the scene comes alive. 'In an evyll tyme bare ye thys bowe' says Lancelot to a self-styled huntress who ought to have her hunting licence revoked, 'The devyll made you a shoter!' (643.39–40; XVIII.21). But Malory's speech is not consistently racy and conversational; more often than not it is patterned and formal, appropriate not to an individual in a given situation but to a person of certain rank with a proper social function. The speech of Malory's characters is dignified, terse, to the point, and not expansive or articulate after French models of eloquence. Malory's knights are not great talkers and the economy of their speech gives it at times a proverbial ring. They are restrained and manly, in a word, knightly. Their speech may frequently sound natural, but it is never careless. They know how to address other people, and do so according to the proper rules. They are not orators, but they are men whom we hear speaking in public. If the occasion should arise, they are not unable to express themselves at length and movingly on an important subject – as Lancelot is able to present his case before the court in defence of Guenevere – otherwise they prefer action to words. Essentially, their speech is typical of the way men speak in front of others. It is not relaxed, unofficial, argotic English; it is formal and considered. They say nothing that you could not quote them as saying. There are no thoughtless asides that slip out and even when their speech is particularly racy there is still much urbanity and polish in what they say. They never sacrifice their dignity. Theirs is less the colourful language of the wit than the restrained understatement of the gentleman, as Lancelot's words to the unsteady-handed huntress show.

Malory's characters frequently speak in a natural way, there is a tone of voice that we recognise, but their speech does not break the bounds of restraint. Their words never precede the thought. In certain contexts they can be thoroughly down to earth, especially when knights are in masculine company, or even in the presence of a lady when the moral indignation is strong enough: 'I had levir kut away my hangers' says Alexander the Orphan (395.32; X.38) than satisfy the fleshly lusts of Morgan le Fay. But there are no verbal slip ups in Malory; because his knights are not great talkers, they can control their tongues. This, of course, is how it should be. There is at least one talker in the *Morte Darthur*: Agravain is 'opynne-mowthed', and we know what that means.

The speech of Malory's characters is appropriate to the public world they inhabit, and this is the speech they take with them to the moments of privacy we witness. Look at the way Lancelot and Guenevere speak to each other when they are trapped together. No modern novelist could get away with presenting the scene in such a way. Fancy Lancelot calling Guenevere 'moste nobelest Crysten quene'. But Lancelot speaks in the only way a court historian can imagine, or is willing to record.

I have mentioned all this at length because I believe that we should not overlook the restraint and formality of speech in Malory by paying too much attention to the more immediately appealing (and more modern) naturalness that can be found. If you like, the naturalness of their speech makes Malory's characters believable, but it is the formality which stops them from being cheapened. They speak like real people, it is true, but they speak like kings, queens, knights, and ladies. The recogniseable ring of their voices attracts us to them; because their speech is appropriate to their rank, it makes us stand back. In this way Malory's characters are credible and impressive at the same time.

This is perhaps an awkward point for us to appreciate. The modern tendency is towards a democratisation of figures of state. An official speech rings hollow and unimaginative; we prefer to see a prince or a Prime Minister interviewed at an unofficial moment, to hear the real voice. The dignity of ceremony is something we appreciate from time to time; otherwise we like to see our rulers off duty, comforted in the notion that – apart from their wealth and importance – they are just like us. For the *Morte Darthur* therefore we must suspend our disbelief and assume another concept of kingship, one which requires us to believe that a king is a king because he is *not* like us. If he were not exceptional he would not be king: *we* would not have been able to draw the sword from the stone. His speech, of course, will be real speech, but the real speech of a monarch.

If we feel that formal discourse is merely clichéd and unimaginative we are hardly likely to accord Malory much talent. If we praise him only when his dialogue is crisp and lively, then we can only accord him intermittent praise. To understand Malory fully we must be ready to see that his dialogues are conventional and stately not because he cannot keep up a natural tone for long, but because a natural tone would spoil the desired effect.

Plain History

Although Malory relies heavily on the broader effects of formal discourse, his dialogues are not without subtlety. The repetitions and coordinated structures can appear simple and artless, it is true, and if our attention lags when the material seems dull, the style will seem dull too. This has indeed led to the idea that Malory was an artless writer, blundering his way through the book, whereas in fact he is more than capable of using verbal nuance. A good example is his handling of the pronouns of address to express precise shades of meaning. Many Europeans notice this immediately, since their own languages have retained this linguistic refinement; an unsuspecting English-speaker needs reminding that *you* and *thou* express more than number. Malory does not always pay attention to the shades of meaning possible here, but he often does, and the result can be impressive. It is through the use of the (improper) singular pronoun that he captures the extraordinary effrontery of the carter refusing to give Lancelot a ride in his cart, or the coldness of Guenevere in her fury 'pulling rank' on Lancelot by speaking to him as though he were a mere subject. There are countless examples, and Malory shows himself capable of being linguistically very precise. Usually, however, his prose is much plainer and unobtrusive, with few effects and manipulations. There is none of the *romancier*'s desire to organise and embellish, rather the sobriety of the chronicle style proper to the historian.

This, of course, is seen in Malory's readiness to add lists and identify names; the historian must record evidence, and evidence is not presented in vague generalities. It is also seen in his respect for the past. Malory does not try to recreate the atmosphere of the past in terms of the present. If we do not understand its assumptions and conventions, Malory is not going to bring them up to date. Rather he states plainly 'custom was those days'. There is nothing more to say.

Moreover, like the historian, Malory writes sparely, with little decoration or description. This, in part, is due to his desire to reduce his source material and write a single manageable history instead of a bulky collection of tales. Description is always easy to remove. But the absence of description is also essential to his outlook. Malory is not presenting an elegant, decorative fiction, but a record of deeds. If information is not essential, it can be taken for granted and overlooked. Consequently, there is little or none of the ordinary business of life in the *Morte Darthur*. Knights appear not to eat unless a meal is an important social occasion and they seek repose when it is convenient in the plot to do so; otherwise they are tireless. The *Morte Darthur* contains none of the mundane affairs of fiction and real life – the French romances are far more aware of the realities of physical surroundings – and Malory rarely takes time to offer any sort of description to set the scene.

Moreover, as we have seen, Malory's use of description tends to be normative not individualising. We may occasionally be struck by an added detail – instead of riding in on a horse, a knight will arrive on a white horse – but the extra information is usually gratuitous, for other knights arrive on white (or black) horses for no apparent reason. We begin to discard the information and no longer pay attention. When, rarely, someone arrives on a dun horse we scarcely even notice, and rightly so, for 'white horse', 'black horse' or 'dun horse' add little more than 'horse'. Descriptive details of the kind seem arbitrary and, remembering Malory's moral bias, far less telling than an appreciative assessment. Had Malory said 'noble horse' we really would have sat up. Malory's concern for group not individual identity, and for moral not physical description is part of his outlook as a traditional writer. He writes not so much to make us visualise, but to help us recognise.

Alliteration

One final detail of Malory's style should be mentioned; it is also linked to his outlook as a traditional writer: alliteration. It is more than likely that the works of the alliterative poets were Malory's initial source of inspiration, and throughout the *Morte Darthur* he is always ready to use alliteration himself, not regularly or structurally, but in particular at moments of high intensity.

Some of Malory's alliteration, perhaps the least important, is the result of direct borrowing from his sources. All of Book II is like this, and there are numerous examples in Book VIII. Some alliteration is not Malory's choice but the nature of the English language. When the king kisses the queen, he cannot help alliterating as he does so. But Malory regularly uses alliteration (or fails to resist its influence) and in this way gives force to what he writes. There is no need to give examples, alliteration can be found throughout the *Morte Darthur*, expecially in passages where the emotional impact is strong.

For us, alliteration can be a dangerous literary feature. It adds a falsely popular ring to our writing and can result in bathos. In Malory there is a long tradition behind it and it adds stateliness and force, the weight perhaps of a popular tradition of proverbial wisdom. It also adds to the deceptively simple appearance of Malory's prose. He does not strike us as a *littérateur*. He has been criticised for being a careless writer, gauche and artless, but his prose at its best is extraordinarily moving. For all his apparent lack of manipulation he has a way of controlling our responses that no modern author could hope to get away with, but he does so less as a man of letters organising and anticipating our reactions, than as a soldier wholly committed to an ethic which commands respect and which, with the force of his own persuasion, he calls on us to admire. He relies less on any literary devices he might have at his disposal, than on the power of a traditional outlook and his own natural good taste. Derek Brewer has described Malory's style as 'the style of a gentleman'. Malory was a knight and, appropriately, his book is, to adapt his own words, 'knyghtly written'.

4

Methods and Materials

The subject matter of the *Morte Darthur* is traditional; Malory's book is not original in the way we expect a modern work of prose fiction to be. Since writers of the medieval period had an entirely different attitude to originality, this in itself is no cause for concern. They were proud to borrow from famous sources, not eager to hide their debts. Malory, for example, even pretends to be borrowing when in reality he is not, preferring to give his narrative the ring of authority than boast its novelty.

The trouble with the *Morte Darthur*, however, is that Malory has not merely borrowed a narrative outline, which he then elaborates and adapts. The whole of his book is second-hand. Moreover, he follows his sources in great detail and there are even parts of his work which are straightforward translation. It is for this reason that most books about the *Morte Darthur* consider the source material to be an indispensible starting point and set out by identifying (as far as possible) the books Malory worked with, his relationship to them, and, in particular, his degree of independence. In other words, the critics approach the *Morte Darthur* through the sources. The only problem is that few new readers do so.

Nor do they wish to, and I am tempted to believe that, for newcomers, the obsession with sources turns out to be a rather negative, fruitless approach. It is hard to muster up much enthusiasm for what a distant French analogue says at any point in the narrative, and the sources that provide what is claimed to be the essential background to the *Morte Darthur* seem often to undermine the book's value not put that value into evidence. If the sources are so essential, so much more complete and authentic, if they are richer, fuller, more sophisticated works which Malory has often abbreviated beyond recognition and even to a point of confusion, and which we need to consult to appreciate the *Morte Darthur* at all, then why bother with anyone called Malory in the first place? There is an obvious reason, but it is not always mentioned clearly enough: however derivative Malory's book may be, however inferior to its sources, none the less, it has survived and they have not. Malory may be the poor relation and they the noble forebears, but – apart from him – their line has died out. It is thanks to Malory that the family name has survived at all.

Malory's Originality

The sources have their importance and they need to be discussed, but the newcomer should be allowed to get to know Malory's own book first. This, of course, is begging the question: some would hasten to point out – precisely – that the *Morte Darthur* is not Malory's own book. His reputation, that is (or what he has of one), seems to depend on the extent of his original contribution. For some, it is difficult to accord him the full status of an author because his borrowings are far too extensive; for others, Malory's individual contribution is perfectly adequate to justify his greatness. In many ways, however, the controversy seems a rather sterile one. Whoever produced the *Morte Darthur*, the work itself exists. Whoever Malory was, he is less important than his book. Indeed, almost all we know about the author of the *Morte Darthur* is his name, and that name lives today only because of the book associated with it. Malory, that is, has no other existence apart from the *Morte Darthur*. Rather than try to isolate degrees of originality, we should perhaps consider the two names as synonyms: when we praise the author, we are in fact praising the book.

And yet it is surely possible to acknowledge the debt – even when extensive – to a source and still judge the impact of a work of literature as a whole. It is not only the original passages of the *Morte Darthur* that are Malory's own. The passages he borrows or adapts, once he has borrowed or adapted them and fitted them into his book, become his own also. It serves no purpose to strip away the borrowings and refuse to judge anything but the writer's original contribution. We rarely treat other major writers in quite this way: is Malory merely being made to pay the price of borrowing in greater bulk?

It is time perhaps to stop approaching Malory through – or reproaching him for – his sources. It is true that his book uses traditional material and that he borrows extensively, but originality is not the only standard of literary excellence, and in the medieval period it is not certain that it was one at all. A novel in which both plot and characters are entirely new can still be depressingly unoriginal. Publishers turn down hundreds every year, while they would relish the chance to publish a traditional story packed with borrowed material that we all know, but rehandled in such a way that its impact was undeniable. Over the years, Malory's borrowed book has proved its worth. If this is not a vindication of its author then nothing is.

Most of all, however, what needs to be pointed out (and is so insufficiently) is that the sources reveal more important things than Malory's debts. They also reveal precisely the opposite: the originality of his turn of mind and his achievement. They corroborate Coleridge's remark that nothing:

> contributes more to a clear insight into the true nature of any literary
> phenomenon, than the comparison of it with some elder production,
> the likeness of which is striking, yet only apparent; while the dif-
> ference is real.

Although Malory borrows material extensively, the book he has produced, as we shall see, is quite unlike his sources. The *Morte Darthur* is not just a translation into English; it has survived because it is a version of the Arthurian tales with an identity of its own. Indeed, Malory's book is so different from his French sources that not infrequently his characters would simply not recognise themselves in the pages of the French text, and if they did, they would surely not approve. Lancelot's lachrymose, love-sick French counterpart would cut a poor figure in the *Morte Darthur*.

A student with an essay to write would do well to keep an eye open for passages original to Malory; they can often round off an argument nicely. But the lack of an original passage does not necessarily invalidate a point of view or condemn a student to silence. Our attention is misdirected when we concentrate exclusively on Malory's additions or inventions. These are important, but a creative response to a source is, in itself, an original contribution worthy of note.

Malory's book has not outstripped all other Arthurian romances because of a small number of original additions, even less because he has merely reshaped the borrowed material into a single book of convenient size (for its shape and size are not convenient; we dip into the *Morte Darthur*, we do not read it from cover to cover). Rather Malory's considerable achievement is that with a judicious mixture of borrowing, paraphrase, reshaping, reinterpretation, and invention he has revitalised traditional material and produced a book which – it is only justice – bears his name.

The Literary Tradition

The origins of the Arthurian legends are lost in time and the material is a mixed bag of history, legend, folklore, fiction and wish-fulfilment. Arthur may well have had a basis in historical fact, but if so, he is from that period of British history which is most obscure. The evidence is scant and often vague, while the documents that speak of Arthur – when they mention him by name, that is – are not what we generally consider to have historical reliability.

In time the historical element was elaborated in oral traditions in which myth and folktale were grafted on. These, of course, have remained an essential part of the material and are evident in Malory – from the magic and the acceptance of magic in the early books to the idea of Arthur as the once and future king, whose return remains somehow a possibility. The legends surrounding Arthur grew, and characters from the pseudo-history of different periods were added on, along with a thriving body of wonders and miracles. The first written versions, full of magic and fantastic events, were in Welsh, and it is probably through Celtic refugees to Britanny that the legends travelled to France. Thanks to the Breton devotion to a British king, the legends became popular there, which explains the not very typical French affection for a king of England.

The legends came back across the Channel with the Normans, and the treatment they received began to change radically. The English reaction to Arthur was to transform legend into history, or rather to dress it in historical garb, for the element of magic, if disciplined somewhat, never disappeared, while on French soil the Arthurian material took a more consciously literary turn in which perceptive psychology and the analysis of refined feeling are essentials. Courtly love is a key feature, the characters are given inner lives, and the concern for sentiment, thought, and motive becomes an important development. All this is found in the texts Malory used, the vast thirteenth century prose romances, which while pursuing the interest in feeling, sought, with an encyclopaedic rather than historical spirit, to provide an all-inclusive body of Arthurian material in which loose ends were tied up and everything was explained and analysed.

This is certainly no place for an account of the literary development of the Arthurian legend, but I take time to mention the literary tradition because of one important point. The Arthurian story was popular, thriving, and well-known throughout the Middle Ages. If, as late as 1485, Caxton published the *Morte Darthur*, it was because several of his noble patrons, no longer at ease reading the French versions available, were eager to have an English book of Arthur, and what you are eager to have, you know about. Malory, who had the linguistic ability to read French texts, most probably had a wide knowledge of Arthurian matters, as his book, indeed, testifies. There were the books he had access to in private collections, those he had read, and those he had heard read which existed in his memory. We have every reason to believe that the memory of medieval men was far more highly developed (because more exercised) than ours, and Malory must have carried a fair stock of Arthurian material with him, including (since the memory can go wrong) incorrect Arthurian material. On top of this, of course, was his general knowledge of the Arthurian legends, things he had picked up without knowing it, and without knowing where.

Any cultured fifteenth century gentleman would have a fair acquaintance with Arthurian matters, in general if not always in detail. Malory, who not only knew French well enough to read it but also to translate it, and who had the time, inclination, and talent to do so, must have been something of an Arthurian specialist. It is true that at times he relies so heavily on his source book that he appears entirely at its mercy and by no means at ease with his task. But this happens infrequently. More often he retains the detachment from his sources that a confident acquaintance with them permits. Nor is Malory's knowledge limited to French Arthurian literature. He made specific use of two English poems, and the occasional name, extra detail or event suggests knowledge of other English works. How well he knew them, or in what form, or if he knew that he knew them, we cannot say. All we can affirm is that the knowledge is there. It took an exceptional man to produce the *Morte Darthur*; it goes without saying that his knowledge was correspondingly exceptional.

The Major Sources

The main sources for the *Morte Darthur* are the group of French romances known as the Vulgate Cycle; the French prose *Tristan*, a separate branch of the material; and two English poems with confusingly similar names, the alliterative *Morte Arthure* and the stanzaic *Le Morte Arthur*. Malory picked up incidental information from other sources, but he did not sit down and systematically adapt them.

The Vulgate Cycle is in five parts. It begins with the *History of the Holy Grail* (*Estoire del Saint Graal*), which explains how the Grail was brought to England after – it goes without saying – quantities of miraculous adventures and entrusted to the first Grail king in preparation for the arrival of Galahad, the Grail knight. It is a book riddled with confusion but shows the clear desire to integrate and provide an explanation for everything. The Grail will be important later; it needs introducing now in the chronologically right place.

The second section is the *Merlin*, to which there is also a continuation or *Suite du Merlin*. This gives the early life and miracles of Arthur's wizard in preparation for the early period of Arthurian history. The third section is the *Lancelot*, the longest and the central portion of the whole. It gives the life of Lancelot from his birth, presents evidence of his nobility and supremacy, but also introduces his adulterous love for Guenevere. It prepares for the next part by recounting the conception of Galahad and introducing the idea of the sinfulness of Lancelot's love. *The Quest of the Holy Grail* (*La Queste del Saint Graal*), the fourth part, is more ascetic in spirit and shows the failure in spiritual deeds of sinful knights, among whom figures Lancelot of course, and the success of the pure. In the final section, the *Mort Artu*, there is a tighter chain of cause and effect: the adultery is not merely condemned as sinful, its discovery leads to disaster and disruption.

The French prose *Tristan* is not a part of the Vulgate Cycle as such, but a parallel volume that does for Tristan what the *Lancelot* had done for its hero. It introduces the wickedness of King Mark and the mockery of Dinadan, but it is principally devoted to a rather aimless knight errantry.

At the beginning and the end of his career, Malory turned his attention to English poems. The alliterative *Morte Arthure* is a martial, heroic poem which tells the story of Arthur's war against the Emperor Lucius, his victory, his coronation as emperor and his downfall through the treachery of Mordred. It is quite un-French in spirit: there is little mention of Lancelot or Guenevere, no love, no sentiment. It is (bogus) military history. The stanzaic *Le Morte Arthur*, on the other hand, is continental in spirit. It tells the story of the final days of Arthur's kingdom, and in abbreviated form covers the material of the *Mort Artu*.

These are Malory's principal sources and his first contribution to the transmission of the Arthurian material should be obvious at once. The vast, all-inclusive sources have been reduced to manageable proportions and the story has been firmly centred on Arthur. Malory sheds most of the early matter and boldly jettisons much of the material altogether: miraculous voyages and diabolical wizardry are not for him. He rejects all of the *Estoire del Saint Graal*, most of the *Merlin*, most of the *Lancelot*, and although he cuts out less from the *Queste del Saint Graal* and the *Mort Artu* he still shows independence of spirit. He systematically changes the tone of the French Grail book, and, refusing to be blindly subservient to one source, he draws on the *Lancelot* and the English *Le Morte Arthur* as well as the *Mort Artu*.

Malory is ready to change the sequence of events to suit his purpose, adapting episodes from the *Lancelot* to his Tristram book and delaying others till the *Mort Artu* section. He removes the tragic ending from the alliterative *Morte Arthure* and fits it in at the end of material taken from the *Suite du Merlin* (preferring the English poem to the French author's treatment of the same episode). He tries to bring the Tristram material more closely into the Arthurian framework by drawing attention to a series of implicit parallels between Tristram's situation and Lancelot's, by narrating the conception of Galahad within the Tristram book, and by first adding a new book, devoted to Gareth, which presents the theme of loyalty to a spiritual brother, in preparation for the theme of troublesome family allegiance that runs throughout the Tristram book, and plays such a part in the final disaster.

Judged by what he borrows, Malory may appear to be a timid compiler; judged by what he abandons, his boldness cannot be denied. He takes a variety of sources, different in aim, tone, genre, and even language and dialect, and handles them with the independence of spirit of an author with a mind of his own. His method was, appropriately for his subject matter, cavalier.

How Malory Worked

We do not know why Malory undertook his task nor how he worked at it, and we probably never will. Since he refers to himself as a 'knyght presoner' at the end of Book I and, at the end of Books IV and VIII, calls on his readers to pray for his release, we are entitled to believe that at least part of the *Morte Darthur* was written in prison. But how much, and which parts we cannot say. Words used at the end of Book I − 'Who that woll make ony more lette hym seke other bookis of kynge Arthure or of sir Launcelot or sir Trystrams' − suggest that Malory's work is being interrupted for want of material, which could suggest imprisonment at this point too. But it was a comfortable incarceration − appropriate to his rank, no doubt − which let him undertake or pursue his task in the first place, and the interruption could suggest disenchantment with the project just as well as a shortage of material to work on. For a solution, we can only rely on conjecture.

Especially if he was in prison, but even if he was not, it is difficult to know where Malory found all the books he needed or chose to use for his work. A number of fascinating attempts have been made to identify the library which contained all the required 'noble volumes' − plus two less noble English poems − Malory had access to. But we do not know whether one such library ever existed or whether Malory found his material in different places over a considerable period of time. Moreover, certain of Malory's sources are so far from the books he makes out of them that he may not have had them before him as he wrote. He might well, in parts at least, have relied on his memory. And if he was in prison, he might have had to.

If we cannot establish how Malory worked we can scarcely hope to be certain about what he was trying to do. We can comment on the effect a book has, but what a book seems to be doing and what its author was intending to do are not the same thing. It is obvious that Malory was aiming to abridge his sources, but that very abridgement makes other matters less than certain. His sources can give us clues about his intentions, but only clues.

Malory's sources use an interwoven narrative structure: the account of one incident is interrupted to present another, which, in turn, is broken off so that we can pass on to a third event, abandoned later in favour of the original story, and so on. It is an elaborate and sophisticated technique, and one which we presume Malory did not care for. He chose to simplify, to unravel the threads; he favoured a more orderly structure, following each adventure to its conclusion as far as possible. And yet we should not go too far. It is true that certain stories are narrated separately in Malory, instead of in interwoven sections as in the French. A good example is found in Book VII: Malory tells the story of the poisoned apple before mentioning the Maid of Astolat; in the French, the two are mixed. It is Guenevere's jealousy over the Maid that makes her banish Lancelot and hence find herself without a champion when the poisoning takes place. But Malory's simplification in structure is obvious here because he reduces (relatively) very little. Elsewhere his apparent unravelling is the inevitable result of the fact that he leaves out much of the material anyway. When you are trying to abbreviate, you are obliged to sort out what it is you are abbreviating: it is easier to see where the knife can be used.

In any case, we must not exaggerate Malory's disgust for interwoven narrative. If we do we must be ready to admit his uneven competence as a narrator, for he does not always succeed in eliminating what he apparently disliked so much. Indeed, he so often fails that few of us – without the prompting of the sources – would have thought of suggesting that interwoven narrative was distasteful to Malory at all. It is one of the features of his book we soon learn to like, so refreshingly unmodern, its leisurely inconsequence a suitable vehicle for the hazardous, arbitrary structure of Arthurian life and narrative. If Malory was trying to eradicate it, many of us are glad he was only partially successful.

In the same way, who, without the prompting of the sources, would ever have suggested Malory's lack of interest in magic? There may be less than in the sources, but it is all the more telling for that. If Malory was trying to eliminate the magic we are all glad he failed; his authorial incompetence has guaranteed the appeal of his book.

And who, without the evidence of the sources, would have thought of suggesting that Malory's book was not a single work? Of course in many ways it is an ungainly book, ill-proportioned and uneven in quality. Of course certain sections can be read independently, and the whole can be read out of sequence if we so wish, but this is because the story is well known, not because the tales are independent. The different books seem self-contained and can be read in isolation precisely because they are not self-contained and isolated, because, that is, there is a stock of information we all have anyway and which provides a background. We can read Book III without reading Books I and II because we all know who Lancelot, Arthur, and Guenevere are to start with.

Moreover, there is no doubt about the unity of matter; Malory's book is all about Arthur and his knights. It is a coincidence that the only two extant versions of the *Morte Darthur* from the fifteenth century both contain the same material, in the same order, and until a manuscript or early edition of a single tale is discovered, the *Morte Darthur* will impress most people as a whole book, however awkward that wholeness may be. It is not a single book in the way that *Middlemarch* is, but nor is it a series of eight separate works published (as the novels of Jane Austen sometimes are) in a bumper edition because they share a common theme and are by the same author. There are different tales but the different tales form a whole. Malory has focused his attention within the Arthurian material and brought it conveniently within one set of covers. For Malory, for Caxton, and for publishers these days apparently that is unity enough.

The question of unity, and the attitude to interwoven narrative and magic are fascinating subjects brought to light by a study of the sources. They can provide fruitful discussion as long as we realise that definite answers cannot be reached. If we try to force evidence out of Malory's sources we are in danger of misrepresenting the *Morte Darthur* by providing neat solutions to questions which the book itself cannot answer and does not make us ask in the first place. No one can be expected to read two books at once. If, in order to understand Malory, we must read with the *Morte Darthur* in one hand and its source books in the other, it may well be that we are trying to answer all the wrong questions.

Malory the Translator

Although we must recall that we do not have the exact manuscripts Malory used, and so all our comments must be guarded, a study of the sources can show us the methods and the variety of methods Malory used, the extent of his original contribution, and – even when he is borrowing material – just how different his book is from the sources that inspired it.

The variety of methods is the first thing that strikes us and there are several possible explanations for it. The suitability of the source to his purpose might have dictated his fidelity or lack of fidelity to it, although this seems uncertain in that the two books he follows closely seem to be the least suitable of all: the religious asceticism of the *Queste del Saint Graal* and the epic violence of the *Morte Arthure* fit Malory's book rather awkwardly.

Malory may have followed his sources closely when he was (literally) free to do so, and been driven to work more generally with them when imprisonment gave him limited access to French manuscripts and made him rely on his memory. Or quite simply the movement from timid reliance to confident independence might indicate the pattern of his experience as a writer and, therefore, the order in which the books were written. None the less, the reasons for the different methods must remain conjecture; it is the methods themselves that we can profitably turn to in order to see something of Malory's art. It is most enlightening to read an extract of Malory and the corresponding passage of his source. Anyone who feels his knowledge of Old French is not good enough can always use a translation – into modern French preferably, to give an idea of the task Malory undertook, but a modern English translation will also help. It will perhaps give an idea of the sort of text Malory might have produced if he had been a subservient translator without a mind of his own.

Book VI represents Malory's work as a translator. Although he severely abridged the *Queste del Saint Graal*, what remains is very much a word for word translation. Whether from lack of experience, from respect for a hallowed source, or from half-hearted interest in a part of his story which could not be omitted but which did not appeal to him, Malory follows his source with extreme fidelity, so much so that he fails to achieve the detachment from a text which guarantees an efficient translation. The structures of his own prose become awkward and at times he barely turns the text into English at all: ploddingly faithful he regularly relies on that fringe of vocabulary which was not entirely assimilated then and which has since been lost.

It is not difficult to see why certain critics have been so dismissive towards Malory's literary talent. Book VI is not, after all, the sort of work we expect of our major authors. Since it has frequently been taken as representative of Malory's art and method, the case against him has been eloquently made. The assumption is that although we do not have such close French manuscripts to compare with other books, if we did, we would see that Malory's method was more or less the same throughout. Perhaps not quite as faithful, but not far. Even recently, and with no intent to deny Malory's talent, Book VI has been taken as perfectly representative of his work with a French text: the introduction to the Penguin edition of Malory gives an extract from the Grail book and its source as a typical illustration of Malory's French-based style.

The student interested in Malory's method – and half an hour with the

French Grail text and Book VI will give him a fair idea – will see the somewhat plodding, unimaginative work of (perhaps) a beginner and will also see why Malory's reputation has suffered. But if he goes on to compare the texts in greater detail, he will soon come to realise that despite his fidelity, Malory felt free to add to his source, and that these additions are in spirit extremely daring. His refusal to sanction any denial of earthly chivalry, and his defence of Lancelot show Malory – if not blissfully misunderstanding his source – refusing to be browbeaten by the asceticism of his original and determined to stick to his guns over the essentials.

When we turn to other parts of the *Morte Darthur*, we quickly see that they are not like Book VI. The Grail book is taken as a convenient representative of Malory's art and method. It is not, and it would be worth challenging anyone to provide source material for any of the rest of the *Morte Darthur* which shows such strict fidelity. The only other source Malory follows so closely is in Book II. It is an English source and even when following faithfully Malory is ready to abandon it when it no longer suits his purpose.

A brief glance at Book II and its source the alliterative *Morte Arthure*, is enough to show how faithful Malory's abbreviated translation is. Indeed, since the translation is between two varieties of the same language, the influence is so much clearer. After all, when Malory borrows the words of French sources he disguises those words as English, when he borrows from the *Morte Arthure* no disguise is needed.

It has often been suggested that Malory began the *Morte Darthur* with Book II. The evidence for this is no stronger than for any other sequence, but the idea has often been taken up. It is, of course, attractive. It is agreeable to think of Malory finding inspiration in an English text and looking abroad for further material for a project he had undertaken under the guidance of the epic, historical spirit of the English poem, devoid of any interest in refined, personal feeling. But whether or not Book II was Malory's first literary venture, it is abundantly clear that he was entirely at home with the alliterative tradition. The poem's dialect was obviously no problem to him and he gives himself up to the spirit of the verse entirely. For not only does Malory use the words of the poem as he gives his abridged rendering of the events, he copies the poem's style when he paraphrases and when he adds material of his own. It is not merely that he cannot break free from the poem's influence, it seems as though he positively does not wish to, as though he were trying to make his version more like the poem than the poem itself.

He combines two lines of the poem into one without damaging the poetic structure; he creates lines of his own, sometimes from the fabric of the poem, sometimes not; he borrows the poem's tags and inversions and then creates others of his own when the poem gives no prompting at all.

Some of the extra alliterative poetic features may have come from the actual manuscript of the poem Malory used – the only extant copy is an imperfect one – but probably very few. Malory has, for some reason, given himself up to his source.

All this is obvious after even a brief comparison of Book II with its source, although a brief glance will inevitably make us understate the influence. Book II is the most extreme example of stylistic influence in the *Morte Darthur*. Nothing else is remotely like this. Both in language and spirit the book is out of keeping with the rest. It is for this reason that Caxton (or perhaps Malory himself) revised Book II, standardised the style and, at the same time, abridged the material further.

Most people pay little attention to Book II: its matter they find rather dull and its thumping rhythms and strange vocabulary soon tire our patience. The newcomer, perhaps, merely needs to recall first that Malory's readiness to yield to the stylistic influence of a source – though never again so extreme – does not entirely die, as the poetic rhythms found in Book VIII remind us; secondly, that the heroic strain of the poem with its martial, even patriotic spirit and lack of interest in private feeling is something with which Malory is entirely sympathetic, and which will colour his treatment of the far more personal, intimate French romances; and thirdly, that although in Book II Malory is carried away by the alliterative patterns of his poetic source, alliteration remains something which is close to him: the sounds of the alliterative tradition are never far beneath the surface of the *Morte Darthur*.

Malory the Adapter

Books II and VI show Malory at the unadventurous (prentice?) stage of ready reliance on a source, but they are the only books that do. Elsewhere, he displays a degree of independence which makes source comparison a much more arduous task.

With Books V and I, and even more so Book III, Malory's abridgement is more radical, as he picks out the essential narrative (and unwinds the interwoven narrative threads) but rarely relies on the precise words of the French text. The verbal parallels are usually those warranted by the coincidence of subject matter, and comparisons between Malory and his sources is often awkward in that a brief extract from the *Morte Darthur* corresponds to a far longer passage from the French, from which much is simply omitted and the rest severely reduced and paraphrased. The words he uses are his own and the structures of his prose are not those of the French texts with their complex subordinations; rather it is a much

more straightforward prose, nearer to the structural simplicity of everyday speech. Stylistically Malory has achieved a measure of independence,
even though the more accomplished French prose draws attention to the
modest competence of Malory's book when he gets into a muddle.

For Malory is still following his sources closely even if he is no longer
merely producing an abridged translation. It is not word for word parallels which betray his reliance on an original, rather his confusions in the
narrative or a lack of assurance in the tone. Some of the errors are inconsequential, some are odd: some add a sense of mystery where the more explanatory French text is without, others bring a hint of moral confusion.
Let me mention a few.

The story of Balin opens with the arrival of a lady wearing a sword.
Only the most virtuous knight will be able to help her unfasten it and
when all the court fails, the unprepossessing looking Balin succeeds. The
lady then asks to have the sword back, but Balin refuses and she, piqued,
goes out. A little later Merlin arrives and denounces her with the words:
'thys damesell that here stondith' (42.15–16; II.4). Malory, reducing his
source but following it closely at the same time, has chosen to omit the fact
that the lady comes back in, and so makes Merlin refer to the presence of
someone who is, in fact, absent. A minor matter, I agree, but one that illustrates a rather rough and ready technique.

Somewhat more odd is the fact that when the Lady of the Lake comes
in to ask for the favour Arthur had promised her when she gave him Excalibur, Arthur declares that he has forgotten the name of his sword. This
is rather shocking. That a young king should forget the name of a magic
sword given to him in such extraodinary circumstances shows a regret-
table lack of attention. The French text, which Malory is following more
faithfully than thoughtfully, explains the oddity. Arthur forgot to ask if
the sword had a name: the king was so overwhelmed by the mysterious
gift that his natural curiosity did not function. This is more fitting than the
absentmindedness of Malory's monarch.

Reading Malory along with his sources, we see the confusions and od-
dities of the *Morte Darthur*, but – and it is an important point – reading
Malory alone, as we should, these features have by no means the same effect. They create a sense of mystery and strangeness, a feeling of the unexplained and inexplicable circumstances of a life on a grander scale. We
come across people who know things they have never been told (because
Malory has omitted the middle part of the story), or who recognise people
they have never met (because their first meeting was part of Malory's reduction). We, understandably, question all this because it is disturbing
that the sense of mystery and meaning should be based on the accidents of
hasty abridgement rather than on intention. But Malory's intentions are
something we can never know. All we can do is work on probabilities

and, most of all, be ready to judge the effect of the book, whatever Malory might have intended.

The dividing line between confusion and mystery is not always clear and there are passages in which the narrative has become muddled in comparison with the source, but which are not without literary force. There is a sense of moral ambiguity which makes Malory's world a richer, more sinister place where we are never quite at ease, or to which we never quite have the key. Perhaps Malory was reducing his source over-hastily, perhaps, quite simply, he misunderstood. Perhaps too, in a real way, he saw the ambiguous possibilities of the changes he was making. Let me take an example.

Arthur's first sword breaks and the Lady of the Lake provides Excalibur. She asks for a favour which she will return to claim. When Balin has successfully removed the sword from the side of the other maiden, the Lady of the Lake returns and asks for the head of Balin, claiming that he killed her brother. Arthur refuses her request and Balin speedily chops her head off because, he says, she killed his mother. Life is never dull in Camelot even though it is confusing. It is surely rather odd that the lady who provides Arthur with his extraordinary word should turn out to be a villainess who goes around murdering mothers and asking for the heads of knights as guileless as Balin. Life at the French court is less confusing: the lady who provides Excalibur and the lady who asks for Balin's head are two. Malory reduces them to one in error, and yet by doing so he gives the powerful impression of a mysterious, intriguing world where everything and everybody is inexplicably and inextricably linked, where logic and the simple forces of good and bad will not work. If Malory has simply misread his source, the result is not without a power of its own; if he has wilfully reread his source as he does elsewhere (Are his changes in Book VI due to misunderstanding or an awareness that he and his source do not understand matters in the same way?), he has added to the evocative power of his world. Either way, the effect of the book is the same.

The reader must not allow comparison with the sources to make him believe that Malory's book is a mass of confusion. It is not. Malory does not always forget to supply essential information from material he omits, and he is careful to anticipate facts if required. The work of reduction and unravelling must be seen as one aspect of Malory's independence. As he reduces and unwinds, he is unable to rely on his text verbally and must reshape. He gives expression to borrowed tales but the expression is his own – and not only at the verbal level. He changes words but he also changes worlds. By comparing Malory with his sources we see how different he has made them.

There is far less magic and fantasy at the opening of the *Morte Darthur* than in its source: Malory turns the French book of Merlin into an English book of Arthur. But the clearest example is perhaps the French *Lancelot*. Anyone who wants to see how adaptation becomes transformation only has to look at Malory's work with the *Lancelot*, not trying to spot borrowed phrases and passages (a method which is of limited service outside Books VI and II), but to see that the two are worlds apart. The character called Lancelot in Malory and in the French text are two different men.

The *Lancelot* is the central (and largest) branch of the Vulgate Cycle and Malory makes use of it throughout his book. There is the Lancelot book itself (Book III), the Lancelot and Elaine section of Book V, and the Knight of the Cart episode in Book VII, along with other reminiscences of the French *Lancelot* in the Urry story and (as we shall see) with the Maid of Astolat. The question to ask is why, when Lancelot is clearly Malory's favourite and most important knight, does Malory merely select a small number of incidents concerning Lancelot and leave out the essentials of his biography. Malory devotes more space to Tristram and describes his boyhood even, whereas he rejects the childhood section of the *Lancelot* altogether. Even Gareth is given a longer book than Lancelot. It could, of course, be argued that Malory never had access to a complete copy of the French *Lancelot* – although he reveals some knowledge of episodes other than those he actually adapts – but I think a more likely argument is that Malory rejected most of the *Lancelot* because it was totally out of keeping with his conception of his hero and of Arthurian affairs. A modern French abridgement of the text has recently been published in two paperback volumes. It makes fascinating reading and we realise at once why Malory borrowed so little.

The *Lancelot* describes the childhood of Lancelot and we discover a young hero of exceptional talent, beauty and personal charm; for modern readers there is something of the Little Lord Fauntleroy in his somewhat cloying virtue. As a young man he is blameless and when he first meets Guenevere, she, the older, worldly, more experienced woman ('J'ai l'expérience de ces sortes he choses') is immediately taken with the handsome youth who is blushing, tongue-tied and full of maidenly modesty. He is a young man of exacerbated sensibility who is in seventh heaven when he feels the touch of Guenevere's hand and who drenches himself in tears ('les larmes lui coulaient des yeux, si abondantes que la soie dont il était vêtu en était mouillée jusque sur ses genoux') when emotion seizes him. Their first kiss is, of course, ecstatic and their first night together is the consummation of a love which will only become a stain if it is revealed. But an adulterous affair it well and truly is; there is no question of being coy about it, and their rendez-vous are organised by a close circle of friends. Their infidelity is plotted and schemed ('nous discuterons, ajoute la reine, de la conduite à tenir'), but since, in this world of sophisticated betrayal, the king is doing the same thing, it counts for little.

Not all of Lancelot's time is spent with Guenevere, and he is naturally a figure of great interest to other ladies because of his exceptional physical beauty – so great that even when he loses all his hair, his fingernails and his skin, a maiden still finds him ravishingly lovely. When four queens abduct him (an incident Malory borrows) they do not recognise him because his hair has not grown back, but his baldness does not reduce *their* appetite either. The emphasis on male beauty is, for us, unusual; perhaps the sort of thing we associate with more specifically feminine literature of a lighter sort.

Lancelot's beauty plays an essential part, however, in his fidelity to Guenevere. He is constantly being tempted by ladies, but he constantly resists, on one occasion beating a hasty retreat (Joseph Andrews-like) from a lady who gets into bed with him (Lancelot wisely does not undress) and tries to take his virtue by storm, and on another, preferring to die rather than offer himself as a reward to the maiden who, in love with him, is the only one who can cure his terrible illness. No one can tempt Lancelot, and when Morgan le Fay imprisons him, he paints the walls of his room with scenes depicting his love for Guenevere and, inspired by his love for her, does so with the skill of a lifetime's experience with a brush. After two and a half years in prison Lancelot sees a rose which reminds him of his lady's beauty. He breaks the bars of his prison to pluck the rose and rides off to offer it to Guenevere, of whom it is, of course, only a pale reflexion. What a pity there were no roses in bloom on the day Morgan locked him up!

It is difficult not to make the *Lancelot* sound like a parody of itself, and although Malory's book can also be made a target of irreverent fun, as Mark Twain has amusingly shown, his Connecticut Yankee would have had a field day in King Arthur's court in the French *Lancelot*. We can, of course, suggest that its gushing sentimentality is no longer to our taste, but less than a hundred years after Malory produced his book, a French writer condemned romances of this kind as being suitable only for young girls.

Malory could have nothing to do with all this. Lancelot in the French text is a sentimental, effeminate youth totally obsessed with his feelings for the queen; Malory's Lancelot is a sterner, more manly figure, not without private feeling, but calling for total discretion about it. He does not move in a circle of worldly infidelity and although most of his adventures in Book III are borrowed from the French text, there is little else to connect the works. Malory has not only reduced, he has transformed. Moreover, he is equally unsympathetic to the spirit of the second half of the French text, where the notions of sin and guilt creep in as a preparation for the Grail adventure and the birth of Galahad.

By a process of skilful omission, Malory changes the nature of his material so that what he borrows becomes, in a real sense, his own. He would never have claimed originality – and is ready to cite a French source to hide his own additions – but his imaginative response to his sources is in itself a considerable personal contribution. Malory's originals are courtly, amatory, explanatory, religious, and magical; he has produced a book which is more manly, military, factual, secular and down to earth. Religion, love, and magic have their proper place, but they are disciplined and without excess. Malory has translated the Arthurian story into his own language with his own outlook; inevitably, as he changed the linguistic medium, he changed its message.

It should be admitted that Book III is an extreme (or extremely clear) example of Malory's method. What he omits makes his book entirely different, and what he borrows becomes part of that entirely different book more than a remnant of the original. But if the example is extreme, perhaps it will serve as an illustration all the more clearly. The unusualness of Malory's method in Book VI has never stopped certain critics from putting it forward as a typical example.

Malory the Maker

Books VII and VIII are the best of Malory's tales; they are also the best to consider along side the sources to appreciate Malory's art. Malory displays a great deal of independence and originality while at the same time borrowing most of his material. The French *Mort Artu* was a more convenient source than the *Lancelot* or the *Tristan*, shorter, less rambling, more unified and with a tighter chain of cause and effect. There was a much smaller mass of extraneous material to sort and cut out, and less exaggerated sentimentality. None the less, even though Malory could have followed his source faithfully, he chose instead to complicate his task by using two other sources at the same time (the English stanzaic poem *Le Morte Arthur* and the French prose *Lancelot*); by rearranging the events in the *Mort Artu* to suit his own purpose; and by adding incidents of his own to make that purpose plain. In Books VII and VIII Malory at once relies on sources like any other medieval adapter/compiler, and at the same time manipulates those sources with the independence of mind of a creative writer.

Once again, Malory's omissions from his source can guide us towards his purpose. He rejects the episode where Arthur, in the castle of his sister Morgan le Fay, sees the paintings that Lancelot produced depicting his love for Guenevere. This episode is omitted not merely because the corresponding episode had been omitted earlier, nor because Malory seeks to eradicate all traces of the excessively sentimental Lancelot, but because he is not concerned with (indeed chooses to ignore) Arthur's private conviction of his wife's guilt. In the French text, the paintings are proof to Arthur that he has been betrayed, and this personal betrayal obsesses him. He is a jealous man out for vengeance, ready to banish Gawain for diplomatically concealing the adultery, and eager to inflict a punishment on the lovers that will be spoken of in generations to come. The French text, that is, sees the adultery in more personal terms – a faithless wife and an injured husband. It is, if you like, far more real, but it is also far more ordinary.

The French *Mort Artu* has, in fact, the kind of surface realism Malory pays little attention to. The daily business of living is not ignored. Characters go from one chamber to another; they are clearly situated in a physical context, a castle with corridors and rooms. Malory's gaze is far more formal. The king's private suspicions of guilt are stifled because of the public honour Lancelot has shown: the realm comes before his love for the woman who is queen of that realm. We see into the minds of the characters in the French text, and what we see – like Arthur's threat of vengeance – is not always flattering; in Malory we remain at a distance from his characters and the story is therefore elevated above the level of the merely personal.

When the *Mort Artu* does not lay the emphasis where Malory wishes, he turns his attention elsewhere. To show that Lancelot's two rescues of the queen are no longer proof of his unsullied devotion, Malory adds a third from the *Lancelot*, the Knight of the Cart episode, and when there is nothing to provide quite what he needs, he relies on his own resources. The Great Tournament section of Book VII is (so far as we know) Malory's own contribution; his French book did not provide a final moment of unity and knightly celebration on the eve of disaster, and the one Malory adds serves the important purpose also of making Gareth excel once again and of underlining his affection for and allegiance to Lancelot. In the same way, Malory added the incident of the healing of Sir Urry because he wished to emphasise Lancelot's virtue and the power of virtue, just before his want of virtue is made public. The *Mort Artu* contained nothing of the sort, and so Malory added a section of his own.

It is no doubt true that Malory did not invent the Urry incident out of the blue, and there is a similar motif – a knight carried in a litter being healed by the best knight in the world – in the *Lancelot*. The whole incident as it appears in Malory cannot be traced to a source, but this central detail can. Even this, of course, is no slight on Malory's creative powers; rather, it is like this that he frequently worked. His reminiscences of Arthurian matters fired his creative imagination, so that even where the most grudging critics are willing to accord him a degree of originality we can probably suggest a distant source somewhere. I would like to give an example of this in some detail because the point I wish to make is important: it is not only when Malory is one hundred per cent original that we can praise his creativity. Even when there are sources in the background, Malory's response to them is part of his own contribution. We no longer, that is, need to live in fear and trembling of a source turning up and destroying Malory's originality, because his contribution to the *Morte Darthur* can include borrowing. The example concerns the Maid of Astolat.

Malory's Maid of Astolat does not resemble in all points her counterparts in the two sources Malory was using (*Le Morte Arthur* and *Mort Artu*) and we can therefore argue that in parts she is an original creation. Without in any way relinquishing this idea of Malory's creativity, I would be ready to suggest that there is an ultimate source even for the points of difference.

The French prose *Lancelot* contains an incident in which Lancelot, poisoned by drinking water from a polluted spring, is nursed back to health by a young lady who almost dies of love for him. Apart from the survival of the lady and the cause of Lancelot's sickness, there are many points of resemblance between this story and that of the demoiselle d'Escalot in the *Mort Artu*. In each case, the lady, who has a brother, falls in love with Lancelot at first sight, has never loved before, and claims to love more strongly than any woman has ever loved a man. Both maidens are reputed to be the fairest in the land and in each case Lancelot is aware of that beauty. Lancelot rejects their love, of course, because his heart is not free, but if such had not been the case, he says, he would indeed have been attracted to them. The maidens themselves realise that socially they are beneath Lancelot. In both stories, members of the court are worried about Lancelot's welfare and set out to find him, and while he is convalescing, in both stories, Bors comes to see Lancelot and before leaving makes a confession to him and asks for forgiveness. In each case a future tournament is announced and Lancelot's illness is inevitably a handicap for him.

The two episodes are not parallel throughout, of course. In the *Lancelot*, the young lady looks after Lancelot and gathers herbs to cure him ('elle va par la prairie, cueille des herbes'); the demoiselle d'Escalot arrives only after Lancelot has been ill for more than a month and, although she stays with him night and day, there is no mention of her nursing him. In the *Lancelot*, the young lady feels she has a right to Lancelot, while he is aware of her virtues not merely of her beauty, and offers to be her knight; in the *Mort Artu*, the maid is insistent in her declarations but expresses no direct claim on Lancelot, while he makes her no offer at all. The maiden in the *Lancelot* story is direct, natural, frank and full of common sense, quite unlike the artful and sophisticated demoiselle d'Escalot. Guenevere urges Lancelot to show kindness to the maid in the prose *Lancelot* and the outcome of the story (a compromise is reached) is one which emphasises the maiden's virginity and leaves Lancelot blameless. In the *Mort Artu*, although the demoiselle dies a virgin, of course, no stress is laid on the point, Guenevere shows no understanding, and Lancelot is blamed not only by the demoiselle but by Arthur too.

It is for the individual reader to decide whether there are enough resemblances between the stories for the one to be reminiscent of the other, or whether the points of difference banish all possibility of comparison. What sounds like an echo to one person will not to another. And yet the point which is, I think, worth making is not that the story from the prose *Lancelot* resembles that of the demoiselle d'Escalot, but that it resembles Malory's story of the Fair Maiden of Astolat. What is interesting is that for each of the differences I have listed above, Malory's story of Elayne of Astolat is closer to the prose *Lancelot* than it is to the *Mort Artu*. Malory, that is, seems to have recognised the similarities between the two stories and the two maidens and remodelled his version of the *Mort Artu* in the light of the prose *Lancelot*.

The demoiselle d'Escalot arrives after Lancelot has been in bed for more than a month, whereas Elayne sets out to find Lancelot, is with him for a month and looks after him with such diligence that Bors' attention is at once drawn to the fact. She may not nurse him back to health as such, but, like the lady in the *Lancelot* story, she too gathers herbs: 'and so sir Launcelot made fayre Elayne to gadir erbys for hym to make hym a bayne' (635.33–34; XVIII.17), its purpose presumably being tonic not cosmetic. Malory tells us 'Than they were ther nyghe a moneth togydirs, and ever thys maydyn Elayne ded ever hir dyligence and labour both nyght and day unto sir Launcelot, that there was never chylde nother wyff more mekar tyll fadir and husbande than was thys Fayre Maydyn of Astolat' (635.26–29; XVIII.17), and adds that 'Elayne never wente frome sir Launcelot, but wacched hym day and nyght, and dud such attendaunce to hym that the Freynshe booke seyth there was never woman dyd never more kyndlyer for man' (633.36–39; XVIII.15). The *Mort Artu* says that the maid stayed with Lancelot night and day, whereas in the prose *Lancelot* the hero tells us 'elle m'a sauvé la vie et fait pour moi plus qu'une demoiselle fit jamais pour un homme'. When Malory quotes the French book, he is, it appears, quoting the wrong one.

The demoiselle d'Escalot is insistent in her plea for Lancelot's love but never suggests that she has a right to him. The lady in the prose *Lancelot* asks her brother 'ne devrait-il pas avec raison m'appartenir?' because of all she has done for Lancelot; and in Malory, Elaine, carried away by passion and anxiety for the man she has served with such diligence, behaves, we have recently been told, as though Lancelot belonged to her already. She threatens to take legal proceedings if Lancelot should die, as a wife had the right to if her husband died in her arms.

Although Lancelot recognises the beauty of the demoiselle d'Escalot, we are given no appraisal of her character. Of Elayne of Astolat we are told 'she ys a passyng fayre damesell, and well besayne and well taught' (635.9–10; XVIII.16), and of the lady in the prose *Lancelot* 'elle est belle, sage et pleine de qualités'. In reply to her request for his love, Lancelot tells the demoiselle d'Escalot 'Je ne puis rien y faire à la vie, à la mort' while he tells the *Lancelot* maiden 'je m'engage à être votre chevalier ma vie durant', and Elaine of Astolat 'This muche woll I gyff you, fayre mayden, for youre kyndnesse, and allwayes whyle I lyve to be youre owne knyght.' (638.32–33; XVIII.19).

The demoiselle d'Escalot is an artful young lady ready to make the most of her feminine charms and clearly at home in the courtly world of refined sentiment. She questions Lancelot indirectly – both in her attempt to get him to wear her token and when she tries to engage his affections – and when she receives a direct, but eminently polite, answer, she at once accuses Lancelot of being harsh and unkind. Her complaint about her sufferings reads like an attempt to force his hand, and her dying accusation is entirely unjust. She bears Lancelot a grudge. Malory's Elayne is a totally different girl. She is guileless almost to the point of naivety and her behaviour throughout is totally unaffected. Hers is not the world of courtly sophistication and this accounts for much of her impact on the reader and, indeed, Lancelot, who is not used to girls like this. When death approaches she insists that her feelings are perfectly natural, but, totally self aware, she bears Lancelot no grudge. She realises the folly and excess of her own sentiments and blames herself. She is like the *Lancelot* maiden who, although her situation is different, is also full of self awareness:

> La demoiselle dit et redit ses doutes, elle chasse Lancelot de son coeur, fait triste figure, puis revient à des pensées plus riantes se rassied et contemple celui de qui dépend sa vie: elle l'aime, qu'elle le veuille ou non, et en plein désarroi maudit l'heure où naquit en elle ce sentiment, dont elle se tient pour folle.
>
> (*Lancelot*. édition 10/18, vol. 2, p. 161).

She blames herself and never offers the slightest criticism of Lancelot. Like Elayne, but unlike the demoiselle d'Escalot, she uses no feminine wiles to entice Lancelot and her requests are open and direct, not couched in courtly insinuations. Although Elayne and the demoiselle d'Escalot share the same story and the same fate, they are entirely different young women; it is Elayne and the French *Lancelot* maiden who, in spite of their different trials, are like sisters.

Malory's version of the Maid of Astolat story shows that he was not ready merely to follow his sources slavishly: the basic material was there, but certain emphases were wrong. As he was reading about the demoiselle d'Escalot he must have recalled this other French maid and found her story in many points more suitable to his vision of the tale. Nor would I even suggest that Malory was doing this consciously; rather, his recollections of other Arthurian episodes have coloured his response to his major source and have led him to take up a position of creative detachment.

Invention is not the only kind of originality, and throughout the *Morte Darthur* (less, admittedly, in certain parts than here), Malory's imaginative handling of his sources amounts to an original contribution. The Maid of Astolat story shows that even when he invents, he borrows, and even when he borrows, he invents a version of his own.

We cannot ignore Malory's sources altogether, even though it is the scholar rather than the general reader who wants to bring the matter up. The sources can be instructive, but never if we approach them in a negative way, constantly minimising Malory's contribution, and ready to accord him the status of an author only where no source exists. Of course he borrowed his material – he would be the first to say so – but he is not merely a compiler/translator however much he compiles and translates. The *Morte Darthur* is not merely shorter than its sources, not merely written in a different language. The stories may not be of his own invention – as if that mattered – but the version he gives of them has his personal hallmark all the same. And it is his version, after all, that has survived. His sources live largely through him and it is certainly not because some of them have recently been edited, translated, abridged, and published in paperback editions that the *Morte Darthur* has anything to fear from the competition. It would be interesting to know how many copies of Malory are sold for every one of his sources today. Publishers' sales figures may not mean much in a world of quick profit, but they probably still mean something.

5

Background and Biography

In its rejection of the personal and private in favour of the public and official the *Morte Darthur* represents a move away from French romance to
English history. Inevitably, therefore, we are prompted to consider the
historical background against which the book was written. Given
Malory's point of view, the social context of his day might be of particular
importance for an understanding of his book. But although Malory is totally committed to the age he describes, although he invites comparison
with fifteenth century society by emphasising its difference ('custom was
those days') and – but rarely – by openly denigrating it (in matters of the
heart and of state his contempories are men of fickle allegiance), Malory
writes with the outlook of the historian not the politician. He can admire
without dissidence: he extols the glory of Arthur's court and despises
modern laxity, but no one political system or group comes under fire.

The *Morte Darthur* is not a pamphlet. The political situation of Malory's
day was no doubt too explosive for an author to risk committing himself
and there is certainly nothing in the *Morte Darthur* to give offence. Malory
refers to himself as a 'knight presoner' but he was certainly not in prison
for writing his book, which is politically so harmless that he was able to
write parts of it while he was under arrest and unlikely therefore to wish
to antagonise the authorities further. Even the most famous authorial
comment – 'Lo ye all Englysshemen' (708.34–41; XXI.1) – is couched in
terms which are vague enough to allow interpretation from both points of
view. It is only understandable that we should want to interpret the historical background as precisely as possible, but it is useful to do so only if
we resist all attempts to provide a key. For there is no conclusive evidence
even for some of the most straightforward questions, nothing to show, for
example, whether the author of the *Morte Darthur*, writing during the
Wars of the Roses, was a Yorkist or a Lancastrian. We might be convinced
that in those divided days you had to be one or the other. Perhaps, but the
division was such that it was surely wiser, and especially in writing, to

keep one's own counsel and leave questions of allegiance open. As far as Malory is concerned, both interpretations are possible: certain details suggest he was a Yorkist supporter, others suggest he was a Lancastrian. But we do not know.

Perhaps, of course, it is subversive to imply criticism at all by offering one's contemporaries an ideal; but subversion is surely the last word that comes to mind when we think of the *Morte Darthur*. Malory is an eminently conservative writer. His book is a plea for order and unity in troubled times, and order and unity are cries to rally round whether the roses you cultivate are red or white.

The Historical Background

The *Morte Darthur* was written during the first decade of the reign of Edward IV, a king who did much to restore the waning prestige of the English monarchy, and who was not loath to trace his ancestry back to King Arthur. It was a period when Edward was having great difficulty winning the confidence of his nobility, and Malory finished his book (and may, indeed, have written all of it) at a time when Edward's authority was being seriously challenged, on the eve, in fact, of the restoration of the mentally unstable Lancastrian king, Henry VI, whom Edward had replaced. Within a few months Edward had regained the throne, and reigned until 1483. His death was followed by the murky events which led to the brief reign of Richard III. It was during Richard's reign, no doubt, that Caxton was asked to print an English version of the Arthurian story, and he did so three weeks before Richard's death at the Battle of Bosworth. The periods immediately preceding the completion and (fifteen years later) the publication of the *Morte Darthur* were both turbulent times in which the notions of rightful and stable kingship were burning issues. Malory's book must have had a relevance for him and for Caxton's noble patrons that it cannot have for us.

The whole of Malory's life was lived in troubled times. He was born during what we call the Hundred Years' War, and no sooner was that over than the Wars of the Roses began, and continued till after his death. He did not live in a period of continual open warfare of course, but life was none too stable, full of rival factions and – perhaps most important – it was an age in which the reputation of England was steadily going downhill. All the Great victories of the Hundred Years' War were behind. Malory may not even have been alive when Agincourt was fought (1415) and if he was, he was only young. The royal leadership of Henry V may have inspired his youth, but Henry died in 1422 and the English inheritance in France, and with it England's prestige, sadly dwindled away during the minority of Henry VI. When Henry was of age to take the throne, he proved unworthy of it, and his long reign was the dismal story of the total collapse of royal authority. It was only when, after bouts of insanity, he was replaced by Edward IV that England found a king who deserved the title, even if his right to it was not undisputed. And even then, not everyone was content. England in Arthur's day had a king who had not only inherited the title, but deserved it through his achievements and capacities, 'thorow dygnyté of his hondys'. When Malory wrote the *Morte Darthur* and when Caxton published it, the situation was neither so fortunate nor so clear.

It is possible that Malory's non-partisan approach reflects not his prudence, but his disenchantment. He reveals no preference for either side because he was indifferent to both – and as a citizen could incur the wrath or indulgence of either or both. If Malory was an old man when he wrote, and had known – or, at least, had been brought up to revere – the triumphant age of Henry V, he might express discontent with both sides in the late 1460s. How dreadful it was that a king should be deposed; how fitting it was that at last a king should be worthy of his crown. Malory's grievances would have no one target, in the way that old people, conditioned by the politics and principles of their youth, are sometimes not quite up to date with contemporary politics. They cannot keep up with the names of such young-looking ministers, and the sudden appearance of an entirely new political party is most unsettling. Unable to take sides, they feel disgruntled in general. Things were different in their day or, for Malory, in King Arthur's day.

But this is supposition. One thing we can be more certain of is that in his book Malory shows himself to be extremely conservative. Like so many military men, he has a passionate commitment to law and order, to king and country. His is a world of discipline, loyalty, and allegiance, where unity is the key concept and the Round Table the symbol of that unity. Hence he can afford to discard the personal suffering of the king to heighten the pathos of the loss of the realm. The French Arthur is tortured by jealousy; in the late 1460s, a king's private jealousy must have seemed somewhat superfluous, considering what was at stake.

Malory never betrays his allegiance to any contemporary political ideal; his total commitment is to Old England, a world (now destroyed) of law, order, and unity. There could scarcely be a greater contrast with the world he lived in, a world of private ambition and greed, a world of power struggles and factions, where brothers were divided and allegiances bought: Edward IV did not have the confidence of his own brothers; it was the men he had enriched that he could rely on most.

The turbulence and unrest of the Wars of the Roses form a strange contrast to Malory's book, and the order and perfection of the Arthurian world, an age of peace and strong government, must have been attractive to Malory and his first readers. But the *Morte Darthur* is never a simple denunciation of contemporary affairs, on which Malory refuses to comment. He withdraws almost entirely, and one aspect of his non-allignment is the absence from the *Morte Darthur* of any everyday world which could provoke criticism and comparison. There is something rarified and isolated about Arthur's kingdom. We have little sense of life going on elsewhere. On the rest of the population, who were not knights and ladies, Malory turns a blind eye.

The real world, or the modern world, does appear at times. There is the strange anachronism of the guns Mordred uses (707.33; XXI.1), but then Mordred represents the threat of a modern world with its shoddy values, a world of dissent. He is a man without an ounce of chivalry or religion, a mere mercenary with whom a truce must be bought. And yet, his greed is not unique. The final battlefield is not merely covered with the corpses of the noble dead, the destruction of the old world, it is alive with the activity of the modern world, the mercenary and materialistic activity of the scavengers. They are the victims of war, perhaps – poor folk desperate to survive or unscrupulous folk eager for easy gain – but they are also a reminder of the modern world of cheap profit and low ideals which Malory uses as a point of reference for the nobility of Arthur's days. And as the Round Table values disintegrate, even a faithful warrior like Sir Bedevere can fall victim to sordid betrayal. He is aware of the market value of a sword which is the symbol of unequalled glory, and he fails to realise that its unexplained mystery is more important than life itself. The sword must return whence it came; there can be no trophies of the Arthurian world, no relics or souvenirs of days gone by, for those days have gone entirely. When Malory writes 'hym thought synne and shame to throw away that noble swerde' (715.28–29; XXI.5) we have sunk extremely low. Is this all the word *shame* means now? Little more than the thrifty housewife's reluctance to let anything go to waste, or the canny soldier's eye for booty: it would fetch a good price in the officer's mess.

The world Malory describes was not perfect and his nostalgia is not shortsighted. There were rival factions then, just as in his own day. None the less it was a better world, and hence Malory's (rare) apostrophe:

Lo ye all Englysshemen, se ye nat what a myschyff here was? For he that was the moste kynge and nobelyst knyght of the worlde, and moste loved the felyshyp of noble knyghtes, and by hym they all were upholdyn, and yet myght nat thes Englyshemen holde them contente with hym. Lo thus was the olde custom and usayges of thys londe, and men say that we of thys londe have nat yet loste that cus-

tom. Alas! thys ys a greate defaughte of us Englysshemen, for there
may no thynge us please no terme.

(708.34–41; XXI.1)

It is a much debated passage; evidence, we are assured, of Malory's political sympathies. Malory must have been a Lancastrian bewailing the
deposed Henry VI back in 1461. As interesting confirmation, Mordred
draws most of his support from regions in the South East, which were
Yorkist. But too much has been made of this by critics who are interested
in using it to identify Sir Thomas Malory. For the complaint is extremely
vague and open to the opposite interpretation. Malory was perhaps a Yorkist bewailing not the deposing of Henry VI many years earlier, but the
growing antagonism to Edward IV that was going on while Malory was
writing. But the political content of the *Morte Darthur* is not precise, and
the fickleness of men during the civil war, constantly changing sides, was
enough to spur Malory's outburst.

It is wiser to avoid drawing too many parallels between the Wars of the
Roses and Malory's book. The essential point to notice is that there was
more uncertainty about the rightful succession than since the twelfth century and that this was the excuse for rebellions in which usurpation was a
key motive. The notion of personal and legitimate kingship – a title both
inherited and merited – is something which was keenly felt, and the figure
of Arthur could only have aroused admiration. Arthur was the man who
was born and deserved to be king, and the whole of the first part of the
Morte Darthur (Books I and II) is devoted to establishing this ideal: rightful
kingship and its nature are Malory's themes.

To what extent Malory found inspiration or recognised similarities in
the kings who had ruled during his lifetime we cannot know. Edward IV
was a noted warrior and the finest commander of the period. The list of
his victories is long. He loved tournaments and fighting and much was
made of tracing his ancestry back to King Arthur. Henry VI was a devout,
well-intentioned recluse who hated combat, had no talent for government
and was a disastrous king and military leader. If we take nothing else into
account it is not difficult to imagine where Malory's sympathies lay.

But Malory may have had no sympathies at all; in writing the *Morte
Darthur* he may have had neither monarch in mind. It is true that in the
late 1460s a Yorkist audience would readily compare Arthur to Edward,
but Lancastrians would be blind to parallels of any sort. Perhaps rightly
so, for the clearest way to see the historical background is as a contrast to
the world of unity, identity, order, and peace that Malory describes. Perhaps it was an ideal. Of course it was too good to be true, or, in this sinful
world, too good to last, and, indeed, it was doomed. It was not a perfect
world, but it was a better one. Not a world that we could restore, how-

ever, if one party or other were brought to power, for the disorder of modern times is a symptom of that fundamental decay that the *Morte Darthur* illustrates: the total abandonment of chivalric values that inevitably occurs when private interests and personal rivalries count for more than the welfare of the realm as a whole.

Who Was Sir Thomas Malory?

It is not the number of obvious and fascinating parallels with the Wars of the Roses, nor any overt political slant which encourages critics to interpret the *Morte Darthur* in terms of its historical background; more often than not it is the desire to identify the author. If we could work out which side Malory was on, we might be able to decide which of the Thomas Malorys available he actually was. Unfortunately we cannot and there is precious little evidence elsewhere to enlighten us. We are, however, reluctant to leave the matter there.

Malory is an unobtrusive writer with no ironic detachment towards his material to make us aware of the narrator's mind. He is reluctant ever to come forward to express an opinion, let alone browbeat the reader, and yet, at the same time, in spite of his apparent narrative reticence, his personality comes across so strongly that we feel a definite desire to know more about the man. Unfortunately, the information available is so scant that this is impossible. The *Morte Darthur* is, to all extents and purposes, an anonymous book. Quite simply, we do not know who Sir Thomas Malory was. But this is a fact that it has been almost impossible to face ever since researchers unearthed information which suggests that perhaps the author of this noble book was a complete and utter rogue. The breath of scandal – we are not surprised – gave the biographical debate new life.

This is not the place for a full account of Malory's life and I have ignored the matter till now because it can only be of academic interest until we know if we are working on the biography of the right man. It is, however, an intriguing subject and one worth mentioning briefly even if only because the student of Malory cannot go far without coming across it. Moreover, some critics fail to mention that a biographical problem exists at all, and identify the author of the *Morte Darthur* without a qualm, or at least they pass from probability to certainty with great speed. Perhaps we know too little about any of the candidates for this to matter much; but that is precisely the point. We know so little – and especially so little that has any real importance for the book that the indentification or identity of the author remains an irrelevance. We are understandably reluctant to abandon Malory without at least trying to track him down first, but until we know more – or more certainly – we might as well do so.

All we know for certain about the author of the *Morte Darthur* is found in the closing words of certain books of the *Morte Darthur* itself. His name was Thomas Malory, he was a knight, he was – at certain stages of the writing of his book at least – a prisoner, and he finished the *Morte Darthur* between 3 March 1469 and 4 March 1470, that is in the ninth year of the reign of Edward IV.

There are other documents from the late fifteenth century concerning Thomas Malorys, but whether this means the author of the *Morte Darthur*, another man, or other men, we do not know. Since Malory was a knight, at least he had the social, legal and financial importance likely to make him appear in records somewhere, but there is always a possibility that despite his love for action in literature, the author of the *Morte Darthur* lived the sort of retiring life that can easily go undocumented.

So far, there are three candidates in the running, three Thomas Malorys alive at the right time and who researchers claim could have written the *Morte Darthur*. The first is generally thought to be the strongest candidate (some think he has definitely won the race and the facts of his life are attributed to the author of the *Morte Darthur* as if no doubt existed); it is certainly he who has caused all the trouble. The second put up a good fight for a short time, but is beginning to drop behind; and the third, after being eclipsed by the first (and then the second) for a long time, has recently made a come-back.

The Warwickshire Candidate – Sir Thomas Malory of Newbold Revel

It is not difficult to see why this Malory heads the field. His name is right, he was alive at the right time (he died on 12 March 1471), and the records state that he was a knight and that he was in prison several times. He fulfilled all the right requirements from the start, whereas, as we shall see, the other candidates did not. The trouble arose when research continued and more facts about his life emerged. The more we learnt, the less suitable he seemed.

Thomas Malory of Newbold Revel was certainly alive when the *Morte Darthur* was completed, but it might be wondered whether he was in a fit state to do the job himself. Since he had seen military action in Calais in 1414 it has been suggested that he was born in 1393 or 1395, but even at a conservative estimate he would have been seventy years old in 1469–70. His most ardent supporters prefer not to mention the year of his birth and they avoid drawing attention to his age throughout his career, but it is something we cannot overlook. In the fifteenth century, seventy was a grand age and it would be extraordinary if a man of such advanced years had written the *Morte Darthur*, although it goes without saying that whenever he was born, Malory was an extraordinary man. Critics who find this Malory's age an embarrassment could always point out that other medieval authors seem to have reached a ripe old age, even if they were not writing or in prison to the last. Dates are often uncertain, but according to the *Oxford History of English Literature* (Volume 2, Part 1), Pecock died aged 71, Trevisa 76, Henryson 79, Lydgate 80, Hoccleve 82, and Hardyng 87.

But it is not age alone which is a hindrance: seventy seems too old for someone who had been in and out of some unpleasant prisons. For the jails this Malory was in and the crimes he committed to get there were not of the sort to allow the gentlemanly kind of incarceration usually thought necessary for his work. Nor do events suggest that he was quite the honourable gentleman who could be trusted to respect the conventions of arrest: on one occasion it took 60 men to secure his arrest, and on another, the penalties imposed on his jailers to ensure he was held securely were extremely high. This Sir Thomas – and there's the rub – was apparently a blackguard with a remarkably chequered career.

The list of crimes of which he was accused is (amusingly) long and varied. He apparently wounded and imprisoned one Thomas Smythe and stole his goods; twice – and at the age of fifty – he was accused of rape on the person of the same lady; he was accused of cattle stealing, horse stealing, of raiding an abbey, and even of ambushing and attempting to murder his patron Buckingham. None of this prevented his becoming a Member of Parliament, but many a rogue has walked the halls of Westminster since then. He was frequently in prison, and after 1452 spent most of the next eight years there, although we have no records to show that he was in prison in 1469–70, when he ought to have been there completing the *Morte Darthur*. His imprisonment might also have been linked to his political affiliations, which seem to have fluctuated. During the Lancastrian king's insanity he was granted a pardon by the Yorkist Protector, but the pardon was refused by the courts. His Yorkist allegiance found expression again in 1462, when he went north to the sieges of the castles of Alnwick, Bamburgh and Dunstanburgh; but between 1468–70 his name appears in lists of Lancastrians who were excluded from royal pardons, although this in itself does not provide the proof we needed of his being in prison at the time.

We once knew too little about Sir Thomas Malory; now it was felt that we knew too much. The life of Thomas of Newbold Revel fitted the criteria imposed by the *Morte Darthur*, but it also surely disqualified the candidate. How could such a blackguard have written a book which has impressed generations of readers for the nobility of its sentiments? How in all decency could this Sir Thomas Malory have written:

> 'What?' seyde sir Launcelot, 'is he a theff and a knyght? And a ravyssher of women? He doth shame unto the Order of Knyghthode, and contrary unto his oth. Hit is pyté that he lyvyth!'
>
> (160.10–12; VI.10).

Different lines of defence have been offered. On paper the crimes he was accused of look bad, but were they really? Cattle stealing, it has been pointed out, was a gentlemanly crime, and rape could mean little more than abduction. Indeed, the fact that Malory favoured the same lady twice suggests that the case was not sordidly simple: he might have been under the impression that he had taken her only 'half be force' the first time. Moreover, even knightly ambush could be interpreted as attempted murder if the prosecuting counsel formulated the accusation; how Malory's defence lawyers would have pleaded the case we do not know. Being accused of crimes is not the same thing as being guilty of them, and although in Malory's case there is rather too much smoke for there not to be a fire somewhere, in troubled times even the most banal acts can be magnified if you are in the bad graces of those in power.

It has also been suggested that Malory's unorthodox career is no problem because the *Morte Darthur* is not quite the noble book it is made out to be. After all, one of its earlist critics considered it full of 'open manslaughter and bold bawdry.' If we stopped idealising the book, we would not need to blush at the author's raffish career. And yet, somehow, this line of argument will not work either. There is brutality in Malory's book; there are times when life seems cheap and when even the finer knights will lop off a lady's head without giving her time to explain herself. But the book's most lasting impression, surely, is one of lofty ideals, of noble sentiments, of total commitment to values we all (in our better moments) respect: mercy, honour, lovingkindness, humility and truth.

In the last resort it must be admitted that the moral problem is a false problem, because, quite simply, a man does not have to be virtuous to admire virtue, nor perfect to write about perfection. The writers of the Gospels would presumably have been the first to admit that they were the chief of sinners. Perhaps Malory, only too conscious of his own short-comings, was able to give expression in the *Morte Darthur* to those loftier ideals which would have been the inspiration of his life if society had not been against him, if he had had the necessary luck, if the adventure had been his, or if he had really tried. And as he wrote he was able to revel in achievements that were never quite his own or, even, express indignation over villainies that were.

We would like to think of Malory as a man of integrity, imprisoned perhaps because of his unbending principles by a corrupt authority, a man totally devoted to the knightly code in his own life. But this may not have been the case. We must even be prepared to admit that since society is full of whited sepulchres, the possibility exists that Malory was one of them – like the mafia leader's pious insistence on his grand-daughter's education in the faith. It would be a pity, but it is not impossible, and the moral question therefore should be laid aside altogether. We are naive if we refuse to admit that many a piller of Victorian respectability has lived a life of hair-raising vice.

The moral question is rarely put aside entirely, however, and it is this which has encouraged the constant search for other Malorys with better claims. It has even led to Sir Thomas Malory of Newbold Revel being split into two – the clean living author from Newbold Revel and his dissolute doppelgänger from Fenny Newbold, which was pronounced to be a separate village in the neighbourhood and not a simple variant of the name Newbold Revel. It is a neat theory. Unfortunately it confiscates the necessary prison record from the author, and makes the number of Thomas Malorys per square mile in that part of Warwickshire uncommonly high.

The Yorkshire Candidate – (Sir) Thomas Malory of Studley and Hutton.

The only indisputable information about the author of the *Morte Darthur* comes from the book itself. It does; but one piece of information had been overlooked: the *Morte Darthur* is written in a regional variety of English which helps to localise the author, and Warwickshire is the wrong locale. Ignoring the moral issue, it was this line of approach that led the American scholar William Matthews to put forward a new candidate, the Yorkshire Thomas. The linguistic evidence of the book pointed to a northern origin and there, at Studley and Hutton, was a Thomas Malory alive at the right time. Matthews devoted a whole book to the subject and gathered a mass of linguistic evidence to disqualify the Newbold Revel man and to support the claims of his own protégé.

The weight of the linguistic evidence was necessary because the Yorkshire Malory did not otherwise fit the requirements: records were lacking to state whether he was a knight or had been in prison. But after all, documents of the period are notoriously incomplete: it is not because the Yorkshire Malory is not mentioned with his title that he did not have one. The real drawback, however, is that this Malory is simply too ephemeral. He was one of fourteen children and possibly illegitimate, but only two references to him have survived. We know that he existed but that is about all. Two of his brothers fought for the Lancastrian party and were killed; if

Thomas had done the same he could have been imprisoned, or knighted, or both. But there are no records. He might have been a prisoner of war in France, but so might the other candidates, and, again, there are no records.

As other scholars considered his claims, the Yorkshire candidate sadly lost ground. The linguistic evidence may well have ruled out a Warwickshire candidate, but there is little in the *Morte Darthur* to warrant a move as far north as to Yorkshire. Lincolnshire at the most. Moreover, it would be surprising if this particular Yorkshireman had written the *Morte Darthur* because, as it turns out, he would have been far too young. His father was born in 1417 and Thomas was the sixth son. Unless his mother brought forth men children only, he could have been the ninth or tenth child, and it is hardly likely that he was born much before 1445. To have completed the *Morte Darthur* at the age of twenty-four is something of an achievement and makes us regret the lack of information concerning this extraordinary young man, as precocious as a Rimbaud or a Keats.

The Cambridgeshire Candidate – Sir Thomas Malory of Papworth St Agnes

The Cambridgeshire candidate was proposed in the same year as the Warwickshire Malory, but since he lacked the obvious qualifications of the Newbold Revel man – there was no evidence for his imprisonment or his title – his claims were overlooked. It is only since the Yorkshireman has weakened the claims of the blackguard from Newbold Revel and has, in turn, been dismissed that the Cambridgeshire man has been given a fair hearing.

First of all, his age is perfect. Born in 1425 he would have been forty-five when he was adding the finishing touches to the *Morte Darthur*. In this he is a far better candidate than the superannuated Warwickshire Malory or the fledgling from up north. Although we cannot be sure, he may well have been in prison and awaiting death in 1469, since the terms of his hastily drawn up will suggest he was expecting to die. Moreover, in times of political unheaval, the crime which brought him to jail may have earned him royal gratitude and a title, for although the records concerning his life never refer to him as a knight, there is one document written shortly after his death in which the title is unequivocally his. And the only passages in which the author of the *Morte Darthur* claims to be a knight were written at the end of his career.

There is, of course, nothing precise to prove that the Papworth man was ever a prisoner, but in those days it was possible to be a prisoner without being in prison, and the absence of documentary evidence here is no more troublesome than the surfeit of inappropriate evidence concerning the Warwickshire man.

Finally, the Papworth man has the right geographical connexions. His family had close ties with Lincolnshire, where he could well have spent his youth being trained, as befitted his station, and as was customary for the eldest son, in the household of a kinsman. Every day he would have heard (and learnt to use) that North-East Midland variety of English he was to use later in the *Morte Darthur*, and – who knows? – it may well have been there that he first became acquainted, in those formative years, with stories of Arthur and his knights through poems which linguistically have strong Lincolnshire connexions, like the alliterative *Morte Arthure*.

His later education may well have been in France, where his taste for Arthurian books could have developed. With his own experience no doubt in mind, Malory thinks to add the detail concerning Tristram's education that he was sent to France to learn French – a point which would have had little meaning in the original text where Tristan spoke French anyway. But this, of course, could be true of all three Malorys.

A La Recherche du Tom Perdu

We had to wait until 1934 for a manuscript of the *Morte Darthur* to come to light. Who knows, if we are patient and if researchers are diligent, documents will be discovered one day to identify the author. But till then, we can only say that we do not know who he was.

Since we know so little about each of the candidates, perhaps we should not worry if the Newbold Revel man seems, for the moment, to be firmly entrenched as the winner. As long as no one writes a study of the *Morte Darthur* using his prison record as a source of enlightenment we need not care. And if Malory is indeed the Warwickshire candidate, the contradiction between the man and his book will be at best fascinating (perhaps embarrassing) confirmation that the author of the *Morte Darthur* was, as we would expect, an exceptional man. Otherwise the moral problem is a red herring: what we know of his life is an irrelevance for his book. Since we know even less about either of the other candidates, if they should turn out to be our man, all we will be able to do is take note, and pass on to more important matters.

The authorship problem is not really – for readers of the *Morte Darthur* – a problem at all, except that our curiosity is such that we inevitably want to know more about the men behind the books we admire. But without the breath of scandal surrounding the Warwickshire man, the whole subject would probably have been abandoned long ago. The scandal has whetted our appetites, but the subject, however fascinating, remains peripheral to any study of Malory's book.

For those who enjoy literary detection, however, the subject is worth following up. It is an extremely complex investigation in the missing persons department involving the study of wills, deeds of property, legal suits, lists of kinsfolk and countrymen, allies and, even, members of juries. But ultimately it is a rather futile quest *à la recherche du Tom perdu* with which Malory himself would have had little patience. He was, it is true, something of a stickler for proper forms of address, but he would pardon my irreverent familiarity because he would, I am sure, share my scepticism.

The chances of our discovering a document telling us which of the candidates – *if any* – was the author of the *Morte Darthur* are very slight, but even if one did turn up, it would not take us far. The information we have about each of the candidates can add nothing to our appreciation of the book. Legal documents do not give life to a man. We have a few facts, a few details from a *curriculum vitae*, but the men themselves are lost. The academic question remains of interest and merits research, but not if it takes attention away from Malory's book. After all, Malory himself was an extremely reticent man, reluctant throughout to come to the fore, to speak in his own name and draw attention to himself. He did not believe that his own opinions or comments could be of interest, and – except when (rarely) carried away – he offers none. He remains constantly in the background, an observer not an actor. I have described Malory as the court historian of the Arthurian world, but he was never himself a courtier – in the way that Chaucer the poet is, at the same time, a Canterbury pilgrim. It was Malory's task to chronicle the deeds of Arthur and his men. What misdirected energy – we feel he would suggest – to waste time on something so unadventurous as the personal history of a mere historian.

6

The Impact of the Morte Darthur

In the medieval period the Arthurian legend was popular all over Europe; today it is so only in the English speaking world. This cannot be explained merely in terms of chauvinism or national pride. Arthur may well have been king of England, but this did not prevent the legend from flourishing all over the continent for centuries, and when Caxton published Malory's book, he complained that Arthur had a greater following in Europe than in England: the French, the Dutch, the Italians, the Spanish, and even the Greeks seemed more interested than the English. He published the *Morte Darthur* in fact because an English book of Arthur was sadly in need: we had to catch up with our neighbours. It was a disgrace that the first of the three Christian Worthies, an Englishman, should be so neglected in his own country – like the proverbial prophet. The English, that is, got onto the Arthurian bandwagon rather late. And then, the legend went out of fashion in Europe. Malory's *Morte Darthur*, however, did not go with it.

For a time, the survival of the legend in England may have been due to a political significance it could not have elsewhere: the English monarchy was eager to bolster its prestige and strengthen its dynastic claims in reference to its Arthurian heritage. Interest in the *Morte Darthur* may have fostered this political interpretation or, in turn, have been fostered by it. But when the English crown lost interest in its supposed Arthurian inheritance, Malory's book still survived.

Not only did it survive, it also inspired, and its impact has been enormous. Nor does the inspiration stem merely from the legend itself, for other Arthurian works have remained without issue and have lost their audience altogether. France had no Malory, and France has had no post-medieval Arthurian tradition. The Arthurian tradition has inspired other writers in England to a certain extent because of the contribution of one man.

This is certainly not how things were expected to turn out, and it is clear that Caxton never suspected that he was publishing the work of

someone who was in any way a major literary figure. His noble patrons
had asked for a book of Arthur in English, and Malory's abridged translation of certain French texts came into his possession at just the right time.
It would do the job nicely, even if some reorganisation was required before the volume went to press. Caxton, in his preface, speaks in some detail of his own editorial role in shaping the book and making it available,
and when he mentions Malory it is clear that he is not unwilling to acknowledge the collaboration of a translator/adapter, but he is certainly
not launching a new author on a literary career. As it turns out, he was
wrong.

The book he was publishing had – as its enduring popularity has
amply proved – an identity of its own. It is with Malory that the Arthurian
legend has survived because it was he who put the material into the form
in which it was most likely to survive. He reversed the medieval process
of expansion and explanation and moved in the opposite direction to produce a single-volume history of Arthur at a time when the production and
dissemination of books was about to change. Had Malory continued with
the encyclopaedic spirit which had expanded the Arthurian material from
its modest beginnings, had he taken the noble French volumes and added
more explanations, tied up more loose ends, making them even bigger, as
the thirteenth century prose writers had made their sources bigger, the
Morte Darthur would no doubt have had a different fate. But Malory's innovation was to strip away excess, to simplify and focus. His one volume
history is – literally – easier to handle. And when the Arthurian legend de-
clined in popularity the *Morte Darthur* contained, in reasonable proportions, all the essentials. It was eminently manageable and convenient,
ideal for private or public reading: whereas those enormous French volumes no longer seemed to justify their existence. An abridgement always
stands a better chance of survival when interest wanes and the whole
work comes to appear needlessly unwieldy.

The convenience of Malory's volume cannot alone explain its survival
of course, since over the years literary expectations changed radically.
Prose fiction developed in other directions and it was clear that in form
and structure, in 'art and combination' the *Morte Darthur* no longer
seemed a modern book, and certainly not a convenient one, at all. It came
to appear like something of a literary ragbag and even admirers of romance like Sir Walter Scott thought it artless and haphazardly written.
Even so, Malory's book survived.

It did so because there is a more important sense in which Malory had
given the Arthurian material the form in which it was most likely to survive: he had chosen the right genre. In this his innovaation is that he
handles his material from a traditional point of view. He looked back to
older modes of narration rather than ahead. He refused the developing in-

terest in the individual and private conscience, and preferred the formal vision of public history.

The romance treatment of the Arthurian legend had brought those distant heroes closer to us by exploring their inner states. They were no longer figures of awesome achievement, but men whose hearts were laid bare. Malory reverses the process and takes us one step away from his heroes. We see how Lancelot acts, how he serves the queen unfailingly, but we see little or nothing of what he feels, of what it all cost him. Malory turns his back on the narrative omniscience that gives the reader an intimate knowledge of great men and concentrates on the history of a nation. He refuses to consider the private behaviour that can tarnish a public image; by keeping us at a distance from his characters he restores all the respect they deserve. Malory's characters are, in this way, bigger men. They are not only heroes, they are heroic.

This approach is very much Malory's own. His sources could only have encouraged him to continue in their direction, to look into the hearts of his characters and write. But with the outlook of a traditional writer – and inspired by such texts, perhaps, as the alliterative *Morte Arthure* – Malory sees the story of Arthur as the history of a nation not of a man. Part of that history is the clash of allegiances that leads to destruction, but the private story merely serves to make the impact of the public history all the greater. The personal ruin of Lancelot and Guenevere and the whole sphere of human experience their relationship implies is a part of a situation which Malory views exclusively in historical terms. In this respect, Lancelot and Guenevere are the exact opposite of another 'pair so famous' who hazard a kingdom for love: Antony and Cleopatra. In a moment of recall Antony declares 'If I lose mine honour, I lose myself' but the play shows us the fascinating individual that this process of loss reveals. Malory never allows his lovers to lose their honour – he even refuses to provide information about them when necessary – and to this end they have already lost their individuality. When what remains of it threatens to come to the fore, they are made to sacrifice it again as they take to a life of penance.

The *Morte Darthur* is not a story in which all is done for love and the world is well lost, it is a romance in the tragic mode and Malory's theme, the ruin of a nation, is one which has increased the impact of the Arthurian material. The private history the tragedy contains is, of course, extremely moving, but it is so only because of all that is at stake. It is the public tragedy that holds Malory's attention and, as events draw to a close, he reorganises his material radically to emphasise the issues involved.

He increases our awareness of what has been (or will be) lost by introducing the episode of the healing of Sir Urry. When events are forcing us

to recognise Lancelot's error, Malory insists on augmenting his reputation, so that we see clearly, with Lancelot, what might have been possible
if his love for Guenevere were not laying him open to attack. The Great
Tournament episode, with its reminder of Gareth's greatness and its re-
statement of Gareth's excellence, underlines, just before his death, the terrible division which results from a failure to place duty before desire. It is
appalling that a knight like Gareth should die at the hands of a knight like
Lancelot, and Malory emphasises the breakdown of allegiances further in
the irony of the situation that follows. The death of the brother who
would have no part in the strife becomes, itself, the excuse for strife. When
Gareth dies, Gawain loses all contact with goodness and restraint, with his
better self. Malory refuses to elaborate on the interweaving personal histories; they are all a part of the wider tragedy of the realm.

The *Morte Darthur* is a romance in the tragic mode – it certainly does
not have the happy ending typical of the romance genre – but it is also,
perhaps, a romance in the historical mode in that it refuses to assert the
importance of the individual over the well-being of the state. This may
well be an inevitable aspect of the feeling of patriotism that the Arthurian
legend arouses in an English audience, but by rejecting the (continental)
tradition in which the arthurian material becomes an ideal vehicle for the
exploration of individual experience, and by concentrating on its historical implications, Malory has given the Arthurian story a firmer hold over
its audience. Interestingly enough, even today we have not quite managed
to dismiss Arthurian matters as mere historical embroidery. The feeling
remains that behind it all, somewhere, there is (or we wish there could be)
a grain of truth – even if it is only the more eccentric members of Arthurian societies who actually keep digging up the countryside in search of
goodness knows what and in order to prove what is probably too slim to
be proved anyway.

It is Malory's outlook as a historian that is responsible for much of what
he omits from his sources. His reduction, that is, is an essential aspect of
his achievement not only because his single-volume history is, in itself,
progress, but because, in a real sense, it is his ommissions which help to
characterise his book.

As we have seen, by refusing to analyse motive and personal behaviour, Malory places a barrier between us and his characters, with the important result that what we lose in intimacy we gain in respect. The more
we know about the people we admire, the more we realise that they too
have feet of clay. Since Malory never allows us to be privy to the lives of
his characters, we inevitably endow them with all the virtue and integrity
that their rank implies.

As a result of knowing less about them, Arthur and Guenevere become
characters of sterling virtue. Malory has removed all the sophisticated in-

fidelities which fill the pages of the French *Lancelot*, for example. In a way, his omissions have cleaned the Arthurian material up. We see nothing of Lancelot and the queen plotting their assignations, nothing of Arthur organising a few little extra marital thrills with willing ladies. By turning his back on private matters Malory has implicitly anticipated the more modern notion that it is natural to expect a sovereign to be virtuous. We are given no reason to doubt that Arthur was a man of irreproachable integrity, just as we know that Guenevere was the epitome of truth in love: it secured her a good end, as Malory takes pains to assure us. We can respect Malory's characters more readily than their French counterparts and the impact of his book is therefore far greater. Malory has given the material a sobriety – and an importance – it clearly lacked. When the French Guenevere claims that she knows all about how to conduct an illicit liaison, we do not stand before her in awe. Sophisticated she may well be, and worldly-wise, but queenly never!

The sentiment and romantic involvement that Malory allows to remain are enough to arouse our interest without being so intense that we find them excessive or cloying. His is never a world of histrionic emotion or trivial makebelieve; it is a sober world of action, adventure and outstanding achievement firmly anchored in a sensible awareness of moral realities. The *Morte Darthur* is a stern book that merits respect. It is a healthy book, not deep and intellectual, perhaps, but noble and heartfelt. Its appeal is, indeed, to the heart not the brain – the only century in which the *Morte Darthur* was not reprinted was, we are not surprised, the eighteenth century – because, although duty, allegiance, and patriotism are not in themselves mindless, they are notions we must feel rather than argue out.

The virtues Malory's Arthuriad concentrates on are those of the soldier not the gentleman and part of the undeniable impact of the *Morte Darthur* is its movement away from the refinements of the heart and intense experience to those values – honour, truth, loyalty, solidarity, service, obedience – that touch us all, even if in more reasonable moments we can find good arguments for a more intelligent detachment. The soldier's trade has lost all its prestige for us, but in troubled times – like those in which Malory was writing perhaps – we can all be moved by a call to rally round and defend the realm. We have all, in moments of emotion, been stirred by the sounds of the National Anthem, even if on other occasions we are able to comment on how dreadful the tune is and raise an ironic smile at what seems to be cheap and sentimental patriotism.

Malory writes as a soldier not a philosopher. His book is not devoted to thought and there is little in the way of an intellectual tradition behind it – confirmation of its arguable importance, I suspect, for certain critics. Malory encourages us to reason things out less often than to feel them. Despite the great restraint of emotion in the *Morte Darthur* – the stiff upper lip attitude and speech of its characters – its emotional force is extremely strong.

Malory's commitment to Arthur and the Round Table code is entirely unquestioning. This is not because Malory is a simpleton, but it is not his chosen role to analyse the effectiveness of systems. Is there ever any point in asking an army officer why his men should have short hair and polished boots? Should we ask him to explain the morality or even the theory behind training men to violence and awarding medals for organised massacre? We ask these questions because we are not soldiers. If Malory had chosen to scrutinise Arthurian chivalry, it is hardly likely that he would have troubled to write the *Morte Darthur* at all.

We must not turn to his book for the reflective wisdom of an enquiring mind, although this does not mean that there is no wisdom in the *Morte Darthur*. There is, and in its own way it is even a didactic book. Its total endorsement of the Round Table code is, in itself, a way of recommending virtue. Malory writes with the sterness of purpose of one wholeheartedly committed to an ethic whose value is beyond dispute. He calls on us to put aside our individual claims on life and to acknowledge the value of allegiance and self denial. The *Morte Darthur* refuses a theme that will be so important in later literature, the human tragedy that comes when public duty thwarts personal fulfilment, and takes an older theme, the larger-scale tragedy that results when personal desire jeopardises the public weal.

In this, Malory's abridgement of the Arthurian material has brought it deceptively up to date. He has produced a modern book, but one which has all the force of an ancient culture. His innovation is to have turned back to traditional modes of perception, and much of the impact of his book resides here. He has brought within a smaller scope issues of a much larger scale; he has reduced the size of his material and magnified its importance.

A Second Reading List

Since this book is intended for those who (in theory) know nothing about the *Morte Darthur*, I have chosen to avoid footnotes. The newcomer to Malory, I believe, is hardly likely to feel an urge to rush off and check a reference or pursue a tangential line of argument immediately. I have referred to theories without troubling to mention their authors and I have plundered the ideas of other writers on Malory without a qualm, but readers who go further in their study of Malory will soon discover to whom the ideas really belong – and I shall give directions here. Those who go no further are not likely to augment or lessen anyone's scholarly reputation anyway.

The standard edition of Malory, based on the manuscript discovered in Winchester College in 1934, is by Professor Vinaver (*The Works of Sir Thomas Malory*, edited by Eugène Vinaver, 3 volumes, Oxford, 1947, second revised edition 1973). With its extensive introductions and copious notes – in the process of being revised by P. J. C. Field – Vinaver's work is a monumental piece of scholarship and an endless source of information. It contains all the details required for a comparison of Malory with his sources, which Vinaver identifies. Scholarly editions of these are listed. The general reader might find it easier to obtain and consult translations. *The Quest of the Holy Grail* (translated by Pauline Matarasso, 1969), and *The Death of King Arthur* (translated by James Cable, 1971), have been published by Penguin books, while translations into modern French of these texts, and a two volume selection from the *Lancelot*, can be found in the paperback series 10/18, published in Paris.

Two editions of part of the *Morte Darthur* are well worth consulting. The introduction to D. S. Brewer's *The Morte Darthur, Parts Seven and Eight* (York Medieval Texts, London, 1968) is an important piece of Malory criticism, in which a number of major topics – Malory's concept of shame and his use of the pronouns of address – are mentioned for the first time. The introduction and commentary to P. J. C. Field's *Le Morte Darthur, The Seventh and Eighth Tales* (*The London Medieval and Renaissance Series*, London, 1978) is also extremely useful. I take exception to Field's interpretations concerning Bors and Guenevere, and Lancelot and Elayne, but many readers will agree with Field rather than with me. Even if one disagrees with details in the commentary, it is always illuminating.

Two essays can be warmly recomended in that they provide the reader with a general assessment of Malory studies. Moreover, they are surveys which are in themselves important contributions to our knowledge. Neither is quite up to date, but both cover a lot of ground. They are: D. S. Brewer, 'The Present Study of Malory' in *Arthurian Romance, seven essays,* edited by D. D. R. Owen (Edinburgh and London, 1972), and Larry D. Benson, 'Le Morte Darthur' in *Critical Approaches to Six Major English Works,* edited by R. M. Lumiansky and H. Baker (Philadelphia, 1968).

Benson's book-length study *Malory's Morte Darthur* (Cambridge, Mass., 1976) is first rate, and Brewer has written several long essays which would appear in even the most selective bibliography. His essay 'The Hoole Book' (*Essays on Malory,* edited by J. A. W. Bennett, Oxford, 1963) was one of the earliest and remains one of the most important discussions of the unity problem, and I have made use of his excellent recent essay 'Malory: The Traditional Writer and the Archaic Mind' from *Arthurian Literature,* volume 1, edited by Richard Barber (Cambridge, 1981).

Useful background material will be found in C. S. Lewis, *The Allegory of Love* (Oxford, 1936, on courtly love, for which the student can always turn to Andreas Capellanus's *The Art of Courtly Love* (translated by J. J. Parry, New York, 1957) to see what a medieval writer had to say. On chivalry, it is worth consulting the work of Malory's contemporary Sir Gilbert Hay. His *Buke of the Ordre of Knychthede* has been published by the Scottish Text Society (Edinburgh, 1914), but extracts can be found in *Later Medieval English Prose* edited by William Matthews (New York, 1963). Richard Barber's *The Knight and Chivalry* (London, 1970) and A. B. Ferguson's *The Indian Summer of English Chivalry* (Durham, N.C., 1960) are full of valuable information. A readable account of the whole period is George Holmes's *The Later Middle Ages 1272–1485* (London, 1962) and a valuable survey of Arthurian literature in general can be found in *Arthurian Literature in the Middle Ages* edited by R. S. Loomis (Oxford, 1959).

Malory's style is admirably dealt with by Brewer in his edition; Mark Lambert (*Malory: Style and Vision in Le Morte Darthur,* New Haven and London, 1975); and P. J. C. Field (*Romance and Chronicle,* London, 1971). Field has also done important work on the life of Malory, in support of the Warwickshire man. The Yorkshire candidate is the subject of William Matthews's entertaining *The Ill-Framed Knight* (Berkeley, Cal., 1966), which considers the question of Malory's library, as does Richard Griffith in his essay in support of the Cambridgeshire candidate ('The Authorship Question Reconsidered' in *Aspects of Malory,* edited by T. Takamiya and D. S. Brewer, Cambridge, 1981).

Extensive bibliographies can be found in Vinaver's edition of Malory and in the list provided by Takamiya in the recent revision of *Aspects of Malory*. The bibliography in Elizabeth Pochoda's *Arthurian Propaganda* (Chapel Hill, 1971) is useful in that it is annotated, as is the more recent and exhaustive *Sir Thomas Malory and the Morte Darthur, A Survey of Scholarship and Annotated Bibliography*, by Page West Life (Charlottesville, 1980). Editions of texts and sources are listed exhaustively, and the contents of each study of Malory are described, sometimes at length.

There are several collections of articles about Malory. All of those in *Essays on Malory* are important, especially the stimulating contribution of C. S. Lewis. *Aspects of Malory* contains some rather specialised essays, but there is a good discussion of adventure by Jill Mann, an original study of the Gareth book by P. J. C. Field, and a consideration of the order of composition by the present writer. I make use of Field's brief essay in *Studies in Malory*, edited by J. W. Spisak (Kalamazoo, 1985) in which he explains the meaning of a legal term. The same volume also contains an essay on language by J. F. Plummer to which I am indebted, and a consideration of Malory's debt to the alliterative tradition by myself.